About Island Press

Since 1984, the nonprofit organization Island Press has been stimulating, shaping, and communicating ideas that are essential for solving environmental problems worldwide. With more than 800 titles in print and some 40 new releases each year, we are the nation's leading publisher on environmental issues. We identify innovative thinkers and emerging trends in the environmental field. We work with world-renowned experts and authors to develop cross-disciplinary solutions to environmental challenges.

Island Press designs and executes educational campaigns in conjunction with our authors to communicate their critical messages in print, in person, and online using the latest technologies, innovative programs, and the media. Our goal is to reach targeted audiences—scientists, policymakers, environmental advocates, urban planners, the media, and concerned citizens—with information that can be used to create the framework for long-term ecological health and human well-being.

Island Press gratefully acknowledges major support of our work by The Agua Fund, The Andrew W. Mellon Foundation, Betsy & Jesse Fink Foundation, The Bobolink Foundation, The Curtis and Edith Munson Foundation, Forrest C. and Frances H. Lattner Foundation, G.O. Forward Fund of the Saint Paul Foundation, Gordon and Betty Moore Foundation, The JPB Foundation, The Kresge Foundation, The Margaret A. Cargill Foundation, New Mexico Water Initiative, a project of Hanuman Foundation, The Overbrook Foundation, The S.D. Bechtel, Jr. Foundation, The Summit Charitable Foundation, Inc., V. Kann Rasmussen Foundation, The Wallace Alexander Gerbode Foundation, and other generous supporters.

The opinions expressed in this book are those of the author(s) and do not necessarily reflect the views of our supporters.

Planning for Community Resilience

Planning for Community Resilience:

A Handbook for Reducing Vulnerability to Disasters

By Jaimie Hicks Masterson, Walter Gillis Peacock,
Shannon S. Van Zandt, Himanshu Grover,
Lori Feild Schwarz, and John T. Cooper Jr.

Washington | Covelo | London

Island Press is a trademark of The Center for Resource Economics.

Library of Congress Control Number: 2014941999

 Printed on recycled, acid-free paper

Manufactured in the United States of America
10 9 8 7 6 5 4 3 2 1

Keywords: climatological events; community planning; disaster recovery; floodplain management; Galveston, Texas; geophysical events; hazard exposure; hazard mitigation planning; Hurricane Ike; hydrological events; land use planning; long-term recovery; meteorological events; natural hazard management; participatory planning; physical vulnerability; social vulnerability

Contents

Acknowledgments

The devastation on Galveston Island and Bolivar Peninsula after Hurricane Ike in 2008 has truly changed the lives of researchers and students involved in the projects at the Hazard Reduction & Recovery Center at Texas A&M University. Our interactions with residents and survivors were remarkable and telling of the resilient spirit of the people. To those who welcomed us into your homes despite the impacts and trauma you faced, we will always be honored to have met you. We raise our glass to the warm southern, Texan, and islander character of Galvestonians.

Thank you also to the City of Galveston staff members who were instrumental in helping us conduct research after the storm.

We also recognize all those involved in the projects and those who collected survey data in Galveston despite rough conditions in the field. Student research played an invaluable role and has certainly enriched the field. Specifically, Rahmawati Husein, Jun-Eung Kang, Gabriel Burns, Dustin Henry, Amie Hufton, and Joshua Gunn are all future giants of disaster planning.

The Texas Coastal Planning Atlas—a vision once dreamt over drinks at our favorite spot—became a reality before Hurricane Ike. A part of that vision has been fulfilled in the pages of this book. A special thanks to all those who worked alongside us to envision and create the website, particularly Doug Wunneburger, Sam Brody, and Wes Highfield.

We are also grateful to the funders of our research after Hurricane Ike; without their support this book would not have been possible. The research described was supported by two grants from the National Science Foundation (NSF) (#0928926 and #0901605) and from a series of grants funded by the National Oceanic and Atmospheric Administration (NOAA) (#NA10NOS4190207 and #NA07NOS4730147), the Texas General Land Office (TGLO) (#11-025-000-4323), and the Coastal Coordination Council (CCC). The authors, and not the NSF, NOAA, TGLO, or the CCC, are responsible for the findings and opinions expressed in this book.

We also appreciate the support of the American Planning Association's Planner's Training Service in developing the two-day workshop. The content and curriculum of that workshop were the main evolutionary acts that spurred the writing of these pages.

Finally, we thank those who helped us compile the book, specifically Michelle Meyer, Chi Ying Huang, Katherine Barbour, and Andrew Wallick.

PART I.
Community Resilience

What does it mean to be resilient? Can a person or a family be resilient? What about a community? The 1900 storm that struck Galveston, Texas, killed more than 6,000 people. The next day, reports say, survivors began to plan how they would reconstruct the city, which indeed they did. Is this resilience? After Hurricane Katrina, a Vietnamese American community fared far better than surrounding communities in similar situations, despite receiving little or no assistance. Is this resilience? What makes a community resilient, and how do we get there?

Community resilience is the ability of a community or its constituent parts to bounce back from the harmful impacts of disasters. Recent years have seen a proliferation of work using the word *resilience* in conjunction with natural hazards and disasters. Knowing that keeping development completely out of hazardous areas is not realistic, researchers have suggested building a disaster-resilient community as a more effective approach to dealing with natural disasters.[1] The concept of resilience has been borrowed and adapted by disaster researchers from the field of ecology, linking resilience to hazard vulnerability and defining resilience as the measure of a system's or subsystem's capacity to absorb and recover from a hazardous event.[2] Many common elements are shared between ecological and hazard or disaster perspectives. Primary among them are notions of the ability of a system to absolve, deflect, or resist potential disaster impacts and the ability to bounce back after being affected. For some, the system is explicitly human or social.[3] For others, although social systems might be the primary focus, they also implicitly include the built environments (e.g., buildings, infrastructure) created by social systems[4] and the ecological systems they depend on or operate in.[5]

Hurricane Katrina, and later hurricanes Ike and Sandy, made visible what many in the broader social science and planning communities have long argued: Natural disasters are far from natural phenomena. Disasters result from the interaction of biophysical systems, human systems, and the built environment. Furthermore, they are largely a function of human action or, more often, inaction. Despite increasing knowledge on natural hazard agents and their potential impacts, disaster losses increase in part because of where and how we design and construct our communities. Many communities continue to develop and expand into high-hazard areas, contributing to increased hazard exposure and often resulting in the destruction of environmental resources such as wetlands that can reduce losses. Short-term technological fixes such as levees, seawalls, and beach renourishment programs may also have detrimental environmental consequences and promote increased development. When major disasters occur, recovery requires massive infusions of external public and private resources, is highly uneven, and is likely to reproduce many preexisting inequities in exposure and vulnerabilities. Who can forget the images of the Superdome and people on rooftops and overpasses after Hurricane Katrina? In Katrina, there were early failures to ensure evacuation of highly vulnerable neighborhoods. We then saw large-scale evacuation of the Houston area for Hurricane Rita, which caused traffic gridlock for more than 24 hours, leaving those who needed to evacuate trapped along miles of concrete. The devastation of New Orleans is a case in point; the vulnerability was well known before the disaster, and therefore the resulting scale of damage from the hurricane was not a surprise—or, rather, should not have been a surprise. These natural disasters have focused attention on the need for forethought and planning in mitigation, preparedness, response, and recovery. Most importantly, they have focused attention on the interaction between biophysical systems, human social systems, and their built environment. The period between disasters presents an opportunity to increase resilience by mitigating against future threats and undertaking recovery that results in a stronger community.

The number and severity of natural disasters are expected to increase over the next hundred years because of a changing climate. At the same time, our world's population continues to expand, and development in high-hazard areas increases. Responding to these changes that are both happening and expected requires communities to become more resilient—better able to anticipate, prepare for, respond to, and recover from the impacts of such disasters. To do so, community stakeholders and leaders must understand the interactions between hazard exposure, physical vulnerability, and social vulnerability occurring in their own communities. In short, many of our communities are becoming ever more vulnerable to natural hazards while simultaneously becoming less disaster resilient.

Part I introduces readers to the concept of resilience and its increasing importance as a standard by which communities can measure their progress toward preparing themselves for the coming environmental changes. Real-life communities that have experience with recent disasters form the basis of our illustrations and explanations of the actions communities can take to improve their resilience. These three chapters make an argument for why communities must act now to ready themselves for the changes to come.

1. The New Era of Catastrophes[1]

In recent years, we have seen the terrifying impacts of natural disasters, including Hurricane Katrina, the Wenchuan and Kobe earthquakes, the Fukushima tsunami and nuclear disaster, and, most recently, 2012's Hurricane Sandy. Globally, the average annual number of natural disasters reported has more than doubled since 1980.[2] These catastrophes are increasing in the number of *meteorological events* (tropical storms, severe weather, winter storms, hail, tornadoes, and local storms), *hydrological events* (flash floods, river floods, storm surge, and landslides), and *climatological events* (heatwaves, freezes, wildfires, and drought).[3] Although *geophysical events*, such as earthquakes and volcanic eruptions, have remained more stable, there has been catastrophic damage to structures and lives, most notably seen in the Kobe earthquake, Wenchuan earthquake, and, more recently, earthquakes in Haiti in 2010 and Japan in 2011. We are experiencing not only an increased number of events but also an increase in their magnitude or severity. The number of "devastating" catastrophes (those with more than 500 fatalities or more than US$650 million in overall losses) and "great" catastrophes (those with more than 2,000 fatalities, 200,000 homeless, severe hits to the gross domestic product (GDP), or the country being dependent on international support) continues to climb globally (figure 1.1).[4]

With the anticipated changes in the global climatic system, continued disregard for vulnerability is likely to worsen the future impacts of hazard events. Recent scientific assessments from climate change researchers suggest that irreversible changes are already under way and will probably result in more frequent extreme weather events. Climate

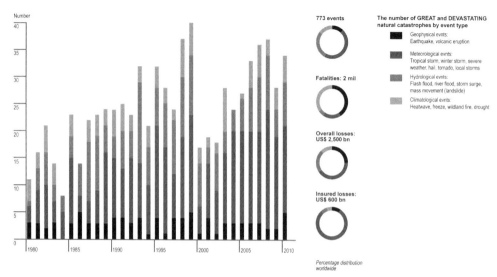

Figure 1.1. Global trends indicate that the frequency and intensity of disaster events are increasing. In 2010, the number of devastating and great catastrophes was more than US$2,500 billion. Devastating catastrophes are those with more than 500 fatalities or US$650 million in overall losses. Great catastrophes are those with more than 2,000 fatalities, more than 200,000 homeless, the GDP severely hit, or the country dependent on international support and aid. (Adapted from Munich Reinsurance Company, *Topics Geo*, 2010.)

change models also reveal that intensity of a number of weather-related hazards is also likely to worsen in the coming decades.[5] As a result, coastal cities will face higher levels of flood erosion, and riverine communities will probably face more frequent and severe floods. These communities will be overwhelmed more frequently as the impacts of global climate change become increasingly evident in the coming decades. Such catastrophic hazard losses can be avoided only through integrated planning at the local level that focuses on mitigating vulnerability from natural hazards across all sectors of local planning.

Disasters are still considered a part of weather systems and as such are treated as singular events ("acts of God") rather than symptoms of a larger trend. Because disasters are treated as extraordinary, the focus of many efforts has been on the *response* to such crises and the ways in which citizens and communities should *prepare* for disasters, rather than the ways in which disaster impacts can be *mitigated* and *recovery* can be shortened or made easier. It is important to recognize that hazards such as droughts, fires, hurricanes, and earthquakes are natural occurrences; they become disasters only when they interact with human systems. In other words, if a forest fire consumes only forest, it is not a disaster. Only when it interacts with homes and structures does it become a disaster. The same with hurricanes: If they strike unpopulated areas, they are not disasters. It is only when they strike populations that a disaster occurs. In this way, disasters are not singular, accidental events; they are symptoms of more chronic problems and are, in fact, social events.

If we understand disasters only as atypical events, then our focus tends to be on response and preparedness initiatives. However, these efforts are largely part of the field of emergency management, not urban planning. Response and preparedness are only a part of an appropriate response to the increase and predictability of natural hazards. Mitigation and recovery are also important, and they fall outside the purview of emergency management. Emergency managers and their allied professions typically have little or no ability to control where and how development occurs, standards to which new construction is held, enforcement of these standards, or long-term recovery activities after a disaster, which can take years. At the same time, municipalities typically do not consider disaster management or recovery to be part of their normal responsibilities. Few comprehensive plans, even in coastal areas, include elements specifically dedicated to planning for and responding to disasters. Even the city of Galveston, a barrier island on one of the most frequently affected coastlines in the world, did not have a recovery plan in place at the time that Hurricane Ike struck in 2008. With the slow onset of climate change impacts, the incorporation of mitigation strategies in comprehensive plans becomes all the more meaningful for communities. A number of catastrophic losses from natural disasters, specifically in urban settings, may be explained by the safe development paradox, which results from well-intentioned, but short-sighted, public policy decisions at all levels of government.[6]

After a disaster, a window of opportunity opens during which rapid changes take place. Communities are rebuilding, meaning that changes in population, land use, density, or industrial composition are taking place at a pace that is not normal. Furthermore, there may be an influx of financial resources and speculators (i.e., outsiders) looking to take advantage of the changes that are occurring. Cities that do not have a plan in place are ill-equipped to guide these changes. Without a vision for the future, goals for development, and policies in place to guide it, cities or communities may find themselves changing in ways that are out of their control, including permanent changes to the composition of the population, rapid changes in land uses, redevelopment, and changes in the economy. Some of these changes may be positive, whereas others are negative.

Fortunately, communities have many tools available to them that have proven to be efficient and more economical than traditional structural mitigation techniques such as dams and levees. Also, levees constructed in low-lying areas can create a false sense of safety from flooding. This sense of safety results from, and perhaps even induces, increased development and growth of population in areas made "safe" by structural mitigation measures. Herein lies the paradox: Flood safety works such as levees can only withstand the impact (with adequate maintenance) up to their design parameters but will undoubtedly fail in events that exceed those parameters. Consequences of this miscalculated sense of safety are evident in catastrophic losses experienced in New Orleans because of high-intensity development, which could have been avoided in the first place by more sensitive development in such high-risk areas. Instead, guiding land development, strengthening building codes, and protecting natural resources are all techniques that are best accomplished with thoughtful and comprehensive city and regional planning. Hazard mitigation and creating resilient communities must be at the forefront of hazard planning and, when done effectively, will save lives and property, making the work of emergency managers more effective.[7]

Two Sides of Increasing Exposure

Natural disasters are an outcome of an interaction between the biophysical systems, our human systems, and the built environment we create. Indeed, we are creating "disasters by design," meaning that as communities grow and develop into hazardous areas—be it along hurricane-prone coastal lines, within floodplains, atop unstable slopes, or along fault lines—we create scenarios that magnify the loss of life and property.[8] As we develop in hazardous areas we significantly affect and diminish the biophysical systems on which we depend and those that can help protect and reduce the impacts of disasters, such as wetlands, barrier islands, and tree stands. If we, as a society, are creating disasters by design, then we have the capability to create communities that are resilient to disaster. How we plan our communities, the patterns of development that occur, and the location of physically vulnerable structures and socially vulnerable populations significantly affect the ability of communities to withstand and even prosper in the face of disaster.

Human action and inaction are damaging our ecological systems and increasing vulnerability to disaster as we continue to develop and expand into high-hazard areas. According to the 2010 U.S. Census data, the United States is most dense along its coastlines. These data also show that there have been population losses in the middle of America and population growth along the coastlines.[9] It is no surprise, then, that we are seeing an increase in damage from hurricanes and floods each year. Despite planners' efforts to manage growth through higher-density development patterns, they may be exacerbating hazard exposure (see box 1.1).

Population growth along the coast has compromised ecosystems and reduced their ability to protect us by providing ecosystem services. Ecosystems provide services such as cleaning drinking water, decomposing waste, cleaning air, or absorbing and redirecting water that would otherwise cause flooding. Therefore, ecosystem preservation and restoration are inextricably related to hazards. The destruction and compromising of

Box 1.1. New Urbanism, Same Old Problems

New Urbanism is an initiative to create more dense development patterns, as opposed to more conventional sprawling growth seen in the United States. By creating more dense structures, communities become more sustainable by increasing opportunities to travel by bike, foot, or transit; encouraging mixed-use development; and providing a variety of housing choices. New Urbanism also promotes a set of design standards as a way to truly create a sense of place, missing from many suburban communities today. In many ways, New Urbanism strives to be an ideal community, a place that is livable, enjoyable, and equitable and accommodates a lower carbon footprint. Although these efforts are changing the ways in which planning takes place, New Urbanism initiatives often fail to consider long-term risk.[a] Instead, studies have shown that they do not differ significantly from conventional sprawling developments in hazard mitigation strategies and reduction of risks. Seaside, Florida, is just one example of a New Urbanism community that is exposed to very predictable hazards. Seaside is a small master-planned community along the Florida panhandle that is located in a hurricane-prone zone. Communities must address the impacts of hazards as a foundation to planning growth and development. Specific strategies New Urbanism developments should include are stormwater management best practices, environmentally sensitive area protection, and structural protection.

a. Berke, Philip R., Yan Song, and Mark Stevens. "Integrating Hazard Mitigation into New Urban and Conventional Developments." *Journal of Planning Education and Research* 28 (2009): 441–55.

ecosystems, such as wetlands, can increase the severity of hazard impacts by increasing exposure to hazards such as surge and flooding.

If vulnerabilities are addressed, solutions more often focus on short-term technological fixes such as levees, sea walls, and beach renourishment programs. These programs themselves can also have detrimental environmental consequences and even promote development in hazardous areas.

Permits acquired for altering wetlands and developing these environmentally sensitive areas are far too easy to come by. Wetlands provide valuable ecosystem services, particularly in hurricane-prone and surge-zone areas. Wetlands act as a sponge for surge waters and have been shown to reduce total damage.[10] When wetlands are altered or destroyed, along with high surge risk, the result is much higher exposure of new infrastructure, housing, and people to hurricane impacts. Preservation and restoration of ecosystems are an important element of hazard mitigation planning; unfortunately, the protection of these natural resources is often neglected.[11] Instead, structural mitigation—the construction of engineered solutions—is still the most popular approach (see box 1.2). While these

Box 1.2. The Ike Dike

Since Hurricane Ike in 2008, there has been much debate about whether a complex gated coastal barrier is a viable option for storm surge protection for the Houston area. The idea is to create a "coastal spine" with large floodgates between Galveston Island and Bolivar Peninsula at the mouth of the Houston Ship Channel and revetments along those islands (figure 1.2). The coastal spine would protect the entire bay from surge waters, instead of smaller levee solutions built in the bay. This floodgate would allow normal ship navigation to occur, as well as the natural water circulation of the bay, but would have the ability to close in the event of a hurricane. The floodgate would be 17 feet above sea level and would use proven technology from the Netherlands. Revetments, or artificial dunes designed to appear natural, would be built along Galveston Island and the Bolivar Peninsula where the seawall is not in place to protect them. These measures are also being considered because of the economic value of the Houston Ship Channel, home to the largest petroleum refining and petrochemical processing plants. If a Katrina-sized hurricane were to hit the ship channel, it would cost Texas an estimated $73 billion in gross product and 863,000 jobs.[a]

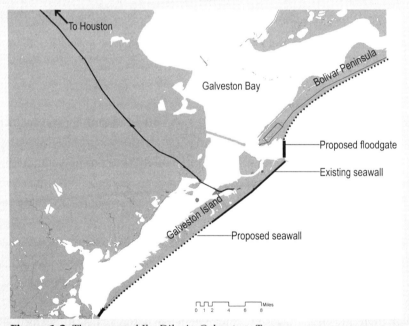

Figure 1.2. The proposed Ike Dike in Galveston, Texas.

a. Texas A&M University Galveston. *Ike Dike*. 2010. http://www.tamug.edu/ikedike/index.html (accessed August 2013).

structural solutions may protect certain areas, they often shift water elsewhere, causing unintended consequences for other communities. Further, they can be very expensive, and are often not the most cost-effective method of mitigating disasters. Finally, they often encourage further development, which can ultimately place more people and property in harm's way.[12]

Case Study: Galveston, Texas, a Living Laboratory

Many national trends, such as coastal population growth, are occurring in Texas.[13] It is one of the most rapidly growing states in the nation, one that experiences both frequent and varied disasters (see box 1.3). Texas is known for a more laissez-faire development approach, with economic development being the driving force behind population growth. It is a property-rights state, meaning that the political will in Texas is in favor of individual property owners rather than progressive planning. Consequently, Texas is a very challenging place to implement planning interventions, causing Texas planners to be creative and to find solutions that will withstand legal challenge. We like to say that if you can plan in Texas, you can plan anywhere. All this makes Texas a fascinating case study and a living laboratory for hazard planning.

The eighteen counties along the Texas coast represent 5.8 percent of the landmass but make up 24.3 percent of the state's 2010 population, roughly 6.1 million people (an increase from 5.2 million in 2000) (figure 1.15). The five northern coastal counties hold only 2.1 percent of the state's landmass but 20 percent of the state's population and nearly 21 percent of the state's housing. These five northern coastal counties were among the hardest hit by Tropical Storm Allison and hurricanes Rita and Ike.

Hurricane Ike affected the Texas coast at levels that had not been seen since the 1900 storm, which caused more than 6,000 deaths and remains the deadliest natural disaster in U.S. history. Hurricane Ike made landfall on Galveston Island—nearly 108 years to the day after the 1900 storm—at the mouth of the Houston ship channel, early on September 13, 2008. On September 9, predictions had its path headed toward the Texas coastline, but it was not predicted to hit Galveston. It wasn't until September 11 that mandatory evacuations were called for Galveston. The storm surge began more than 24 hours before it made landfall. The historic sea wall of Galveston, which was first constructed in 1904, helped protect the east end of the gulf side of the island, believed to be the most exposed (figure 1.16). However, because of the path of the storm, the surge actually came from the bay side of the island. A surge of 17 feet came across the island from Galveston Bay, where the seawall was not there to protect residents or structures. Hurricane Ike was a Category 2 hurricane based on wind speed but was a Category 4 storm based on storm surge. Because of the nature of this storm, storm prediction

Box 1.3. Texas Vulnerability

Texas is a fascinating case study to understand planning for natural hazards because it is a hotspot in hazard exposure, physical vulnerability, and social vulnerability.

Texans experience nearly all kinds of natural and technological hazards. Texas is second in the United States in the number of direct hits by hurricanes, and it far exceeds the other states in the number of tornadoes and flood damage (figures 1.3, 1.4, and 1.5). A third of all crop damage from wildfires and about a quarter of all U.S. property damage from drought occurs in Texas (figures 1.6 and 1.7). It is estimated that 5,700 acres of wetlands are lost annually, and more than half of all wetlands have been destroyed since the 1950s. Environmental concerns are also a threat, with more than 4,000 active offshore platforms along the coast.

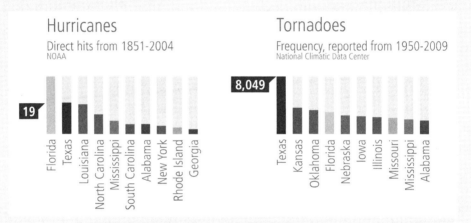

Figure 1.3. *(left)* Texas is second in the United States in the number of direct hits by hurricanes. (NOAA, *The Deadliest, Costliest, and Most Intense United States Tropical Cyclones from 1851 to 2004 [and Other Frequently Requested Hurricane Facts]*. Miami, FL: 2005.)

Figure 1.4. *(right)* Texas far exceeds the other states in frequency of tornadoes and flood damage. (NOAA, *State of the Climate: Tornadoes for Annual 2009*, published online December 2009. Asheville, NC: National Climatic Data Center, NOAA, 2009.)

Texas has the second highest GDP in the nation (figure 1.8). It has high physical vulnerability, with the most farms in quantity and land area and as one of the leading states in manufacturing, wholesale trade, and retail trade. It houses fifteen military bases, including Fort Hood, the largest military base in the world. The Texas coast is home to a large, growing population and a vibrant economy (figure 1.9). The City of Houston has the highest GDP in the state and is home to more than 3,600 energy-related companies, producing 40 percent of the nation's chemicals. The port of Houston handles the most

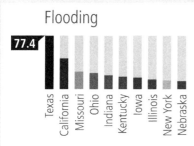

Flooding

77.4

Texas "consistently *outranks all states in deaths, injuries, and property loss* resulting from flood events"
– Zahran, Brody, Peacock, Vedlitz, Grover, 2008

On average, Texas is impacted by *400 floods annually*, making it the *most vulnerable state to flooding*, outranking the second highest state by twofold
– State of Texas Hazard Mitigation Plan, 2010-2013

Median damage in millions of USD 1995
Reported from 1955-1978 and 1983-1999
University Corporation for Atmospheric Research

Texas | California | Missouri | Ohio | Indiana | Kentucky | Iowa | Illinois | New York | Nebraska

Figure 1.5. Texas is the U.S. state most vulnerable to damage from flood events. (Hazards & Vulnerability Research Institute. The Spatial Hazard Events and Losses Database for the United States, Version 12.0 [Online Database]. Columbia: University of South Carolina, 2013. S. Zahran, S. D. Brody, W. G. Peacock, A. Vedlitz, and H. Grover. "Social Vulnerability and the Natural and Built Environment: A Model of Flood Casualties in Texas." *Disasters* 32, no. 4 (2008): 537–60.)

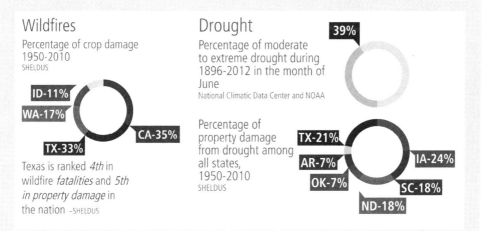

Wildfires

Percentage of crop damage
1950-2010
SHELDUS

ID-11%
WA-17%
CA-35%
TX-33%

Texas is ranked *4th* in wildfire *fatalities* and *5th* in *property damage* in the nation –SHELDUS

Drought

39%

Percentage of moderate to extreme drought during 1896-2012 in the month of June
National Climatic Data Center and NOAA

Percentage of property damage from drought among all states, 1950-2010
SHELDUS

TX-21%
AR-7%
OK-7%
ND-18%
IA-24%
SC-18%

Figure 1.6. *(left)* A third of all crop damage from wildfires occurs in Texas. (Hazards & Vulnerability Research Institute, The Spatial Hazard Events and Losses Database for the United States, Version 12.0 [Online Database], Columbia: University of South Carolina, 2013.)

Figure 1.7. *(right)* Almost a quarter of all property damage from drought occurs in Texas. (Hazards & Vulnerability Research Institute, The Spatial Hazard Events and Losses Database for the United States, Version 12.0 [Online Database], Columbia: University of South Carolina, 2013.)

foreign tonnage in the United States and is the second busiest port overall (figure 1.10). Houston also has the second most Fortune 500 headquarters in the United States.

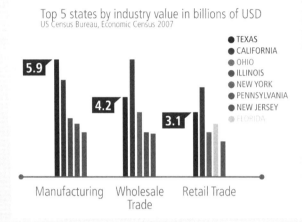

Figure 1.8. Texas has the second highest GDP in the nation and has high physical vulnerability, with the most farms in quantity and land area and as one of the leading states in manufacturing, wholesale trade, and retail trade. (U.S. Census Bureau, *2007 Economic Census*, 2007. https://www.census.gov/econ/census07/www/get_data.html [accessed December 2012].)

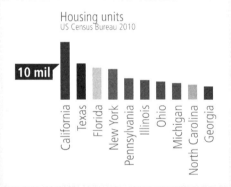

Figure 1.9. The Texas coast continues to increase in social vulnerability, particularly in transportation and housing needs. (U.S. Census Bureau, U.S. Census data, 2010.)

Texas's population is expected to increase by 82 percent in the next 50 years (figures 1.11 and 1.12). It is the ninth most impoverished state and is ranked forty-ninth in percentage of the population with a high school education or higher. It is a majority mi-

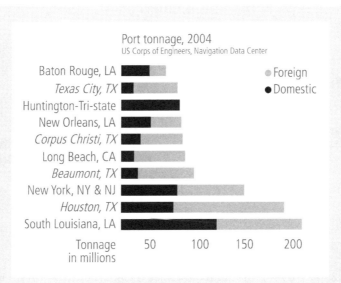

Figure 1.10. Texas has some of the most active shipping ports in the United States. (U.S. Army Corps of Engineers, Waterborne Commerce Statistics Center, 2004.)

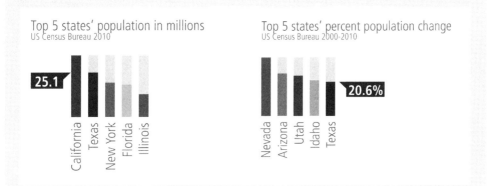

Figure 1.11. *(left)* Texas is the second most populous state in the United States. (U.S. Census Bureau, U.S. Census data, 2010.)

Figure 1.12. *(right)* Texas's population is expected to increase by 82 percent in the next 50 years. (U.S. Census Bureau, U.S. Census data, 2010.)

nority state, and nearly 15 percent of the total population is non–English speaking. The Texas coast continues to increase in social vulnerability, particularly in transportation and housing needs (figures 1.13 and 1.14).

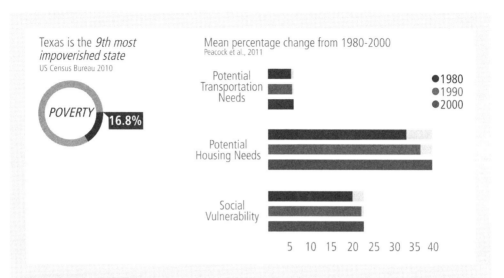

Figure 1.13. *(left)* Texas is the ninth most impoverished state. (U.S. Census Bureau, U.S. Census data, 2010.)

Figure 1.14. *(right)* The housing and transportation needs of Texans continue to increase, along with social vulnerability. (W. G. Peacock, H. Grover, J. Mayunga, S. Brody, S. D. Van Zandt, and H. J. Kim. *The Status and Trends of Population Social Vulnerabilities along the Texas Coast with Special Attention to the Coastal Management Zone and Hurricane Ike: The Coastal Planning.* College Station, TX: College of Architecture, Texas A&M University, Hazard Reduction & Recovery Center, 2011.)

Figure 1.15. The eighteen counties along the Texas coast contain nearly a quarter of the state's population and are exposed to hurricane winds, surge waters, and sea level rise. Coastal communities such as Galveston are particularly vulnerable.

has been modified to include separate predictions for wind and surge. Hurricane Ike resulted in the following:

- Damage to 75 percent of all buildings in Galveston
- A loss of 17 percent of the island's population
- The loss of 47 percent of the century-old tree canopy due to saltwater intrusion
- Property losses that made it the third most costly natural disaster in U.S. history

As of 2014, Galveston is still recovering and rebuilding. Recovery of the island has been uneven. The most affected populations have been much slower to recover, and even now, more than 500 units of public housing have not been rebuilt, permanently displacing this vulnerable population.

Figure 1.16. Piled debris along the seawall in Galveston, Texas, after Hurricane Ike in 2008. (Robert Kaufmann, *FEMA Disaster Photo Library*, Galveston, TX, 2008. https://www.fema.gov/media-library [accessed March 1, 2014].)

Our Research on Community Resilience

Over the past 10 years or so, researchers from Texas A&M University's Hazard Reduction & Recovery Center have been actively engaged in communities along the Texas Gulf Coast and beyond. As urban planning faculty members, we have focused on studying how communities prepare for, respond to, and recover from natural disasters, including coastal hazards such as the hurricanes that are frequent in this area, as well as inland flooding, fire, drought, tornadoes, and even technological disasters. Our research has involved, first, the development of data standards and sources to be used to assess social, economic, physical, and environmental conditions and change in communities, at the smallest level of geography possible. Second, our research has sought to identify drivers of change in land use, in development patterns, and ultimately in both physical and social vulnerability. Finally, when faced with a disaster in our own backyard, our research has sought to understand how these conditions affected the magnitude and patterns of damage, losses, and recovery (figures 1.17, 1.18, 1.19, and 1.20). In September 2008, the Texas Coast experienced what we call a "focusing event." Hurricane Ike followed other hurricanes that struck earlier in the summer, causing flooding in the Rio Grande Valley of South Texas. Though tragic, these events not only provided the opportunity to conduct research on resiliency but also catalyzed planning activity to act on the sometimes temporary political will to make positive changes in the aftermath of a storm. Our belief is that the research described in this book will be valuable to anyone working to create a more resilient community.

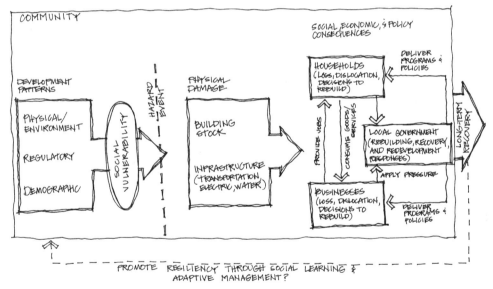

Figure 1.17. There are a variety of social, economic, and policy consequences after a disaster. Depending on the scale of the consequences, the length of long-term recovery will expand or contract. Such consequences are a result of the physical damage experienced, depending on the building stock and infrastructure. A piece often missing is the effect of development patterns—the built or natural environment, regulations, and demographic characteristics—that generate social vulnerabilities. We studied these components after Hurricane Ike.

Figures 1.18 and 1.19. Student researchers document damage on Galveston Island. Credit: Richard Nira.

Figure 1.20. Three months after Hurricane Ike, the destruction was still apparent. Credit: Richard Nira.

A Fact Basis Should Be Developed through Mapping

Before Hurricane Ike, the Texas Coastal Communities Planning Atlas (http://coastalatlas. arch.tamu.edu/), a Web-based, user-friendly geographic information system (GIS) mapping interface that covers coastal communities along the Texas coast, documented the physical, environmental, regulatory, and social development patterns present. In the months that followed Hurricane Ike, data were collected to provide immediate insight on impact, dislocation, and early repair and rebuilding decisions. The combination of research data and previously mapped data in the Texas Coastal Communities Planning Atlas has allowed us to understand how predicted responses compared with actual responses and has allowed us to gauge community recovery at multiple scales over several years. Identifying and mapping such data in a community is the fact basis for sound decision making on actions to be taken or policies to be implemented by both policymakers (local officials) and resident stakeholders. Identifying and mapping specific components and characteristics is described in part II.

Land Use Practices and Policies Can Be Applied to Disaster Planning

A survey of all Texas coastal jurisdictions on land use practices undertaken in 2010 has allowed us to better understand the tools that are available to planners to mitigate hazards through a variety of techniques, including limiting development, strengthening building codes, protecting natural resources, and educating residents about the impacts of disasters. This survey helped us understand the extent to which these tools were being used and make recommendations about which may be most effective and feasible. Furthermore, through participatory observation analysis, qualitative interviews, and documentary analysis, we have tracked policy changes by county and city governments to assess adaptive management and social learning. These results inform part III of this handbook.

The research findings on community recovery and land use practices along with the mapping tool, available to planners and others working in communities along the Texas coast, have provided a means to help planners and stakeholders visualize and assess hazard exposure, physical vulnerability, and social vulnerability to a variety of hazards. They have also provided a means to train planners across the country. In 2012, our team was asked to develop a curriculum on building resiliency for the American Planning Association's Planners Training Service (PTS). The PTS provides in-depth training in two-day workshops around the country. Drawing from the research described earlier, we developed 14 hours of training materials and brought on Lori Feild Schwarz, at that time senior planner for the City of Galveston, who had lived through Hurricane Ike and with whom we had been collaborating throughout the recovery period. Her direct experience facing, recovering from, and learning from such an event provided incredible insight and ground-truthing to our research. She shares examples and stories throughout to help readers understand the applications of our research and see how it did or did not make a difference along the Texas coast. Here, we capture these efforts in a user-friendly guide aimed at bringing our collective research and knowledge to a wider audience.

Purpose of the Book

As the impact of natural disasters continues to increase in severity, communities are exposing potentially millions more people to the adverse impacts of meteorologically based disasters. The purpose of this guide is to educate communities and citizens on approaches to becoming more resilient to natural disasters. It is meant to encourage and facilitate community learning that is interactive, collaborative, and participatory. We hope that the reader leaves this guide

- understanding that hazards must be a part of city and regional planning processes
- able to explain the components that make communities vulnerable
- understanding which land use tools can decrease vulnerabilities
- knowing the elements of good plan quality
- able to find ways to engage the public in the hazard planning process

Who Is This Book For?

Although resiliency can be addressed at multiple scales, including the individual, neighborhood, community, city, region, state, and even nation, this handbook focuses on processes at the neighborhood, community, and city scale. All these scales are interconnected, but here we address those that can be dealt with in a single community. Because community resilience is a product of processes going on at both the individual and higher levels, our efforts have focused on identifying the key decisions made by public authorities regarding disaster preparedness, response, recovery, and mitigation planning and policy development.

This handbook is intended for city planners, elected officials, appointed officials, neighborhood leaders, and nongovernment organizations. It is intended for business people, retired people, and even youth. This handbook is intended to enable local communities and professionals involved in the design, regulation, and management of the built and natural environments to construct communities that are more socially and physically resilient.

Although most of the examples in this book come from the authors' work along the Texas coast, the lessons learned are not exclusive to Texas, nor is it exclusively for coastal hazards. The lessons we've learned in our work are broadly applicable and focus on building a fact basis for decision making, assessing the utility of planning tools available for building resilience, and engaging community members in planning for their own futures. Some strategies may change based on the hazard, but the various exercises in this handbook are applicable to all communities.

How to Use the Handbook

This handbook is intended to be used as a participatory approach to hazard planning. Some exercises and activities will involve GIS and similar online mapping tools. Even if you do not have the capacity to produce GIS maps, you should still take time to understand its relevance and the process of uncovering community hazard patterns. Most importantly, the book is intended to guide a community—which may include professional planners, stakeholders, community groups, or a combination thereof—through the steps of an inclusive plan-making process and ultimately to become more resilient (figure 1.21). Community participation in the plan-making process is generally accepted by planners as being critical to producing enduring and effective plans.[14] These steps of planning are common to most plans prepared to direct and manage local development policies. These steps are further explained throughout the book and are as follows:

1. **Organize:** Gather together a core team of stakeholders who are likely to have the most capacity, whether in time, interest, ability, resources, or networks.

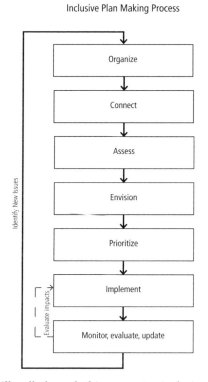

Inclusive Plan Making Process

Figure 1.21. This book will walk through this seven-step inclusive plan-making process.

2. **Connect:** Reach out and involve as many community members as possible in the strategizing and planning process.

3. **Assess:** Collect pertinent data to be used as the foundation of decisions going forward.

4. **Envision:** Interactively engage the public in setting goals to mitigate hazards.

5. **Prioritize:** Identify a range of promising policies and actions that align with other strategies.

6. **Implement:** Identify manageable tasks and responsible parties.

7. **Monitor, evaluate, and update:** Create feedback loops as a way to adapt to changing conditions.

We believe this framework provides an inclusive effort to collaboratively and adaptively solve complex problems. The steps are woven throughout the book along with a series of examples, stories, tools, and exercises to help you learn by doing. The exercises are intended to be completed as you read through the book and alongside city officials, staff, or citizens. The book can be used to guide a course or a series of workshops engaging the public or as a resource for city staff, businesses, or individual citizens. If there is limited knowledge on the topic, it is helpful to start at the beginning to gain insight into the many concepts and principles throughout. In general, the guide should be used as a reference in policy decisions and implementation.

The book is divided into three parts. Part I describes resilience and peels back the many layers that make a community resilient. It describes the disaster phases, introduces the disaster impact model, and provides details on Steps 1 and 2: Organize and Connect. Part II investigates how to assess your community's hazard exposure, physical vulnerability, and social vulnerability. It explains Steps 3 and 4: Assess and Envision. Part III provides detailed information on effective and promising mitigation strategies and consistently incorporating policies throughout other plans, and it describes Steps 5, 6, and 7: Prioritize, Implement, and Monitor, Evaluate, and Update.

At the end of each chapter we provide sample exercises that you may use with your stakeholder group, city staff, elected officials, and others to undertake a process that addresses the specific needs of your community. These exercises are intended to guide your group in developing an approach to identifying and understanding your community's assets and capabilities.

In short, our nation and many of our communities are becoming more vulnerable and less resilient. If we are going to address this increasing vulnerability and become more sustainable, we must increase our resilience. Disasters such as Ike, Katrina, and Sandy are a matter of when, not if. Let's plan for the expected and the unexpected.

2. What Is Resilience?

To begin tackling the problem of increased vulnerability to natural disasters, we must understand what we are trying to achieve. In recent years, the term *resilience* has gained popularity, but it is used in widely varying ways. All communities should strive for resilience, but what does it mean? Resilience has different definitions arising from a range of disciplines that use the concept, including natural hazard management, ecology, psychology, sociology, geography, psychiatry, and public health.[1] These different perspectives mean that *resilience* is a widely used term that can take on different meanings in different contexts. The following is an in-depth look at the ecological and social aspects of resilience as defined in various fields of research.

Biophysical Systems and Community Systems

Perhaps the definition of *resilience* most relevant to disaster management comes from the field of ecology. Ecology's well-defined concept of resilience has evolved over the years (see box 2.1). A number of common elements emerge from these definitions. First, the unit of analysis is generally an ecosystem. Second, there is a notion of resilience being defined as either the ability of systems to absorb changes and yet maintain themselves or the ability to rapidly bounce back from some form of impact. These two notions suggest that resilience may be measured by the amount of shock a system is able to absorb and the rapidity with which it rebounds after the shock. From these perspectives, a more resilient system is one that can absorb larger shocks and bounce back in a shorter period of time. A third theme emerging from these definitions is a subtle shift focusing on the capacities of a system to resist or absorb impacts and its ability to maintain or return to largely the same form, function, structure, or qualitative state. So a resilient system not only has the ability to resist impact, but when impacted it can return to its previous state, and the focus is on the capacities of systems that provide the abilities to absorb, resist, and bounce back.

Box 2.1. Definitions of Resilience from Ecology

"An ecosystem is the measure of the ability of an ecosystem to absorb changes and still persist." Holling, 1973[a]

"The speed with which a system returns to its original state following a perturbation." Pimm, 1984[b]

"A buffer capacity or ability of a system to absorb perturbation, or the magnitude of the disturbance that can be absorbed before a system changes its structure by changing the variables and processes that control behavior." Holling, 1995[c]

"The potential of a particular configuration of a system to maintain its structure/ function in the face of disturbance, and the ability of the system to re-organize following disturbance-driven change and measured by size of stability domain." Lebel, 2001[d]

"A potential of a system to remain in a particular configuration and to maintain its feed-backs and functions, and involves the ability of the system to reorganize following the disturbance driven change." Walker et al., 2002[e]

"Resilience for social–ecological systems is related to three different characteristics: (a) the magnitude of shock that the system can absorb and remain in within a given state; (b) the degree to which the system is capable of self-organization, and (c) the degree to which the system can build capacity for learning and adaptation." Folke et al., 2002[f]

"The capacity of a system to absorb disturbances, to undergo changes, and still retain essentially the same function, structure, and feedbacks." Walker and Salt, 2006[g]

"Ecosystem resilience is the capacity of an ecosystem to tolerate disturbance without col-lapsing into a qualitatively different state that is controlled by a different set of processes. Thus, a resilient ecosystem can withstand shocks and rebuild itself when necessary. Re-silience in coupled social–ecological systems, the social systems have the added capacity of humans to learn from experience and anticipate and plan for the future." Resilience Alliance, 2007[h]

a. Holling, C. S. "Resilience and Stability of Ecological Systems." *Annual Review of Ecology and Systematics* 4 (1973): 1–23.

b. Pimm, S. L. "The Complexity and Stability of Ecosystems." *Nature* 1984: 321–6.

c. Holling, C. S. "What Barriers? What Bridges?" In *Barriers and Bridges to the Renewal of Ecosystems and Institutions*, edited by L. H. Gunderson, C. S. Holling, and S. S. Light, 3–34. New York: Columbia University Press, 1995.

d. Lebel, L. "Resilience and Sustainability of Landscapes." *ASB Partnership* 2001. http://www.asb.cgiar.org/docs (accessed August 5, 2007).

e. Walker, B., et al. "Resilience Management in Social–Ecological Systems: A Working Hypothesis for a Participatory Approach." *Conservation Ecology* 2002.

f. Folke, C., S. R. Carpenter, T. Elmqvist, L. Gunderson, C. S. Holling, and B. Walker. "Resilience and Sustainable Development: Building Adaptive Capacity in a World of Transformations." *Ambio* 31 (2002): 437–40.

g. Walker, B., and D. Salt. Resilience Thinking: Sustaining Ecosystems and People in a Changing World. Washington, DC: Island Press, 2006.

h. Resilience Alliance. *Assessing and Managing Resilience in Social–Ecological Systems: A Practitioner's Workbook*. Stockholm: Author, 2007.

More recently, the ecological literature has sought to expand its notion of a system to include coupled social–ecological systems (SESs). The addition of social systems adds an important new dimension in that now a resilient system is a system that has the ability to learn from experiences and adapt (see box 2.2). Thus, the idea is that systems can modify themselves in response to impacts and thereby become more resistant to future impacts.

Box 2.2. Definitions of Resilience with a Social System Perspective

"The measure of a system's or part of the system's capacity to absorb and recover from occurrence of a hazardous event." Timmerman, 1981[a]

"The capacity to cope with unanticipated dangers after they have become manifest, learning to bounce back." Wildavsky, 1991[b]

"The capacity that people or groups may possess to withstand or recover from the emergencies and which can stand as a counterbalance to vulnerability." Buckle, 2000[c]

"A measure of how quickly a system recovers from failures." FEMA, 1998[d]

"Local resiliency means that a locale is able to withstand an extreme natural event without suffering devastating losses, damage, diminished productivity, or quality of life without a large amount of assistance from outside the community." Mileti, 1999[e]

"The capacity to adapt existing resources and skills to new systems and operating conditions." Comfort et al., 1999[f]

"Social resilience is the ability of groups or communities to cope with external stresses and disturbances as a result of social, political, and environmental change." Adger, 2000[g]

"The qualities of people, communities, agencies, and infrastructure that reduce vulnerability. Not just the absence of vulnerability rather the capacity to prevent or mitigate loss and then secondly, if damage does occur to maintain normal condition as far as possible, and thirdly to manage recovery from the impact." Buckle et al., 2000[h]

"The amount of disturbance a system can absorb and still remain within the same state . . . the degree to which the system is capable of self-organization . . . the degree to which the system can build and increase the capacity for learning and adaptation." Klein et al., 2003[i]

"The ability of social units (organizations, communities) to mitigate hazards, contain the effects of disasters when they occur, and carry out recovery activities in ways that minimize social disruption and mitigate the effects of future earthquakes. Characteristics of a resilient system: 1) Reduced failure probabilities; 2) Reduced consequences from failures, in terms of lives lost, damage and negative economic and social consequences; and 3) Reduced time to recovery (restoration of a specific system or set of systems to their 'normal' level of performance)." Bruneau et al., 2003[j]

"Resilience is the capacity to survive, adapt and recover from a natural disaster. Resilience relies on understanding the nature of possible natural disasters and taking steps to reduce risk before an event as well as providing for quick recovery when a natural disaster occurs. These activities necessitate institutionalized planning and response networks to minimize diminished productivity, devastating losses and decreased quality of life in the event of a disaster." Walter, 2004[k]

"The capacity of a system, community or society potentially exposed to hazards to adapt, by resisting or changing in order to reach and maintain an acceptable level of functioning and structure. This is determined by the degree to which the social system is capable of organizing itself to increase this capacity for learning from past disasters for better future protection and to improve risk reduction measures." UN/ISDR, 2005[l]

"Resilience is a measure of how well people and societies can adapt to a changed reality and capitalize on the new possibilities offered." Paton and Johnston, 2006[m]

"The ability to survive future natural disasters with minimum loss of life and property, as well as the ability to create a greater sense of place among residents; a stronger, more diverse economy; and a more economically integrated and diverse population. . . . Applies to the process of recovery planning in which all affected stakeholders—rather than just a powerful few—have a voice in how their community is to be rebuilt." Berke and Campanella, 2006[n]

"Social resilience is the capacity of a social entity e.g. group or community to bounce back or respond positively to adversity. Social resilience has three major properties, resistance, recovery, and creativity." Maguire and Hagan, 2007[o]

"A community that anticipates problems, opportunities, and potentials for surviving; reduces vulnerabilities related to development paths, socioeconomic conditions, and sensitivities to possible threats; responds effectively, fairly, and legitimately in the event of an emergency; and recovers rapidly, better, safer, and fairer." Wilbanks, 2008[p]

"The ability of social systems, be they the constituent element of a community or society, along with the bio-physical systems upon which they depend, to resist or absorb the impacts (deaths, damage, losses, etc.) of natural hazards, to rapidly recover from those impacts and to reduce future vulnerabilities through adaptive strategies." Peacock et al., 2008[q]

a. Timmerman, P. "Vulnerability, Resilience and the Collapse of Society." *Environmental Monograph 1* (Institute for Environmental Studies, University of Toronto), 1981.

b. Wildavsky, A. *Searching for Safety.* New Brunswick, NJ: Transaction, 1991.

c. Buckle, P. "Re-defining Community and Vulnerability in the Context of Emergency Management." *Australian Journal of Emergency Management,* 2000: 8–14.

d. Federal Emergency Management Agency (FEMA). *Homeowner's Guide to Retrofitting: Six Ways to Protect Your House from Flooding.* Washington, DC: Author, 1998.

e. Mileti, D. S. *Disasters by Design: A Reassessment of Natural Hazards in the United States.* Washington, DC: Joseph Henry Press, 1999.

f. Comfort, L., et al. "Reframing Disaster Policy: The Global Evolution of Vulnerable Communities." *Environmental Hazards* 1, no. 1 (1999): 39–44.

g. Adger, W. N. "Social and Ecological Resilience: Are They Related?" *Progress in Human Geography* 24, no. 3 (2000): 347–64.

h. Buckle, P., G. Mars, and S. Smale. "New Approaches to Assessing Vulnerability and Resilience." *Australian Journal of Emergency Management* 15, no. 2 (2000): 8–15.

i. Klein, Richard J. T., Robert J. Nicholls, and Frank Thomalla. "Resilience to Natural Hazards: How Useful Is This Concept?" *Environmental Hazards,* 2003: 35–45.

j. Bruneau, M., et al. "A Framework to Quantitatively Assess and Enhance the Seismic Resilience of Communities." *Earthquake Spectra* 19, no. 4 (November 2003): 733–52.

k. Walter, C. "Community Building Practice." In *Community Organizing and Community Building for Health,* edited by M. Minkler. New Brunswick, NJ: Rutgers University Press, 2004.

l. United Nations Office for Disaster Risk Reduction (UN/ISDR). "Hyogo Framework for 2005–

2015: Building the Resilience of the Nations and Communities to Disasters." 2005. www.unisdr
.org/wcdr/intergover/official-docs/Hyogo-framework-action-english.pdf (accessed January 4,
2007).

m. Paton, D., and D. M. Johnston. *Disaster Resilience*. Springfield, IL: Charles C. Thomas, 2006.

n. Berke, P. R., and T. J. Campanella. "Planning for Postdisaster Resiliency." *Annals of the American
Academy of Political and Social Science* 604, no. 1 (2006): 192–207.

o. Maguire, B., and P. Hagan. "Disasters and Communities: Understanding Social Resilience."
Australian Journal of Emergency Management 22 (2007): 16–20.

p. Wilbanks, T. J. "Enhancing the Resilience of Communities to Natural and Other Hazards: What
We Know and What We Can Do." *Natural Hazards Observer* 32 (2008): 10–11.

q. Peacock, W. G., H. Kunreuther, W. H. Hooke, S. L. Cutter, S. E. Chang, and P. R. Berke. *Toward
a Resiliency and Vulnerability Observatory Network: RAVON*. HRRC reports: 08-02R, 2008.

There is much to be gained from the applications of these definitions to the study of
social systems and the hazard context. However, we must also be wary about the simple
application of these definitions or approaches to social systems. For example, the notion
of bouncing back to roughly the same form or state as before a disaster event may not
be necessarily advantageous or desired. The analysis of disasters often finds that disasters themselves represent failures of social systems to properly adapt to the biophysical
environment, inappropriate development, and land use patterns and that systemic weaknesses in the form of social vulnerabilities are often generated by the systems themselves.[2]
Returning or bouncing back to the predisaster state is not necessarily resilient or adaptive
but rather lays the seeds for future disasters. Nevertheless, these definitions help us to
understand the nature of resilience and what it might mean for disaster management.

Dimensions of Resilience

Our definition, which draws from various disciplines and takes a more holistic and inter-
dependent approach, suggests that "resilience is the ability of a community and the bio-
physical systems upon which they depend, to:
- Resist or absorb the impacts (deaths, damage, losses, etc.) of natural hazards;
- Rapidly recover from those impacts; and
- Reduce future vulnerabilities through adaptive strategies."[3]

More recently there has been increasing emphasis on more formally identifying these
dimensions of resilience. For example, it has been suggested that addressing the ability
of a system to absorb, deflect, or resist potential disaster impacts implies a reduction or
diminishing of impacts, a reduction of failure probabilities, or reducing the consequences

of failures. Some researchers use the terms *resistance* or *robustness* for this dimension of resilience.[4] The bounceback after being impacted is of course associated with restoration and recovery or some notion of reducing the time to restore or return to "normal" functioning. This time dimension is sometimes called rapidity, and it is associated with the slope of the trajectory of recovery: how quickly the social system returns to normal. Furthermore, the trajectory of recovery may stabilize (i.e., flatten out) at a point short of the predisaster trajectory or surpass it.

The potential for surpassing the original (predisaster) trajectory suggests the ability to increase resiliency through system learning or adaptation. This potential is often a critical element in notions of resilience in the disaster literature.[5] Communities that stress learning and adapting in response to disasters have the potential to build capacity, become more sustainable, and develop higher states of resiliency. Common themes are improving a system's mitigation status, enhancing robustness, and reducing future loss potential or failure probabilities; reducing preexisting physical and social vulnerabilities; and promoting sustainable disaster recovery by increasing economic, ecological, and social sustainability.

Figure 2.1 captures these resiliency themes drawn from the literature and our working definition of resilience. System resiliency implies robustness, rapidity, and enhancement in response to natural disasters. A resilient system is, relatively speaking, robust with respect to its ability to absorb and resist the impacts of a hazard agent, implying a reduction in potential disaster impacts. Furthermore, having experienced a disaster, a resilient system is able to bounce back quickly, reaching restoration levels in rapid fashion, relatively speaking. Finally, as part of the recovery process, a resilient system enhances its capacities by improving its mitigation status, reducing preexisting vulnerabilities, and improving its sustainability. Enhancements may include adaptations that acknowledge the community's cultural and natural attributes and symbolize its endurance in the face of disasters. Box 2.3 describes how citizens in Galveston used their skills to transform the landscape and adapt and embrace their new community after the disaster.

We Need an Inclusive Effort

Disasters are not one-time events. Although certainly some communities are more vulnerable than others, disasters are not a matter of if; they are a matter of when and what. Planning for hazards cannot and should not be the sole responsibility of emergency managers. Emergency managers are well equipped to address preparedness and response functions, but they are ill equipped for mitigation and recovery, the other two stages of disaster management, and the ones that take place between disasters. When they occur, disasters magnify and accelerate processes already taking place in our communities.[6] Treating them

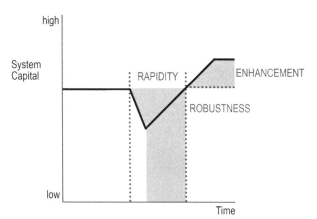

Figure 2.1. Critical dimensions of resilience. Resilience implies system robustness, or the ability to withstand potential hazard impacts; rapidity, or how quickly restoration or recovery levels are achieved; and enhancement, or the quality of recovery processes in terms of learning and adapting. (Adapted from Bruneau et al., 2003)

Box 2.3. Symbols of Resilience

Before Hurricane Ike, one of Galveston's most notable environmental features was the Broadway Avenue esplanade of live oak trees that welcomed visitors to the city and led them to the island's Gulf Coast beaches. It also created a stately backdrop for the city's unparalleled-in-the-state stock of historic Victorian homes. The saltwater incursion that accompanied Ike's surge killed the trees, destroying more than 75 percent of the island's tree canopy and destroying the natural habitat for migratory birds that have used the island as a winter destination.

The loss of the trees dealt a psychological blow to island residents. They were irreplaceable, and their loss changed the face of the island. Although tree-planting campaigns initiated a decades-long road to recovery, the dead trees stood as a reminder of all that had been lost.

Rather than take the trees out, community members elected to create sculptures from them (figure 2.2). Up and down Broadway Avenue, and in the blocks off of it that make up the historic district and beyond, tree sculptures now stand where dead trees once did. The initiative to create the tree sculptures was a spontaneous, grassroots effort led by the Galveston Island Tree Conservancy. The range of sculptures is impressive, and many of the images represent the island's culture and natural attributes, including pelicans, mermaids, dolphins, and more (figure 2.3). Some are simple, some are very elaborate. Many were created by professional artists, but others were created by property owners themselves. The result is a touching and spontaneous but lasting testament to the resilience of the people and the place.

Figure 2.2. Seventy-five percent of the 100-year-old tree canopy on Galveston Island was lost after Hurricane Ike. Today, you can find the remnants of the beautiful trees that have been transformed into art. (Credit: Dustin Henry.)

Figure 2.3. Birds carved from the trees that did not survive the surge waters and salt intrusion. (Credit: Dustin Henry.)

The tree sculptures remind us that resilience is not about a return to prestorm conditions. It is about adapting to circumstances as they arise, working with what you have, appreciating the change in situation, celebrating the essence and way of life of the community, and creating strength and beauty in unexpected places.

as unpredictable, improbable, and unique events takes the responsibility for mitigation out of the hands of community members and decision makers. Resilient communities will be those that incorporate disaster planning and management into everyday actions, taking care to move people out of harm's way and create capacity and networks that allow community members to respond quickly and effectively. Research and experience have shown that the key to community resilience is a strong community fabric, where citizens and organizations with a stake in reducing the impact of disasters are acting in concert. Therefore, planners must be skilled in designing and executing inclusive planning programs. By involving citizen and organizational stakeholders in determining community land use patterns and maximizing adaptive community capacity in the implementation of land use strategies, planners play a significant role in increasing community resilience.

The Importance of Public Participation

Citizen participation begins with community building, or the work of organizing people with common interests and focusing their efforts to achieve common goals. True community building takes place when all are informed, included, and respected.[7] In addition, there are a range of choices planners can make to influence this participation.[8] These choices can yield authentic dialogue, for example, which in turn motivates and empowers all to change the future for the interest of the whole.[9] Therefore, community building is key to planning processes. However, promoting citizen participation programs can be messy and result in unintended negative consequences if it is not done well. The benefits of community hazard planning include the following:

- Increasing public awareness and understanding of vulnerabilities
- Building partnerships with diverse stakeholders, increasing opportunities to leverage data and resources in reducing workloads
- Expanding understanding of potential risk reduction measures
- Informing development, prioritization, and implementation of mitigation projects
- Unifying and coordinating with other community plans, such as comprehensive plans, transportation plans, parks and recreation plans, school district strategic plans, and county strategic plans
- Expediting the delivery of internal and external support before and after disasters

Two months after Hurricane Ike, the Galveston City Council began the process of appointing a Long-Term Recovery Committee. Initially, the thirty-member steering committee for the underway comprehensive plan update was selected. However, there was great interest from the community to participate in the recovery process. Over the next six weeks, the Long-Term Recovery Committee expanded to include 330 Galveston residents. Because of the large size of the committee, significant coordination was needed to manage the multiple topics being considered for the recovery plan. The committee was assisted in this process by city staff and the FEMA Long Term Community Recovery Team (Emergency Support Function 14 [ESF-14]).

One of the first actions of the steering committee was to develop a communication subcommittee to ensure that citizens had an opportunity to contribute to the development of the recovery plan. To gain more input and participation from Galveston residents, ten open houses were held in the last two weeks of January 2009 (4 months after the storm), including off-island locations for displaced citizens. More than 800 people attended these open houses and provided more than 2,700 comments to consider in the recovery planning process. There was also substantial outreach by electronic communication, primarily through e-mail and on the city's website. A dedicated website was also developed to serve as a source for recovery information and to share information with the public about the committee's planning activities.

After the primary public outreach efforts, the steering committee met from February 2 to March 23, 2009 for three hours every Monday night. The public was invited to all steering committee meetings and were given the opportunity to speak to the committee formally at the beginning of each meeting or to participate informally in the smaller group work sessions. This large-scale planning effort totaled more than 4,200 volunteer hours to create the Recovery Plan. The steering committee determined to focus on six recovery areas: the environment, economic development, housing and community character, health and education, transportation and infrastructure, and disaster planning.

Over the six-week planning process, the committee developed a vision and goals and identified forty-two projects that would lead the recovery process for the city. The Long Term Community Recovery Plan was presented to the public at a community open house at the end of March 2009 and to the Galveston City Council on April 9, 2009. Ultimately, the responsibility for completion of these projects was assigned to various organizations throughout the community, with the City of Galveston taking the lead on numerous recovery initiatives. Many of these initiatives were incorporated into two significant planning projects: the Hazard Mitigation Plan and the Comprehensive Plan. No one in Galveston will forget the 330 citizen committee members and the countless hours to improve and transform their community. This example of citizen engagement promotes collaborative governance and yields community members who support and seek to follow through on implementation and action.

Tapping into Community Capacities

Another component to consider when planners set out to engage the community is tapping into community capacities that often go unnoticed or underused but are critical.

Capacity generally denotes notions of containing or storing and of ability, talent, competence, or experience.[10] *Community capacity* therefore refers to the sum of individual and organizational capacities within a community and, more specifically, the extent to which individual and organizational capacity is aligned to achieve community goals. In recent years the major forms of capital (social, economic, physical, and human) have been recognized as important factors in building community capacities to deal with disasters.[11] The hazard literature suggests that the sustainability and resilience of a community depend on its ability to access and use the major forms of capital.[12] The following discussion summarizes the four major forms of capital and how they can contribute to building community disaster resilience.

Social Capital

Many definitions of *social capital* exist in the literature.[13] Social capital has been defined as the features of social organization such as networks, norms, and social trust that facilitate coordination and cooperation for mutual benefit. Although social capital has been defined in a variety of ways, there is a common emphasis on the aspect of social structure, trust, norms, and social networks that facilitate collective actions.[14] In the context of community disaster resilience, social capital reflects social cooperation or community connectedness, which provides an informal safety net during disasters and often helps people access resources.[15] For instance, community ties and networks are beneficial in building disaster resilience because they allow people to draw on the social resources in their communities and increase the likelihood that such communities will be able to adequately address their disaster concerns.[16] Similarly, social networks such as friends, relatives, and coworkers are important in building disaster resilience because they provide resources that can assist households during disaster response and recovery.[17] Also, social bonds have been shown to influence adoption and implementation of hazard adjustment.[18] Furthermore, research has demonstrated that, in circumstances where characteristics of social capital or connectedness are lacking in a community, members of that community tend to have less capacity in terms of networks for dealing with disasters.[19] With regard to organizations, ties are linkages between the organizations and individuals, other local organizations, and government agencies such as social services, public health, emergency management, and community development. These local or internal networks enable communities to act collectively for mutual benefit and adapt to change in disasters.[20] Furthermore, community linkages to external capacity through federal and state agencies and nongovernmental organizations that deal with disaster relief (e.g., Red Cross, philanthropic organizations, and faith-based organizations) and development (Department of Housing and Urban Development, Habitat for Humanity, and the Small Business

Administration) can facilitate the delivery of external support when necessary.[21] There-fore, the work of assessing, cultivating, and coordinating the human and social capital in a community is fundamental to increasing community resilience.

Economic Capital

Fundamentally, *economic capital* is the financial resources people use to support their live-lihoods.[22] It includes savings, income, investments or businesses, and credit. The impor-tance of economic capital in building community disaster resilience is perhaps straightfor-ward in the sense that economic resources increase the ability and capacity of individuals, groups, and communities to absorb disaster impacts and speed up the recovery process. People with access to financial resources recover more quickly from disasters.[23] Also, access to credit and hazard insurance are associated with the level of household preparedness and ability to take protective measures.[24] The hazard literature suggests that a more stable and growing economy will generally increase community disaster resilience, whereas an unhealthy or declining economy is an indication of increasing vulnerability.[25] Further-more, the planning literature clearly suggests that economic resources can be critical for effective hazard mitigation planning.[26]

Physical Capital

Physical capital refers to the built environment, which includes residential housing, com-mercial and industrial buildings, public buildings, and dams and levees. It also includes lifelines such as electricity, water, sewer, transportation, telecommunication facilities, and critical facilities such as hospitals, schools, fire and police stations, and nursing homes.[27] The hazard literature suggests that physical capital is one of the most important resources in building a disaster-resilient community. A primary element of this capital is hous-ing,[28] of course, but other features of a community's physical infrastructure, such as roads, bridges, dams, levees, and communication systems, are essential elements for proper functioning of a community.[29] Furthermore, critical facilities play an important role in ensuring that people have resources and support arrangements during disaster response and recovery. In general, lack of physical infrastructure or critical facilities may have a direct negative impact on a community's capacity to prepare for, respond to, and recover from disasters.

Human Capital

Economists have defined *human capital* as the capabilities embodied in the working-age population that allow it to work productively with other forms of capital to sustain eco-nomic production.[30] Sometimes human capital is simply called the labor force or the ability to work. However, two main components of human capital are frequently mentioned in the literature: education and health of the working population group.[31] Education, which includes knowledge and skills that are accumulated through forms of educational attainment, training, and experience, is an essential component of human capital. Health of the working-age population is another important component of human capital. Health is considered a critical component of human capital because an unhealthy population may not be able to harness other forms of capital.[32] As a result, a community cannot fully engage in the process of building disaster resilience without human capital. For instance, knowledge and skills of local people on types of hazards, hazard history, and hazard risk in their community can be an important asset in building community disaster resilience. An individual's access to resources—whether financial, political, or logistical—or ability to move out of harm's way can determine his or her level of disaster resilience.[33] In general, the literature suggests that human capital in the form of knowledge, skills, health, and physical ability determines a person's level of disaster resilience more than other types of capital.[34] Likewise, when networks of individuals and organizations pool their collective human capital, it can have a positive effect on community disaster resilience.

Conclusion: Pulling the Pieces Together

The consensus of the scientific community is that natural disasters are not wholly "natural" events but rather the outcome of the interaction between biophysical systems, human systems, and their built environment.[35] Furthermore, they are in large measure a function of human action or, very often, failure to act. Many of our nation's communities continue to develop and expand into high-hazard areas, contributing to increased hazard exposure. So not only are the number and severity of disasters increasing, but our exposure to them is also increasing, making our communities less resilient. Therefore, it is important to understand that social and ecological systems play a part in absorbing and deflecting impact, in rapidly recovering from those impacts, and in providing flexibility to adapt, learn, and ultimately enhance previous conditions.

Research and experience are starting to show that, by engaging the public and understanding the various interests, abilities, knowledge, and resources in a community, planners can make themselves and their communities better able to manage all phases of disaster management. Unfortunately, although many local planners and aid providers are well intentioned, they often have limited capacity of their own to design and manage inclusive citizen participation programs, which could exacerbate the effect of the existing limited capacity of communities to cope with losses.[36]

The ability of a community to withstand, absorb, and bounce back from a disaster depends on the capacity of that community to act at each phase of disaster to mitigate, anticipate, protect, respond, deflect, and recover. Capacities may be understood as capital assets (social, human, economic, and physical) that are needed to mobilize the necessary resources. The next chapter describes the disaster phases through the lens of capital assets.

Exercise 1. Peeling Back the Layers of Your Community

Now that you've read chapter 2, take a moment to answer these questions. They are intended to be used as brainstorming questions to begin thinking about your community's resilience.

1. What characteristics embody an ideal resilient community? First, imagine what makes a strong community. Elicit answers from your work group on flip charts or through a focus group. After the group completes their responses, take a moment to reflect. Are there themes that emerge? Are any of these characteristics missing from your community? *Example: Where folks know their neighbors.*

2. Do characteristics refer to ecological systems or social systems? Second, evaluate the responses to determine whether your answers address social systems or ecological systems. If your list is not balanced, take a moment to identify a few more characteristics or ideas of community resilience. Take a moment to reflect on how your own idea of resilience might have changed. *Example: Social system.*

3. Which characteristics identified increase robustness, rapidity, or enhancement? Third, knowing that there are three dimensions of resilience, determine whether the responses could provide robustness, foster rapidity, or promote enhancement. Which dimension is missing most from your list? If your list is not balanced, meaning you do not have an equal number of characteristics that address all three dimensions, take a moment to add additional elements to create a more balanced list. *Example: Rapidity: One may recover more quickly if he or she can connect to people with other resources.*

4. Are there groups or organizations that could participate? Fourth, we should consider not only social and ecological systems and the robustness, rapidity, and enhancement of each but also whether there are groups that can participate in building a resilient community. Look back at your list of the elements you feel contribute to a resilient community. Are there groups or stakeholders associated with each element that could participate, engage, or collaborate to increase resilience? *Example: Homeowners' associations, neighborhood groups, school district, Adopt-a-Highway, churches, local bowling league.*

5. Which provide human, physical, social, or economic capital? Fifth, which characteristics are associated with the four possible community capital resources (human, social, physical, and economic)? You may find that multiple capital assets apply to each characteristic. Which capital assets are recurring more often, and which are not? Are there other components of resilience you haven't addressed or included yet? If your list is not balanced, think about what other characteristics of a resilient community could be included. *Example: Social capital.*

6. Which apply to your community (strong, need work, weak, nonexistent)? Lastly, look at the first list one more time. Which of your ideal community characteristics pertain to your community? Identify the elements your community is currently strong in, needs work on, or is weak in. Remember, your list is only a fraction of the components that could be added to increase resilience. Do you see how complex this is becoming? *Example: Weak: I occasionally see my neighbors when I get the mail.*

3. Organizing and Connecting through the Disaster Phases

With the previous chapter's definitions of resilience and community capital assets in hand, we now turn to a broad conceptualization of the disaster management phases. Actions taken to build resilience in a community can occur at any of the four phases of disaster management: mitigation, preparedness, response, and recovery.

The Disaster Phases

The four phases of disaster are seen in figure 3.1. These phases should be understood as part of an ongoing cycle of actions that take place continuously, both during and between disasters. Whereas emergency managers are typically focused on preparedness before a disaster and response immediately after a disaster, urban planners have the potential to address both mitigation and recovery in ways that significantly reduce exposure and increase resilience. Interestingly, each disaster phase has the opportunity to increase and support each community capital area. In a sense, the four capital areas can be applied to almost every community project, program, activity, and endeavor. Let's briefly examine each disaster phase to better understand the kinds of actions, stakeholders, and community resources involved.

Hazard Mitigation

Hazard mitigation generally refers to efforts undertaken before an event to reduce or eliminate the risks from natural hazards that may affect human life and property.[1] Activities

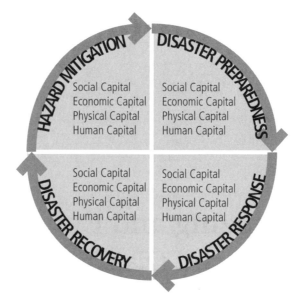

Figure 3.1. The four phases of disaster management are hazard mitigation, disaster preparedness, disaster response, and disaster recovery. Each disaster phase has the opportunity to increase and support each community capital area.

generally focus on preventing disasters or reducing the probability of or severity of impacts, through actions taken before hazard agents strike. Lindell and Perry[2] discuss mitigation actions or practices as passive protection against casualties and damage at the time of impact. In other words, once mitigation is in place, there is no action necessary before an event.

Mitigation approaches are characterized as being one of two forms, structural or nonstructural:

- *Structural:* generally thought of as engineering solutions such as dams, levees, and seawalls
- *Nonstructural:* policy-related solutions focusing on land use planning and management to limit development in hazardous areas and provide passive protection

And yet this classification is overly simplistic, because many forms of mitigation actions do not easily fall into one and only one category. In their important work drawing on more than 30 years of scholarly work on emergency and environmental hazard management, Lindell, Prater, and Perry adopted a modified classification used by the Federal Emergency Management Agency (FEMA)[3] that identifies several forms of mitigation actions, including the following:

- *Hazard source control:* Strategies designed to control the source and spread of the hazard agent such as chemical spills or leaks, as well as flammable materials

- *Community protection works:* Usually large engineered structures such as dams, levees, and seawalls designed to protect areas from hazard agents
- *Land use practices:* Various forms of development regulations and zoning approaches designed to keep development out of hazardous areas
- *Building construction practices:* Building codes and special utility codes designed to lessen structural damage due to flooding and high winds
- *Building content practices:* Examples include attaching bookshelves and water heaters to the wall to prevent damage and possible injury during an earthquake

In two classic books that specifically address mitigation issues to promote sustainability and resilience, Godschalk et al. and Mileti focus attention on three general categories of actions:

- Strengthening buildings and infrastructure exposed to hazards by means of building codes, engineering design, and construction practices to increase the resilience and damage resistance of structures, as well as building protective structures such as dams, levees, and seawalls (most of these would be classified as structural)
- Avoiding hazard-prone areas by directing new development away from known hazardous locations through comprehensive plans and zoning regulations (these would be classified as nonstructural)
- Maintaining protective features of the natural environment by protecting sand dunes, wetlands, vegetation cover, and other ecological elements that absorb or reduce hazard impacts (these actions are also called nonstructural mitigation measures)[4]

The first two actions are similar to traditional notions of structural and nonstructural approaches to hazard reduction, but the last action represents an all-too-often neglected set of mitigation actions that focus on protecting natural environmental resources because of the *mitigation services* these often fragile ecosystems can provide human communities. Increasingly researchers and environmental stakeholders from various groups have pointed out that many naturally occurring ecosystems such as dune systems, marsh areas, and vegetation in riparian zones can provide important mitigation services for flood-related hazards by acting as buffers that absorb flood waters and slowly release them, reducing flood damage and deaths. Brody, Highfield, and Kang[5] summarize more than 6 years of research in the book *Rising Waters*, which clearly shows the effectiveness of preserving wetlands, among other policies, to reduce flooding damage and losses.

In chapters 7 and 8 we will address in more detail hazard mitigation planning and various forms of policies and strategies, but the point here is that hazard mitigation encompasses a wide array of planning activities and specific actions that a community can undertake to significantly reduce the impacts of hazard agents. Research and experience have also shown that undertaking hazard mitigation planning and, most importantly,

implementing many of these mitigation strategies demands involvement and commitment from local citizens and stakeholders who may have vested interests in mitigation
strategies. Resources not only from the local level but also from the state and federal levels
can be key for undertaking mitigation planning activities and for developing and implementing mitigation strategies and policies. These resources include not only financial
resources but also human and social capital in the form of trained professionals, citizens,
businesses, and nongovernmental organizations with particular interests and knowledge.
It is vital that we begin thinking of and identifying our own community's key constitu-
ents and stakeholders, as well as resources that should be included and called on to formulate an effective mitigation plan (table 3.1).

A sound understanding of disaster potentials can better enable individuals and households to undertake voluntary mitigation actions, such as putting shutters on their homes,
purchasing flood insurance, and developing their own disaster plans. Furthermore, they
are more likely to be supportive of the community undertaking mitigation strategies such
as open spaces and hazard setbacks for development.

Disaster Preparedness and Response

In many respects disaster preparedness and response are two sides of the same coin. Preparedness is about doing the things that need to be done to make a community ready to
respond when threatened or hit by a disaster. Response is the activation of the plan and
preparedness activities in response to the threat or disaster event. Both are vital to help
minimize the physical impacts.

Disaster or emergency preparedness focuses on "preimpact activities that establish
a state of readiness to respond to an extreme event that could affect the community."[6]
Preparedness is all about setting in place practices to protect human lives and property
in conjunction with threats that cannot be controlled by means of mitigation or from
which only partial protection can be achieved.[7] Much of preparedness is associated with
determining the needs and solutions to what Lindell, Prater, and Perry[8] identify as the
four key emergency response functions:

- Emergency assessment (establishing a hazard and risk profile, key sources for detection and monitoring impact, damage and population at risk)
- Hazard operations (determining what kinds of resources and actions will be needed
  for each hazard type in your community's hazard and risk profile and ensuring their
  availability)
- Population protection actions (knowing what and where populations are likely to be
  at risk given the community hazard and risk profile and developing contingency for
  protective actions such as warning, evacuation, and sheltering)

Table 3.1. Identifying Hazard Mitigation Activities, Stakeholders, and Community Resources

Hazard Mitigation Activities	Actors and Stakeholders	Community Resources
Building dams, levees, dikes, floodwalls or seawalls, and stream channelization	Department of transportation (state and local) U.S. Army Corps of Engineers Construction companies Community Building department or permit office Emergency management agency (state and local) Public works Public safety Geographic information system (GIS) department Regional planning council State coastal department or agency State sea grant State natural resources and environment department or agency Federal Emergency Management Agency (FEMA) regional office Housing and Urban Development (HUD) National Flood Insurance Program (NFIP) coordinator or floodplain management office	Transportation employees Engineers Construction employees Local population Budget, revenue, or finance agency Business groups College or university Council on aging Developers and homebuilders Disaster volunteer groups Economic development Environmental groups Faith-based groups Farmers and landowners Neighborhood groups Philanthropic groups Public health agency School district Water and sewer utilities Electric utilities Professional associations or organizations (e.g., Association of State Floodplain Managers, American Planning Association) Youth groups
Land use planning to prevent development in hazardous areas	Planners Developers Construction companies Local population GIS department	Planners Construction employees Economic incentive (e.g., tax benefit and insurance discount) Council on aging Disaster volunteer groups

Table 3.1. continued

Hazard Mitigation Activities	Actors and Stakeholders	Community Resources
Land use planning to prevent development in hazardous areas	NFIP coordinator or floodplain management office Building department or permit office Emergency management agency (local) FEMA	Economic development Faith-based groups
Protecting structures through strong building codes and building standards (e.g., installing window shutters for buildings located in hurricane-prone areas)	Planners Developers Department of insurance Homeowners Business owners Emergency management agency (local) HUD NFIP coordinator or floodplain management office Fire department or emergency medical service (EMS) Building department or permit office Police department Regional planning council GIS department Construction companies FEMA	Legal officers Building inspection officers Planners Homeowners Business owners Neighborhood groups Philanthropic groups Public health agency School district Council on aging Disaster volunteer groups Economic development Faith-based groups Water and sewer utilities Electric utilities
Acquiring and relocating damaged structures, purchasing undeveloped floodplains and making them open spaces, acquiring development rights, and enacting zoning regulations	Federal, state, and local governments Planners Developers Homeowners Business owners Regional planning council GIS department NFIP coordinator or floodplain management office Fire department or EMS Parks and recreation department	Community financial resources Local population Homeowners Business owners Neighborhood groups Philanthropic groups Public health agency School district Council on aging Disaster volunteer groups Economic development

Table 3.1. continued

Hazard Mitigation Activities	Actors and Stakeholders	Community Resources
Acquiring and relocating damaged structures, purchasing undeveloped floodplains and making them open spaces, acquiring development rights, and enacting zoning regulations	Environmental Protection Agency (EPA) College or university FEMA	Faith-based groups Farmers and landowners Social service agency
Preserving the natural environment to serve as a buffer against hazard impacts	Environmental nongovernmental organizations (NGOs) U.S. Army Corps of Engineers Forest department Parks and wildlife department Developers Local population Regional planning council GIS department NFIP coordinator or floodplain management office	Environmental experts NGOs Council on aging Disaster volunteer groups Economic development Faith-based groups Farmers and landowners Philanthropic groups Public health agency
Educating the public about hazards and ways to reduce risk	Emergency management agency (local) Local population Homeowners Business owners Developers Fire department or EMS Police department Public health agency	Trained personnel Emergency managers Planners NGOs Faith-based groups School district Regional planning council GIS department College or university Media

- Incident management (developing or adopting procedures and standards for coordination and communication among the personnel and organizations that will be involved in emergency responses)

Meeting these functional areas involves a host of preparedness activities, including the following:

- Developing plans for activating and coordinating emergency response organizations
- Devising standard operating procedures to guide organizations in performing their emergency functions
- Training personnel in the use of those procedures
- Conducting drills and exercises and critically evaluating performance
- Stockpiling resources such as protective equipment for emergency workers and medical suppliers for the injured
- Assembling community resources for use as needed in an emergency

Even in the communities that can afford a well-staffed emergency management department with the most elaborately equipped emergency operation center, emergency management will only be a small, albeit critical, part of preparedness. Effective preparedness means helping organize and coordinate the community with all its different groups and organizations. Obviously, emergency management should include fire, police, and emergency medical service (EMS) organizations in preparedness planning. However, it is equally important to include businesses that can help households prepare for disasters, such as hardware, home improvement, and grocery stores, and businesses that deal with hazardous materials (manufacture, storage, and transportation). Also, including schools, churches, food pantries, shelters, and elder care facilities will be important for addressing the needs of the most vulnerable in the community. Finally, although it is popular to characterize EMS, fire, and police personnel as first responders, research has shown over and over again that the true first responders are family, friends, and neighbors. Therefore, initiating and including Community Emergency Response Teams[9] (CERTs) and simply working with community and neighborhood groups can be an important element of effective preparedness.

Table 3.2 presents a number of different disaster preparedness activities, actors and stakeholders, and resources.

Disaster response is the other side of the preparedness and response coin, representing in some sense the activation of preparedness plans. Response activities are conducted during the time period that begins with detection of the event and ends with the stabilization of the situation after the impact.[10] Again, emergency managers and first responders are critical players; however, there should also be substantial involvement and cooperation with the multitude of other organizations that should have been involved in the

Table 3.2. Identifying Disaster Preparedness Activities, Stakeholders, and Community Resources

Disaster Preparedness Activities	Actors and Stakeholders	Community Resources
Developing response procedures	Emergency managers Fire department and EMS Faith-based groups GIS department Regional planning council FEMA regional office U.S. Department of Homeland Security School district	Emergency managers Fire department and EMS College or university Disaster volunteer groups GIS department
Designing and installing warning systems and detection and monitoring systems	Emergency managers National weather service National Hurricane Center National Oceanic and Atmospheric Administration Budget, revenue, or finance agency Community	Emergency managers
Developing plans for evacuation	Emergency managers Department of transportation Local population School district Public transit authority Fire department and EMS Police department GIS department	Emergency managers Transportation employees School district Public transit authority GIS department
Testing emergency operations (exercises and drills)	Emergency managers Fire department and EMS Police department Public and elected officials Disaster volunteer groups NGOs Local population School district Public transit authority	Emergency managers Fire department and EMS Police department Public officials Volunteers NGOs Media

Table 3.2. continued

Disaster Preparedness Activities	Actors and Stakeholders	Community Resources
Training emergency personnel	Emergency managers Fire department and EMS Police department School district Public transit authority	Emergency managers First responders
Stockpiling of resources (e.g., medical supplies)	EMS personnel Emergency managers Fire department and EMS Police department Business owners Local and national retailers	EMS personnel Hospitals Fire department and EMS Police department Business owners Local and national retailers

preparedness planning activities. Disaster response activities often focus on protecting the affected population, attempting to limit the damage from the initial impact, and minimizing damage from the secondary impacts.[11] According to Lindell, Prater, and Perry[12] such activities should include the following:

- Securing the impacted area
- Warning the population
- Evacuating the threatened or impacted area
- Conducting search and rescue for the injured
- Providing food and emergency medical care
- Sheltering evacuees and other victims

The way in which these activities play out will be influenced by many factors; primary among them is the nature of the hazard threat or disaster itself. As discussed earlier, some hazard agents, such as hurricanes, generally have a lead time that enables response activities to happen well before landfall. Therefore, population warning and evacuation activities are major activities in gearing up to impact. For sudden situations such as a hazardous materials event, evacuation occurs at the same time as impact zones are established and secured, compounding activities in potentially conflicting ways.

The critical impact of having all potential responding organizations and groups involved in and committed to preparedness becomes critical when we consider all of the many possible actors and resources potentially needed to undertake response. Table 3.3 presents important disaster response activities and some of the potential actors, stakeholders, and resources that communities can draw on to address response activities.

Table 3.3. Emergency Response Activities, Stakeholders, and Community Resources

Emergency Response Activities	Actors and Stakeholders	Community Resources
Securing the affected area	Police department Fire department	Police officers Firefighters EMS personnel Firefighting vehicles
Warning	Police department Media Peers Public officials	Police officers Firefighters Television Radio Newspapers Internet Telephone and cell phone carriers Family and friends
Evacuating the threatened area	Local population Transportation departments Public officials	Personal vehicles Social networks (family and friends) School district Public transit authority
Conducting search and rescue for the injured	Police department Fire department NGOs CERT Volunteers	Police officers Firefighters CERT Volunteers
Providing emergency medical care	EMS NGOs (e.g., Red Cross)	EMS personnel Hospitals Ambulances Firefighting vehicles
Sheltering evacuees and other victims	NGOs (e.g., Red Cross) Faith-based organizations (FBOs) (e.g., Salvation Army)	NGOs FBOs NPOs

Table 3.3. continued

Emergency Response Activities	Actors and Stakeholders	Community Resources
Sheltering evacuees and other victims	Nonprofit organizations (NPOs)	Hotels and motels Churches and schools Family and friends

A key factor when engaging in preparedness and response planning is not to think of it as producing a final end product—usually a three-ring binder or electronic document that no one ever opens again, until it is too late. Lindell, Prater, and Perry[13] note that it must be viewed as a process, "a continuing sequence of analyses, plan development, and the acquisition of individual and team performance skills achieved through training, drills, exercises, and critiques." If the plan is allowed to become stale, contacts will wither and commitments will wane, and the next hazard threat has the potential to become larger in scale, much like Hurricane Katrina.

Disaster Recovery

Disaster recovery consists of actions taken to repair, rebuild, and reconstruct damaged properties and to restore disrupted community social routines and economic activities.[14] Peacock and colleagues[15] have defined community recovery as a process in which groups and organizations, making up the community, attempt to reestablish social networks to carry out the routines of daily life. Often disaster recovery activities begin after the disaster impact has been stabilized and extend until a community has returned to its normal activities.[16]

Given the nature of human communities, composed of many different types of groups and organizations, recovery is fundamentally a multidimensional process that takes place at many different locations with varying times and varying speeds. While some households and businesses are still responding to events, others may be well on their way to recovery. In addition, there may also be numerous restoration and rebuilding activities associated with public and private infrastructure involving everything from power, water, and sewage networks to transportation and communication networks. And the resources needed will come from a variety of sources, including savings, insurance, and various forms of grants, just to mention a few.

The disaster literature categorizes disaster recovery into two phases based on time frame:

1. Short-term recovery (relief and rehabilitation)

   a. Restoration of access to affected areas

   b. Reestablishment of economic activities (commercial and industrial)

   c. Provision of temporary housing, clothing, and food for the victims

   d. Restoration of critical infrastructure such as lifelines (water, power, and sewer)

   e. Restoration of essential government or community services

2. Long-term recovery (reconstruction)

   a. Rebuilding housing

   b. Rebuilding major structures (e.g., buildings, roads, bridges, and dams)

   c. Revitalizing the economic system

Table 3.4 presents important disaster recovery activities, actors and stakeholders, and resources.

Although short-term recovery is more a function of emergency management, long-term recovery through reconstruction is not. Long-term recovery in the United States is left largely to the private market, particularly in terms of housing recovery.[17] The federal government does not take an active role, and until recently there was very limited recovery capacity (see box 3.1). Although local investment may address the reconstruction of infrastructure, the recovery of individual housing units and businesses is left to the market, although federal and state policy may supplement individual resources such as private insurance and charity. Allowing the market to manage recovery strongly indicates that the goal of recovery is restoration of preexisting conditions—in other words, putting things back just the way they were.[18] Insurance payments to homeowners and business owners will cover only replacement of the original conditions of the home or business and typically will not allow improvements to be made, including improvements that may reduce physical vulnerability, such as elevation, roof straps, and reinforced walls. Perhaps more importantly, market-based recovery scenarios typically accentuate or exacerbate preexisting social inequities. One of the most durable findings in the disaster literature is that low-income households and racial and ethnic minorities are more likely to experience damage, and they recover more slowly.[19] Slower recovery times result from a lack of insurance or being underinsured, having fewer savings, and generally having fewer resources with which to undertake recovery and rebuilding. As a result, neighborhoods and communities may see shifts in their population demographics, their housing stock, and their business composition.[20]

The postdisaster recovery period is a window of opportunity for change. Stakeholders are generally more open to making community improvements that will increase resilience and thus will be more engaged and supportive of such initiatives. Furthermore, there is usually at least a temporary influx of financial resources that can be used to

Table 3.4. Disaster Recovery Activities, Stakeholders, and Community Resources

Disaster Recovery Activities	Actors and Stakeholders	Community Resources
Relief and rehabilitation activities		
Restoration of access to affected area	Police department Fire department Department of public works Department of transportation (state and local) Debris management Water and sewer utilities Electric utilities Public safety	Police officers Fire fighters personnel Volunteers Construction workers
Reestablishment of economic activities (commercial and industrial)	Business organizations Water and sewer utilities Electric utilities Local and national retailers Construction companies FEMA	Businesses organizations Volunteers Construction workers Local population
Provision of housing, clothing, and food for the victims	NGOs (e.g., Red Cross) FBOs (e.g., Salvation Army) NPOs Family and friends Housing agency Social service agency FEMA Regional planning council Emergency management office HUD	NGOs FBOs NPOs Family and friends Local and national retailers Planning department
Restoration of critical facilities within the community	Utility company Department of public works Local and national retailers	Utility employees Volunteers Local and national retailers Construction workers Necessary equipment
Restoration of essential government or community services	Federal, state, and local governments	Local government employees

Table 3.4. continued

Disaster Recovery Activities	Actors and Stakeholders	Community Resources
Relief and rehabilitation activities		
Restoration of essential government or community services	Local population	Civic organizations and emergency groups Local population
Reconstruction activities		
Rebuilding of major structures (e.g., public buildings, roads, bridges, and dams)	Federal, state, and local governments Department of public works Department of transportation (state and local) Building department or permit office	Private sector businesses Local population
Revitalizing the economic system	Local government Economic groups or business	Businesses organizations
Reconstruction of residential housing	Federal, state, and local governments Insurance companies Construction companies Family and friends HUD Housing agency Social service agency FBOs	Household income Property insurance Family and friends

implement projects if the projects are ready to go ("shovel-ready"). The problem is that it's hard to predict how wide the window will open and how long it will stay open. Communities that have strong plans (especially comprehensive plans) in place are in a much better position to act quickly and decisively after a disaster to enact positive change. Comprehensive plans are critical in the postdisaster period because they guide decision making. In a postdisaster situation, decisions must be made rapidly, often without adequate time for gathering evidence or doing proper planning. Resources not normally available to communities are suddenly available, and opportunities (and threats) arise that necessitate immediate action. Having a comprehensive plan in place that addresses some of

Box 3.1. The National Disaster Recovery Framework

When a disaster occurs that exceeds the capacity of state and tribal resources, the federal government uses the National Disaster Recovery Framework (NDRF) to support local recovery efforts. It was first developed in September 2011 and was to be paired with the National Disaster Response Framework. The NDRF provides guidance and support to state, tribal, and local jurisdictions. It establishes a Federal Disaster Recovery Coordinator, State or Tribal Disaster Recovery Coordinators, Local Disaster Recovery Managers, and Recovery Support Functions (RSFs). The RSFs include Recovery Planning and Capacity Building; Economic, Health and Social Services; Housing; Infrastructure Systems; and Natural and Cultural Resources. These RSFs are different from the Emergency Support Functions (ESFs) found in the National Disaster Response Framework. ESF time frames occur within days to weeks after a disaster, whereas RSFs may overlap with ESFs, but their time frames are months to years after a disaster. The NDRF is meant to be scalable and adaptable depending on the disaster itself.

these concerns before a disaster occurs makes it possible to maximize opportunities and minimize threats by guiding decisions that are supported by evidence and agreed upon by the community.

The Disaster Impacts Model

The ability of a community to withstand, absorb, and bounce back from a disaster depends on the capacity of that community to act at each disaster phase to mitigate, anticipate, protect, respond, deflect, and recover. The Disaster Impacts Model,[21] seen in figure 3.2, is a heuristic device to help us picture and understand how community characteristics set the stage for how a disaster will affect the community and what actions can be taken at the different stages of a disaster to minimize impact and hasten recovery. The model articulates the importance of considering planning, policies, and actions associated with mitigation, preparation, response, and recovery, for addressing the physical and social impacts of hazards and, equally importantly, for addressing recovery outcomes.

Through the center of the Disaster Impacts Model (DIM), we see the direct impacts of a disaster: the physical and social impacts. The physical impacts are those most familiar to us, those we see in the media and that are highly visible. These may include casualties, as well as injuries and illnesses resulting from primary impacts, those caused by wind, floodwaters, unstable structures, and so on, and secondary impacts such as the impacts that result from exposure to mold, compromised air or water quality, and so on. Physical impacts also include property destruction and loss, including structures

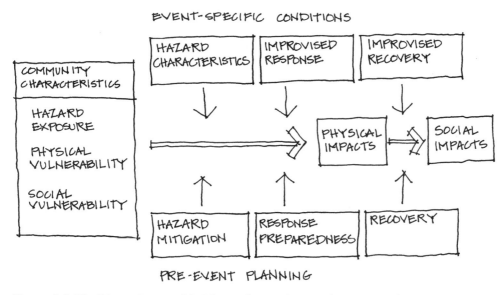

EVENT-SPECIFIC CONDITIONS

PRE-EVENT PLANNING

Figure 3.2. The Disaster Impacts Model provides insight into the various influences on physical and social impacts experienced after a disaster. (Modified from Lindell, Prater, and Perry, *Introduction to Emergency Management*, 2007.)

themselves, as well as their contents (furniture, equipment, and supplies), vehicles, animals, and crops. Losses to the community's infrastructure, including roadways, water or sewer facilities, interruptions to power and telecommunications, and disruptions to transportation systems are all physical impacts. Along with these impacts, there will probably be damage to the environment, which may result in habitat loss, wetland loss, or erosion, for example.

Physical impacts also create various social impacts. Social impacts are often less obvious but may be just as damaging to a community. They may include changes to the population, such as temporary displacement, long-term dislocation, or even population loss. For instance, in Hurricane Katrina, because of the overwhelming destruction of homes, more than a million people were displaced. Individuals and families may also experience psychological impacts such as posttraumatic stress disorder, anxiety, depression, substance abuse, or other mental health problems. Children who experienced the traumas of Katrina had difficulty adjusting to new schools and were reported to have more anxiety, depression, and academic struggles. Political impacts often include a change in leadership or a loss of local leadership, and may also—in extreme cases—include instability and violence. Finally, social impacts include economic impacts, including business losses or changes, interruptions in some kinds of goods and services, market instability, and an overall change in the economic structure of a community. Again, after Katrina, the damage to structures included that of businesses, and to this day economic growth is slow. However, it is worth noting that some changes that occur may be positive.

The goal of planning for disasters is to reduce these physical and social impacts. A resilient community will have fewer physical and social impacts after a disaster. In fact, we know that disasters do not necessarily create these physical and social impacts. Instead, people and communities create the magnitude of disasters, or the magnitude of the physical and social impacts that result.

In figure 3.3 we see the community characteristics with regard to hazard exposure, physical vulnerability, and social vulnerability on the left side. Hazard exposure is the likelihood of a community experiencing a particular type of natural hazard, such as flooding, hurricane, fire, or drought. It is typically expressed as a probability. Physical vulnerability is the extent to which the community has development, including structures, infrastructure (e.g., roads, water, sewer), and critical facilities such as hospitals, fire stations, schools, or police stations, that are vulnerable to the hazard in terms of their location and the strength or quality of those structures. Whether or not the structures are elevated, the building code to which they were constructed, and their age may all be important determinants of physical vulnerability. Social vulnerability is the variation in the community's population in terms of their ability to anticipate, prepare for, respond to, and recover from a disaster.[22] Social vulnerability considers population factors including age, race or ethnicity, income, education, family composition, and other characteristics. The community characteristics will be explored in depth in part II.

It is important to recognize that these three aspects of communities interact with one another, as seen in figure 3.4. A hazard does not become a disaster unless it interacts with

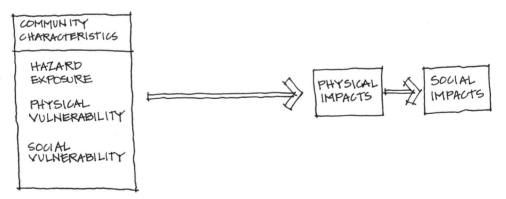

Figure 3.3. Community characteristics change the nature and magnitude of the physical and social impacts that occur after a disaster. (Modified from Lindell, Prater, and Perry, *Introduction to Emergency Management*, 2007.)

Figure 3.4. The community characteristics of the Disaster Impacts Model are interacting components. When a community is exposed to hazards, physically vulnerable, and socially vulnerable, it is considered a hotspot for risk and vulnerability and ultimately will expect increased levels of physical and social impacts.

the built and social environment. Indeed, if a fire occurs in a forest or a river floods a valley, it's not often called a disaster if no one is affected. More often than not, these are considered to be only natural processes. Although humans may cause ecological disasters, such as oil spills, these disasters still have wide-ranging impacts on both the environment *and* communities. Ecological disasters represent an interaction between social and ecological systems. Similarly, households can increase or decrease their physical vulnerability. If a community's population is housed in structurally sound, elevated structures, it may experience little or no damage from a surge event. Consequently, the overlaps between these three elements represent areas that are ripe for interventions. The extent to which these overlaps can be minimized or even eliminated represents the reduction of risk and increasing resilience.

The physical make-up of a community—the location and quality of facilities and infrastructure—and the demographics of a community are, to a large extent, knowable and regularly used by community planners. Unfortunately, they are often ignored in planning for hazards today. The coordination and collaboration of emergency managers and community planners are critical. These characteristics must be the basis for resiliency planning when it comes to mitigation and recovery planning, as well as other emergency management interventions. Indeed, they are the fact basis for all comprehensive community resiliency planning. Plans must be based on an understanding and assessment of these preexisting community characteristics. Each one affects the others and has the potential to increase or decrease damage and loss. In areas where all three come together, damage is expected to be the greatest and recovery the most extensive. These overlaps represent potential hotspots that are prime targets for resiliency planning issues, whether mitigation, recovery, or other planning activities are considered.

The model also recognizes a number of other important factors that will influence the nature of the physical and social impacts. The boxes along the top row refer to *event-specific conditions* that influence outcomes. Symbolized by the *hazard characteristics* box, as shown in figure 3.5, are the characteristics of the hazard or disaster agents themselves, which are of course key factors in determining physical impacts. Earthquakes, floods, tornadoes, wildfires, and hurricanes, to name but a few natural hazards, have many unique characteristics that pose particular threats to a community. These characteristics change based on the length of forewarning, magnitude of impact, geographic scope of impact, duration of impact, and speed of onset. Some hazards, such as hurricanes, can have long lead times and, given modern forecasting technologies, can yield warning times that provide opportunities for all types of emergency preparations, including evacuation. Other hazard agents, such as earthquakes, give essentially no warning and hence do not allow for emergency preparation. Still others, such as drought or sea level rise, can be almost imperceptible, as they grow increasingly worse over extended periods of time, making it difficult at times for people to recognize environmental cues to the looming and growing threat. The nature of these hazards also varies widely, meaning that their threats to life and property can be quite different. For example, hurricanes can generate multiple hazard

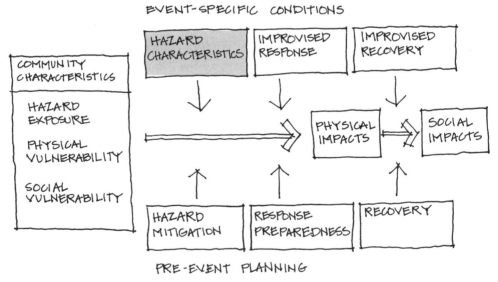

Figure 3.5. Disaster Impacts Model. Hazard characteristics are key for understanding disasters impacts. (Modified from Lindell, Prater, and Perry, *Introduction to Emergency Management*, 2007.)

characteristics, including destructive winds, ocean surge, and precipitation that can result in inland flooding. Finally, all natural hazards can vary in their intensity or magnitude. Indeed, whether using the Fujita (F0–F5) scale to measure tornado strength, the Moment Magnitude Scale to measure earthquake size, or the Safford–Simpson scale (Category 1–Category 5) to measure hurricane strength, all express the greater the potential physical impacts the higher you move up the scale.[23]

Many people have come to believe that the disaster itself creates the physical and social impacts we see, when in fact they are describing the hazard characteristics. This understanding results from the view that disasters are singular events, with rapid onset or with a short course—"acts of God," if you will. We now understand that disasters are a part of more chronic problems. It can be easy to come to the former conclusion when we see the devastating effects. This backward notion even penetrates our language and descriptions of disaster events. For example, we say that Hurricane Katrina *caused* tens of billions of dollars in damage and *killed* more than 1,800 people. And we describe Hurricane Sandy in 2012 as *causing* billions of dollars in damage, including thousands of homes, and *resulting in* millions of people without electricity. These physical impacts are products of more than the disaster agents themselves. They result from the expansion of human settlements into high-hazard areas, exposing more and more people and property to the impacts from these hazards.

The other *event-specific conditions* on the DIM include the improvisation of response and recovery. These components, as discussed previously, refer to the disaster conditions that often are unpredicted or unanticipated. Response improvisations typically fall into the purview of rescue operation personnel. These unanticipated conditions can lead to slow response rates or conditions that make rescue operations difficult. For instance, the collapse or destruction of a hospital indicated in the response plan to provide needed medical services and mass care during a disaster will certainly result in improvised emergency response and may well increase the magnitude of physical impacts as a result of a lack of appropriate medical care. Recovery improvisations will probably not affect the physical impacts we see but will influence the social impacts. Because many jurisdictions do not have recovery plans in place, we often see an increased reliance on recovery improvisation. Large lag times of displacement, or the slow rate in receiving insurance claims or building permits to rebuild homes, can certainly result in psychological, political, or social impacts.

Figure 3.6 highlights three important pre-event planning and implementation activities that can play critical roles in lessening the physical and social impacts or hazard characteristics. These are *mitigation, response preparedness*, and *recovery planning* as well as implementation of these plans by adopting policies, implementing strategies, and

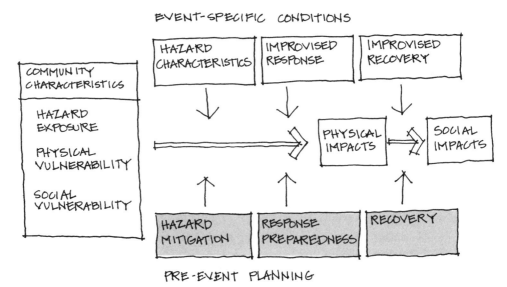

Figure 3.6. Disaster Impacts Model. Pre-event disaster planning and implementation focusing on mitigation, response preparedness, and recovery can play critical roles in helping reduce the physical and social impacts of disasters. (Modified from Lindell, Prater, and Perry, *Introduction to Emergency Management*, 2007.)

practicing plans. As seen in the DIM[24] in figure 3.6, the hazard mitigation plans that implement actions, practices, and policies can influence the hazard characteristics. Ideally, if hazard mitigation plans lessen the exposure of social and ecological systems to hazards by limiting critical facilities, lifelines, and other structures as well as socially vulnerable populations, then the burden on emergency managers will be lessened because fewer people and less property will be in harm's way. Furthermore, the recovery process will be eased because fewer people will be affected. Unfortunately, mandated hazard mitigation plans do not take into account all community characteristics during planning, often are not aligned with other community plans, focus on structural mitigation projects, and have little in the way of land use management policies, as described in detail in part III.

Response or emergency preparedness planning is another pre-event input that influences the extent of physical and therefore social impacts. These plans are an important component of emergency management for agencies that provide support, but they are not the focus of this book.

Recovery planning is the final input in the DIM. As you can see, recovery plans influence the magnitude of long-term social impacts. Recovery plans should provide a guide for communities rebuilding after a disaster as a means to reduce lag time and seize the window of opportunity mentioned previously. Recovery plans should address many of the disaster recovery issues discussed previously in this chapter. Unfortunately, recovery plans often don't exist in a community, and when they do, along with hazard mitigation plans, they may actually be in conflict with other community planning products, such as comprehensive plans, land use plans, economic development plans, and capital investment plans. Chapter 9 discusses how to achieve consistency in goals and strategies among a variety of plans normally undertaken by communities.

It's About Mitigation and Recovery Planning

There are specific strategies and policies that can increase a community's robustness, influence the rapidity of recovery, and enhance future conditions. A range of disaster plans exist. In particular, this book focuses on mitigation and recovery planning because we believe that mitigation is key for reducing disaster impacts. When we learn from a disaster and adapt our social systems and their built environment to reduce future losses through mitigation practices during recovery, we are working to achieve resilience. Another way to think about the four disaster phases and the importance of mitigation and recovery is shown in figure 3.7, which illustrates the temporal relationships of the different disaster phases. As you can see from the diagram, hazard mitigation and long-term recovery

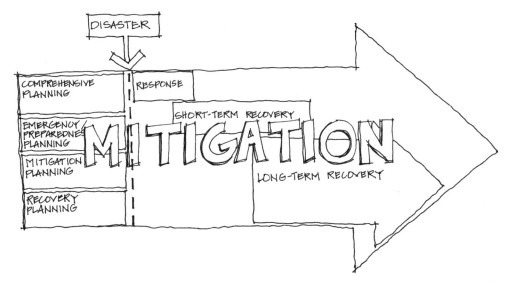

Figure 3.7. The four phases of a disaster are arranged temporally around the disaster event. All four phases are essential to reducing risks and becoming more resilient, but mitigation activities and practices should be part of every phase of disaster and community planning. (Modified from Schwab, 1998; Lindell, Prater, and Perry, *Introduction to Emergency Management*, 2007.)

efforts dominate the timeline and should be an ongoing practice in every community. Therefore, city and regional planners should be heavily involved in mitigation and recovery planning processes and should work with emergency managers when drafting mitigation and recovery plans. This will yield plans that can be implemented and are consistent with citywide efforts. In a sense, we are suggesting that many of the things city and regional planners are already doing can be applied in a new way to increase community resilience to natural hazards. Part II will more specifically describe the *community characteristics* of the DIM, which provides the fact basis for decision making and the foundation of planning efforts.

As described in chapter 1, the book is intended to actively engage the public in hazard planning. Here we describe Steps 1 and 2 to inclusively plan for disasters.

Step 1: Organize

The first step to inclusively plan for disasters involves forming a core team of three to five people with responsibility for managing disasters and representatives of agencies and organizations with a mission to increase community disaster resilience. These are the folks who will probably have the most capacity (time, interest, ability, resources, and networks) to meaningfully contribute to the design and execution of a broader community engagement strategy. The members of this group should clarify the purpose of the group and the roles and responsibilities of all parties. They should also determine whether others should be invited to fill any gaps in roles and responsibilities or to improve the efficiency or equity of the group. Then they should begin working on a strategy to involve the public.

Step 2: Connect

The second step is to connect to other groups. A simple way to introduce the hazard planning process to the public and invite members of the community to participate is to host open information meetings. The point of an information meeting is to provide an overview of the project to potential team members, to discuss roles and responsibilities of team members, and to determine whether others should be actively recruited to join an advisory group or taskforce to provide ongoing feedback to the core team. A taskforce would ideally include eight to fifteen people who can serve as hubs and information brokers to community members.

With regard to the kind of person to invite to an open information meeting, many helpful guides are available. The field of public health has been at the forefront of community engagement, and in 2011 FEMA developed a whole-community approach.[25] Leaders of faith-based, civic, and voluntary institutions that are trusted in the community are important points of connection, especially those with a mission to provide a safety net to the most vulnerable citizens of a community. These groups not only are able to reach those most likely to be negatively affected by a disaster, but they are often activated in the hours and days after a disaster. Involving these groups in the planning process allows them to contribute to the plans that will ultimately influence their ability to help others. The following list of groups that could contribute to a meaningful set of core decision makers and taskforce is a good place to start for planners considering the stakeholders to include in a public participation process.

Local Government
- Budget, revenue, or finance agency
- Building department or permit office
- Emergency management agency
- Fire department or EMS
- Health department
- Social service agency
- Housing agency
- Executive's office
- Parks, land conservation, or environment agency
- Planning or community development agency
- Police department
- Public works
- Public safety
- Transportation agency
- Geographic information system department

Regional Government
- Regional planning council
- Transportation agency

State Government
- State coastal department or agency
- State emergency management department or agency
- State natural resources or environment department or agency
- State planning department or agency
- State sea grant
- State transportation department or agency

Federal Government

- FEMA
- Housing and Urban Development
- National Flood Insurance Program coordinator or Floodplain Management Office
- National Oceanic and Atmospheric Administration and National Weather Service
- Army Corps of Engineers
- Emergency Support Functions (ESF) #14 community recovery agencies:

    American Red Cross

    U.S. Chamber of Commerce

    Department of Agriculture

    U.S. Department of Commerce

    U.S. Department of Defense

    U.S. Department of Education

    U.S. Department of Energy

    U.S. Department of Health and Human Services

    U.S. Department of Housing and Urban Development

    U.S. Department of Homeland Security

    U.S. Department of Interior

    U.S. Department of Labor

    U.S. Department of Transportation

    U.S. Department of the Treasury

    Environmental Protection Agency

    National Voluntary Organizations Active in Disaster (VOAD)

    Small Business Administration

    Tennessee Valley Authority

Independent or Quasigovernmental

- Area agency council
- Business groups
- College or university
- Council on aging
- Developers and homebuilders
- Disaster volunteer groups
- Economic development
- Environmental groups
- Faith-based groups
- Farmers and landowners

- Libraries and museums
- Media
- Neighborhood groups
- Philanthropic groups
- Public health agency
- School district
- Water and sewer utilities
- Electric utilities
- Professional associations and organizations (e.g., Association of State Floodplain Managers, American Planning Association)
- Youth groups

The next step in connecting is to invite these potential taskforce members to a connecting meeting. This meeting will describe the purpose of the team, the importance of the plan, the roles of the core team and taskforce, and the anticipated timeline and commitment involved. Through the course of the meeting you will need to determine whether taskforce members are willing to accept their roles and responsibilities. Ask the group whether there are other people who need to be represented, and make a point to follow up with them later.

Finally, convene the core team and taskforce again in a second connecting meeting to begin the work. At this point, it would be a good idea to present preliminary data or data as described in part II. Take the time to set up the issues and hazard concerns in the community.

Exercise 2. Organizing the Team and Connecting to the Community

As discussed, a range of disaster plans exist. For this exercise, let's focus on mitigation and recovery planning. With the definitions, concepts, and tables provided in this chapter, identify potential stakeholders in your community who could make up the core team to begin the planning process and list them in table 3.5. Remember, the core team should have three to five members and should involve stakeholders who have a primary or fiduciary responsibility to the plan-making process. Refer to the disaster phase lists at the beginning of the chapter or the examples listed at the end of the chapter. The list is not exhaustive, so think outside the box.

Table 3.5. Organizing the Core Team

Institution or Agency	Name	Phone E-mail	Role	Skills

Make a list of community members who could participate in the planning process using table 3.6. This table can help ensure that there will be a diverse taskforce. The majority of team members should be from institutions connected to disadvantaged communities. Be sure to also include team members who are from geographic areas that are often excluded in the planning processes, who have a diverse set of skills, and who can connect with other networks and act as hubs for information dissemination.

Table 3.6. Connecting to the Taskforce

Name	Phone E-mail	Institutional Affiliation	Community or Area	Role	Skills	Other Networks	Race and Gender

PART II.
Knowing Your Community

It is difficult to build a resilient community if there is no understanding of the current conditions within it. In other words, you can't get where you want to go without knowing where you are. Knowing your community means understanding the complex, interconnected community characteristics that define it. Every community is an emergent system with an almost endless network of interactions, mainly biophysical, human, and the built environment.

In part I we introduced the interactions between community characteristics—hazard exposure, physical vulnerability, and social vulnerability—as a Venn diagram. We illustrate them this way to help readers understand that each of these aspects of the community can be assessed individually and that the degree of overlap between them can be influenced by a variety of actions taken by planners and other professionals. Not only can the circles be moved—closer or further away from one another—but they can also be changed in size; the circles can be made smaller or larger through actions of community actors. In other words, the overlaps between these three elements represent areas that need attention and action before, during, or after a disaster. The extent to which these overlaps can be minimized or even eliminated represents the reduction of risk and ultimately an increased level of resilience. This risk analysis is an important component of hazard mitigation planning. Part II describes the process of identifying and analyzing the dangers to individuals, businesses, and government agencies posed by potential natural disasters.

Before we begin part II, let's pause to understand the third step to inclusively plan for disasters: Assess.

Step 3: Assess

The third step to inclusively plan for disasters involves assessing your community by developing a fact basis for decision making. It is important to base recommendations for your community on facts. A thorough fact basis should include information related to hazard identification, vulnerability assessment, and emergency management. Increasingly, a number of communities are partnering with local community leaders, nonprofit organizations, and other stakeholders to collect datasets. Creating partnerships at this stage ensures adequate attention to different analytical perspectives from various stakeholders. In addition, the process of collecting and analyzing information about community vulnerability can anchor the work of the local taskforce in a clear understanding of the realities of their community's unique circumstances and the potential for improvement. For example, members of a taskforce can work with planners to ensure that maps depicting the location of hazards and the built environment are up to date in light of anecdotal or indigenous knowledge about the history of hazards in the community. Members of the taskforce can also help planners identify and map critical natural or culturally significant resources worth protecting in the community. Most importantly, members of the taskforce can help planners gain a better understanding of the estimated need for shelter capacity, evacuation clearance time, and the full extent of social vulnerability. Completing the vulnerability assessment should reveal which hazards deserve the most attention in the community.

The three chapters in part II describe ways to get to know your community better, specifically by understanding and assessing the hazard exposure, physical vulnerabilities, and social vulnerabilities of your community.

4. Assessing Hazard Exposure

Disasters occur when physical and social systems interact with natural or technological hazards. The characteristics of the hazard itself are typically the most significant determinants of damage and loss. For example, in our work in Galveston, the exposure to storm surge (proximity to the bay side of the island) was the most important predictor of damage. Hazard exposure depends, to some degree, on the geographic location of the community.

Assessing Current and Future Risk

Based on the geographic area, specific and predictable hazards can be expected. For instance, coastal communities in the southern and eastern United States are more likely than western coastal communities to be affected by storm surge, flooding, tropical storms, and hurricanes. Communities in the Great Plains of the United States have a higher frequency of tornadoes, which is why this area is called Tornado Alley. The midwestern United States has experienced frequent flooding from the Mississippi River, along with severe winter storms. The western United States sits atop active fault lines, exposing millions of people to earthquakes and landslides. Most populations are exposed to some sort of hazard.

Communities are often faced with more than one hazard type. It is important to identify the potential hazards to which your community is likely to be exposed and assess the likely impact. Some things to identify are as follows:

- Hurricane risk zones (SLOSH models and wind fields)
- Hurricane surge zones
- Tsunami risk zones
- Flood zones (Flood Insurance Rate Maps [FIRMs])
- Coastal erosion and accretion
- Seismic hazards and fault lines
- Hazardous material sites, or areas with high quantities of chemicals that are ignitable, reactive, corrosive, or toxic
- Wildfire risk areas
- Drought-affected zones
- Probability of severe weather
- Landslide risk
- Sea level rise
- Fog risk
- Avalanche risk zones or regular avalanche tracks

Given the threat of changing climatic conditions, it is important to include climate change sensitivity analyses in the overall community risk analysis. Although the present state of climate change science cannot predict specific impacts at the community level, there is increasing confidence in regional impact projections. These regional projections can be used to inform hazard risk analysis at the community level. For example, the projected increase of 2–4°F in annual mean temperature by midcentury under the Intergovernmental Panel on Climate Change (IPCC) commitment scenario in Buffalo, New York, seems inconsequential. However, the significance of this change lies in the high likelihood of a shift in precipitation from snow to rain. The community is likely to be highly sensitive to anticipated climatic changes, because a number of residential communities next to creeks and water bodies already experience frequent flooding. It would be beneficial to incorporate similar climate change sensitivity analyses into the overall community hazard risk analysis (see box 4.1 for resources). This will ensure that communities are sensitive to the known hazards and future risks from climate change.

Spatial Analysis of Hazards

Many, but not all, hazards will affect areas in predictable ways based on geography. Floods, surges, and earthquakes are particularly predictable, wildfires are somewhat less predictable, and tornadoes and winter storms are quite unpredictable in terms of the specific areas that will be affected. Mapping can be a very useful tool for understanding, visualizing, and communicating risk. However, maps should be used with some important caveats. First, maps are only as good as the data that underlie them. Particularly for

Box 4.1. Resources to Help in Identifying Community Hazard Exposures

National Oceanic and Atmospheric Administration (NOAA) National Weather Service Storm Prediction Center, with the latest maps on severe weather and tornadoes: http://www.spc.noaa.gov/wcm/

Intergovernmental Panel on Climate Change (IPCC): http://www.ipcc.ch/publications_and_data/publications_ipcc_fourth_assessment_report_synthesis_report.htm

U.S. Global Change Research Program: http://www.globalchange.gov/

Environmental Protection Agency (EPA): http://epa.gov/climatechange/index.html

NOAA: http://collaborate.csc.noaa.gov/climateadaptation/Lists/Resources/AllItems.aspx

The Nature Conservancy (TNC) has developed a Coastal Resilience Web mapping tool. You can explore areas that should be restored, areas that are most at risk, community planning characteristics (which include storm surge models and sea level rise), and future habitat growth: http://maps.coastalresilience.org/gulfmex/#

The Spatial Hazard Events and Losses Database for the United States (SHELDUS) includes all counties in the United States and 18 different hazard types: http://webra.cas.sc.edu/hvri/products/sheldus.aspx

small areas, maps can be based on sparse data, old data, or incomplete data. Data are often aggregated and may not represent the actual distribution of a characteristic. Second, a line on a map can give a false sense of security. Because of the varying scales of a map, the width of a line on a map may represent anywhere from a few feet to a few hundred feet. Although a residential area may appear to be on the safe side of a line, it doesn't mean that the water (or fire, or seismic risk) will actually stop right at that line. Third, many maps are based on geographic units that may or may not be appropriate for the analysis being done. For example, much of the demographic data that we use is available only at the block or block group level. Other data are available at a tract or county level. Data at these levels don't always match the level of specificity we would like to see. Furthermore, the larger units, such as tracts and counties, can sometimes distort data for less populated areas, making it appear that a large area is affected by a hazard, when in fact very few residences or people are there.

The benefits of using maps outweigh the risks, however. Although smaller or low-capacity communities (such as many in Texas) may not have their own mapping or geographic information system (GIS) capabilities, there are resources available. Most hazard mitigation plans developed by emergency management offices include thorough analyses of community hazard exposure. Regional councils of government are a resource for small communities and more often have mapping capabilities. Furthermore, there has been a proliferation of online mapping services such as those listed in box 4.1. These mapping portals can provide very detailed looks at local areas.

To help readers understand how to use hazard maps, we use the Texas coast as an example. The Texas coast has exposure to several hazards, including flooding, surge, wind, fire, and drought (not to mention a host of technological hazards related to the oil industry). In figure 4.1, we look at the Texas coast's wind exposure.

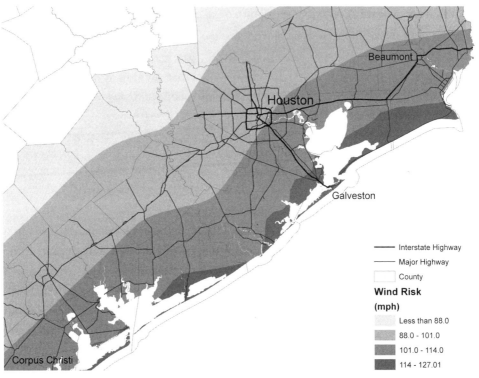

Figure 4.1. Generating a wind risk map is an example of the fact basis developed to determine the hazards a community is exposed to. This map shows the wind risk along the coast of Texas.

- Thirteen of the eighteen counties along the coast have 80 percent or more of their area exposed to hurricane force winds of more than 100 miles per hour.
- All coastal counties fall into wind zones 2, 3, or 4.

Even with just this one simple layer, we can start to understand that a large portion of the Houston metropolitan area, with a population of more than 6 million, is likely to be affected by high winds. This suggests a need for stronger building codes and incentives for wind-resistant adaptation, such as roof straps and impact-resistant windows.

Figure 4.2 displays the surge risk zones along the Texas coast.[1] Surge is an unusual rise of water generated by a storm, above the usual astronomical tides. Surge zones are determined by models based on storm strength; thus a Category 2 hurricane would be expected to produce a surge shown as surge zone 2. Storm surge is sensitive to the shape of the coast and to changes in the storm track, intensity, speed, and overall size. It is also the most devastating part of most hurricanes. In hurricanes Charley (2004), Katrina (2005), and Ike (2008), the traditionally used Saffir–Sampson Hurricane Wind Scale failed to accurately predict the storm surge because it depends primarily on models of wind. The potential for surge depends on different factors than wind. After Ike, forecasters began issuing predictions for wind and surge separately. The Saffir–Simpson scale is still used for wind, but a new scale, based on integrated kinetic energy (IKE) models, assigns separate 0–5 ratings for surge.[2] For example, Hurricane Ike had a Category 4 surge but only a Category 2 wind. When Hurricane Sandy struck the northeast in late fall 2012, a full moon amplified its storm surge and flooded much more of New York and New Jersey than wind models predicted.

Surge is more than just flooding. It involves both a rise in water levels and powerfully

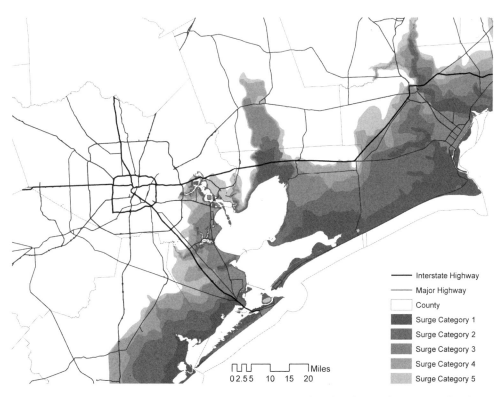

Figure 4.2. Coastal communities should generate surge and sea level rise risk maps as a fact basis for decision making. This map shows surge risk for Galveston Bay and the Port of Houston.

destructive wave action. In Hurricane Ike, the Bolivar Peninsula, opposite Galveston Island, was scoured by the surge, and most structures were simply dragged into the sea. If a community lies within a surge risk zone, precautions should be taken no matter the size of the storm. Along the Texas coast, like many coastal areas, the surge can reach far inland because of the flat topography and river deltas. For the Texas coast, on average, 47 percent of coastal county areas are located in hurricane surge risk zones.

Flooding affects more people than any other hazard in the United States. Most communities can determine their flood risk easily by collecting the community's FEMA Q3 maps, which designate the 100-year floodplain (see box 4.2 and figure 4.3). Communities that do not have Q3 maps should consider partnering with the U.S. Geological Survey (USGS) to develop and validate flood inundation map libraries.[3]

In Texas, coastal counties have more—sometimes substantially more—than 20 percent of their area in flood risk zones 3 (500-year floodplain, Zone 500X), 4 (100-year floodplain, Zone A), or 5 (surge).[4] All coastal county areas are at risk of flooding. It is important to note that these flood zones are notoriously conservative in their assessments. Just because a community is on the "safe" side of a hazard zone does not mean it is not exposed. Mindful planning can incorporate the probabilities of disaster impacts without focusing on a hard line drawn on the map.

Box 4.2. Defining Flood Zones

Zone A: The 1-percent-annual-chance flood event areas (or 100-year flood). No hydraulic analyses have been performed, and so no base flood elevations (BFEs) or flood depths have been calculated.

Zone AE: The 1-percent-annual-chance flood event areas (or 100-year flood). Hydraulic analyses have been performed, and BFEs or flood depths are available. On older maps these areas were known as zones A1–A30.

Zone AO: The 1-percent-annual-chance shallow flood event areas (or 100-year flood). These areas typically have 1- to 3-foot sheet flow depths on sloping surfaces.

Zone V: The 1-percent-annual-chance flood events for areas along coasts that experience storm-induced waves. No hydraulic analyses have been performed, and so no BFEs or flood depths have been calculated.

Zone VE: The 1-percent-annual-chance flood events for areas along coasts that experience storm-induced waves. Hydraulic analyses have been performed, and BFEs or flood depths are available. On older maps these areas were known as zones V1–V30.

Zone B or Zone X: 0.2-percent-annual-chance flood areas (or 500-year flood).

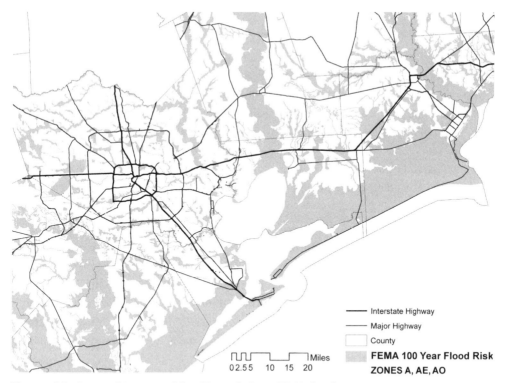

Figure 4.3. Geographic maps of flood hazards from FEMA flood maps are an important component of understanding a community's exposure to flood hazards. This map shows the 100-year floodplain around Galveston Bay and the Port of Houston in Texas.

To help communities of all sizes understand, visualize, and communicate their exposure to coastal flooding, surge, wind, and other hazards, our team has developed a user-friendly, Web-based GIS interface called the Coastal Community Planning Atlas (see box 4.3). This tool is one of many that have been developed by local, state, and federal agencies and institutions. As technology continues to make this type of spatial information available, even low-capacity communities like many found in Texas can accurately assess their exposure to a wide range of hazards. Online mapping tools can be an effective way to engage the public in hazard awareness.

Identifying and mapping hazards should be part of a community's participatory approach to planning (see box 4.4). Again, it is important to note that a community does not need the latest technology to engage in these techniques, and many low-resource communities have conducted wonderful analyses with traditional pen-and-paper approaches, as seen in box 4.4. The message of this chapter is to become aware of hazards, identify the probability of those hazards, and determine which areas in your community are adversely affected (figure 4.4).

Box 4.3. The Texas Coastal Communities Atlas

The Texas Coastal Communities Atlas (https://coastalatlas.arch.tamu.edu/) is an Internet-based spatial decision support system that allows users to identify and visualize critical issues related to numerous dimensions of development, including environmental degradation, natural hazard risks, and significant changes in land use patterns. This is an Interdisciplinary Initiative supported by funds from various agencies, including NOAA/Texas Sea Grant, Texas General Land Office, and Coastal Services Center/NOAA. It brings together partners from various research groups and institutions with the common goal of guiding and managing growth along the Texas coast in a sustainable and equitable manner.

In the later phase of the project, users will be able to query data and create custom maps based on multiple development scenarios. Communities can use this educational tool to guide future decisions about growth in a sustainable manner, such that the need for economic development is balanced with priorities associated with environmental protection and human health, safety, and welfare. The system will also help address important research questions related to where future growth will occur in Texas coastal zones, the impact of this growth, and the usefulness of Web geographic information systems (GISs) in facilitating sustainable planning.

Box 4.4. Participatory GIS

Contributed by Dr. Michelle Meyer

A participatory geographic information system (GIS) is a method of geospatial science and spatial planning that attempts to increase community participation in the production and use of geospatial information. This method targets the incorporation of disadvantaged or marginalized populations who normally lack access to such technologies.[a] With this public involvement, participatory GIS can be context- or issue-driven to advocate for specific concerns identified by participants. For example, community groups have used GIS to provide information to elected officials and community leaders in order to address housing stock improvement or livability and to map crime.[b]

Doing analysis and generating maps with GIS often involve expensive software and specialized expertise, which has generated critiques about the uneven access to GIS data, lack of diversity in knowledge incorporated in digital geospatial databases, and lack of participation in data creation and use. Participatory GIS works to democratize spatial data and GIS tools. This includes the integration of local knowledge with expert knowledge, allowing community groups to have control and ownership in the data that are created.[c]

The amount of public participation in these projects varies from input on expert-generated maps to creation of research questions and data sources. For example, community members hand drew polygons where various land uses occurred on professionally printed maps.[d] These printed maps were digitized and combined by professionals to delineate crucial conservation areas using local knowledge. In Minneapolis, a neighborhood group hired a GIS consultant to perform mapping based on their identified concerns. They mapped vacant housing and walkability using Global Positioning System (GPS) devices to determine which portion of the neighborhood would receive their limited improvement funds.[e] New developments in publicly available GIS tools, such as those in free smartphone or tablet applications, and training on how to upload geographic data allow people to produce maps and other data more easily. For example, recent research has developed smartphone apps that allow people to upload transportation information to assess commuting and livability in U.S. cities.[f] With smartphones, pictures, audio, and video can all be easily geocoded and uploaded to spatial databases. Even with new technologies, the emphasis remains on participation; thus, participatory GIS should be used as part of an empowering, respectful, and engaging public dialogue.[g]

a. McCall, Michael K. "Seeking Good Governance in Participatory-GIS: A Review of Processes and Governance Dimensions in Applying GIS to Participatory Spatial Planning." *Habitat International*, 2003: 549–73.

b. Craig, William J., and Sarah A. Elwood. "How and Why Community Groups Use Maps and Geographic Information." *Cartography and Geographic Information Systems*, 1998: 95–104.

c. Dunn, Christine E. "Participatory GIS--a People's GIS?" *Progress in Human Geography*, 2007: 616–37.

d. Ramirez-Gomez, Sara, and Christian Martinez. "Indigenous Communities in Suriname Identify Key Local Sites." *ArcNews*, n.d.

e. Craig, William J., and Sarah A. Elwood. "How and Why Community Groups Use Maps and Geographic Information." *Cartography and Geographic Information Systems*, 1998: 95–104.

f. Schlossberg, Marc, Cody Evers, Ken Kato, and Christo Brehm. "Active Transportation, Citizen Engagement and Liveability: Coupling Citizens and Smartphones to Make the Change." *Journal of the Urban & Regional Information Systems Association* 24, no. 2 (2012).

g. McCall, Michael K., and Peter A. Minang. "Assessing Participatory GIS for Community-Based Natural Resource Management: Claiming Community Forests in Cameroon." *Geographical Journal*, 2005: 340–56.

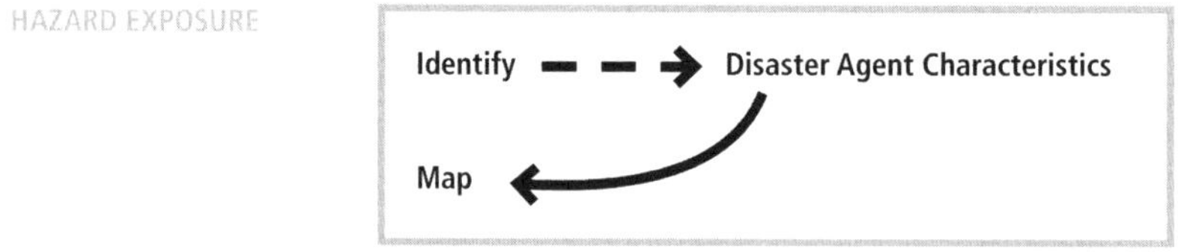

HAZARD EXPOSURE

Identify - - → Disaster Agent Characteristics

Map ←

Figure 4.4. First identify, then map hazard characteristics. For hazards that can be mapped, mapping can reveal patterns.

Exercise 3. Examining and Mapping Community Hazards

List the various hazards your community is exposed to. Look back over the past 100 years to determine the historical precedents of hazards in your community. Refer to resources online or in box 4.1. List your answers in the first column of table 4.1.

Table 4.1. Hazard Exposure

What Hazards Are You Exposed To?	Historical Precedents	What Are the Hazard Characteristics?	Hazard Effects	Priority Level
Example: hurricane	4 hurricanes over the last 100 years	Flooding and surge waters, high winds, high temperatures, tornadoes	Loss of electricity, reduced mobility limits access to resources, high demand and low staff in hospitals, limited access to clean drinking water	High

Determine the known hazard characteristics. Remember, from chapter 3, that hazard characteristics are characteristics that the hazard generates. For instance, the high winds and intense rainfall of a hurricane may lead to storm surge, exacerbating flooding. High winds could also cause trees to fall on power lines, resulting in a loss of electricity and reduced mobility as roadways are blocked by debris. As another example, if your community is exposed to drought, a characteristic could be high temperatures and lack of rainfall. It results in dust storms, reduced crop production, loss of green infrastructure and vegetation in urban areas, or limited access to clean, drinkable water sources. Each hazard should have several hazard characteristics associated with it. Add this information to table 4.1. Now think about the potential effects or consequences of these hazards in your community. What might occur as a result of the impact? Imagine possible scenarios and add your information to table 4.1.

Based on the information collected in table 4.1, fill in table 4.2. What is the likelihood of impact based on the historical precedents? What is the severity of impact based on the hazard exposure? Hazards that both are likely and have high impacts should be addressed first. We suggest you use the highest-priority hazards in the exercises and activities in the remaining chapters.

Table 4.2. Prioritize

	Not Likely	Very Likely
Low Impact		
High Impact		

Now that you've taken the time to brainstorm potential hazards and the associated hazardous components that will affect your community, take the time to analyze hazards that are most appropriately understood through the display of spatial information. For instance, all communities should have flood maps. If you have limited mapping capacity, select hazards that are appropriate to map on your prioritized list. You don't have to learn GIS in order to do this. There are many online mapping tools that can give you a picture of your exposure. Also, remember that this task may be most appropriate for a municipal staff, but it can also be used as a public participatory engagement tool. Engaging the public in mapping and identifying hazardous areas can be part of a public awareness campaign.

After you have completed this exercise and tables 4.1 and 4.2, look back over the information. Are there any hazards on this list that you did not realize your community was exposed to? Do you think your community will be concerned about or fearful of these data? Do you think your community will be skeptical of these data? Which hazards have occurred most often?

5. Assessing Physical Vulnerability

The fact basis for both hazard mitigation and comprehensive planning has long been based on hazard exposure and physical or structural vulnerability.[1] As discussed in chapter 4, hazard exposure is a function of the nature of the hazard agent and its potential to affect the geography of urban areas captured in risk maps. Physical or structural vulnerability, on the other hand, is a function of the location of the population and the built environment relative to the hazard. In other words, hazards become disasters when they interact with populated areas. When they strike communities, hazards interact with physical systems that include elements of the built and natural environment that are often taken for granted (figure 5.1). How often do we think about the pipes that carry our water or electricity? Do we ever consider the investment and value of wastewater or sewage facilities and the strength and integrity of our schools or fire stations? Thus, physical vulnerability is the susceptibility to damage and loss based on the interaction between exposure and physical characteristics. These include the following:

- Structures, namely homes and businesses
- Infrastructure, such as roads, water and sewer systems, and critical facilities
- The natural environment, often that which protects or buffers the community

Structures

In our ongoing example of Hurricane Ike, the primary forces of the hazard were winds,

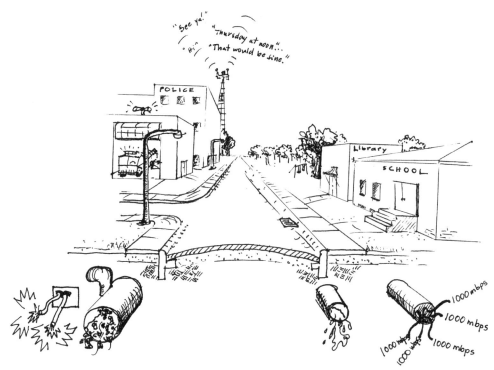

Figure 5.1. There are a number of physically vulnerable components that we often take for granted in our communities. The drawing portrays the variety of services communities provide that are invaluable during disaster impact, response, and recovery.

flooding, and surge. Hurricane Ike was unique in that it was only a Category 2 wind event, but its surge levels were equivalent to a much more powerful storm. To assess the physical vulnerability of Galveston, we needed to identify each structure's location relative to various flood zones. Of particular significance were locations in flood zone A, which represent 100-year flood zones, and flood zone V, which represent 100-year coastal flood zones likely to experience velocity or wave action (see box 4.2 in chapter 4).[2] The latter zones are those primarily subject to ocean surges associated with hurricanes, which not only are associated with major damage to structures because of the velocity and wave action but also are the major cause of death. Indeed, it was the surge associated with the 1900 storm that killed thousands. The extraordinary loss of life associated with the 1900 storm was one of the primary reasons Galveston undertook to build its now famous sea-wall as an attempt to prevent powerful ocean surges from ever entering the city again. The seawall is a classic example of structural mitigation, much like levees and dikes. All of these are considered infrastructure and are physically vulnerable themselves because of the risk to human life and property downstream in the event of a breach. In Hurricane

Katrina, more than 20,000 housing units were damaged by flood waters from breached levees in St. Bernard Parish.

Simply put, physical vulnerability results from the encroachment of urban growth into hazardous areas. For this reason, it is an area over which we have a lot of control. Indeed, cities and communities can directly influence a community's vulnerabilities because, in large part, they determine how and where a community builds. To assess our existing physical vulnerability, we must take into account the nature or characteristics of physical infrastructure and populations in terms of their susceptibility to impacts in light of the hazards to which they are exposed. The focus is on the quality and nature of construction (e.g., building codes, roof types, elevation, free-board) and on the location of critical facilities (e.g., hospitals, police stations) in particularly high-hazard areas.

In our hurricane example, damage can be a result of high winds that penetrate the envelope of a structure, storm surge that can flood interiors and scour foundations, or often a combination of both. Although the pathway may be different, both cases may result in various levels of damage ranging from superficial exterior damage to complete structural failure and destruction (figures 5.2 and 5.3). The characteristics of the structure—its roof, foundation, exterior materials, and standard of building—act in concert with these forces, resisting or succumbing to damage. Numerous characteristics have been identified as potential determinants of increased damage from a hurricane. For example, gabled roofs are more vulnerable to high winds, and hip roofs are the preferred type in hurricane-prone areas. Elevated homes on piers are also preferred, if not required for flood insurance, for areas that are prone to storm surge; they tend to suffer less damage than low-lying pier and beam structures or structures simply built on at-grade foundations. Like many communities, Galveston has examples of all forms of housing. Although some of its older housing is built using low-lying pier and beam foundations, much of that housing was raised using fill after the 1900 storm to increase its elevation. However, historic structures have a host of other vulnerabilities in disasters, as seen in box 5.1. That general pattern continued until the late 1950s, and especially in the 1960s and 1970s, when homes were built on simple slab-on-grade foundations (figures 5.2 and 5.3). Most newer homes (1980s onward) built outside the urban core and not protected by the seawall, toward the west end of Galveston Island, were built and elevated on 6-foot, 12-foot, and even higher piers.[3]

The changing nature of building customs, standards, and codes can be important for understanding physical vulnerabilities. Strong building codes, especially in hazard-prone areas, have shown repeatedly that they reduce damage from a range of hazards and are an important tool available to local communities for hazard mitigation.[4] Studies

Figure 5.2. Single-family housing destroyed on Galveston Island. (Credit: Shannon Van Zandt, *Destroyed Structure*, 2008.)

Figure 5.3. Multifamily housing destroyed on Galveston Island. (Credit: W. G. Peacock.)

Box 5.1. Galveston's Historic Properties

Galveston was first settled in 1816 and contains many historical gems for the state of Texas and the nation. There are many nationally registered historic buildings and sites on the island, which made recovery efforts particularly complex (figure 5.4). See the FEMA Standard Operating Procedures of the National Register of Historic Places Standard Section 106 for more information on how to handle historic properties after a disaster. All federal agencies must take into account the impact on historic properties based on Section 106 of the National Historic Preservation Act of 1966. The Advisory Council for Historic Preservation (ACHP) is an independent federal agency that advises the president and Congress on national historic policy. ACHP and other organizations have developed a Prototype Programmatic Agreement (PPA) to assist FEMA after a disaster. FEMA is still responsible for following the rules and regulations of Section 106, which can make disaster recovery difficult, tedious, and extensive. To learn more about ACHP, go to http://www.achp.gov. The following is a list of common historic preservation concerns in a disaster:

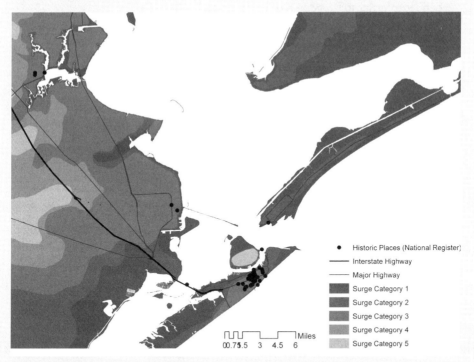

Legend:
- Historic Places (National Register)
- Interstate Highway
- Major Highway
- Surge Category 1
- Surge Category 2
- Surge Category 3
- Surge Category 4
- Surge Category 5

Miles
0 0.75 1.5   3   4.5   6

Figure 5.4. Historic places in surge zones. Hurricane surge zones 1–5 are shown overlaid with the National Register of Historic Places. Historic properties affected by disasters have recovery implications that municipalities and states should anticipate.

Predisaster Preparation

- Inventory historic properties and cultural resources, include periodic photographs of properties, and incorporate them into the geographic information system (GIS) if possible (figure 5.4).
- Determine whether expedited historic preservation review procedures are warranted, particularly if there are not strong administrative approval policies.
- Integrate historic preservation into local emergency management processes.

Postdisaster Concerns

- Restorable buildings are torn down.
- Irreplaceable and significant architectural elements that could be salvaged are removed as debris.
- Historic trees are destroyed rather than salvaged or replanted.
- Property owners make hurried decisions, resulting in inappropriate repairs.
- Archaeological resources are damaged or disturbed by heavy equipment.
- Normal design review procedures for changes to historic properties may be suspended in order to expedite repairs.
- Construction applications may overburden officials, because there may be insufficient staff to carefully review all the applications.
- Inspections of damage or repairs to historic structures may be carried out by people without appropriate qualifications with respect to the preservation of historic structures.

Source: Nelson, Carl L. *Protecting the Past from Natural Disasters.* Washington, DC: Preservation Press, National Trust for Historic Preservation, 1991.

after Miami's Hurricane Andrew found problems not only with code enforcement but also with the changing nature of the code itself.[5] The Miami area had experienced many powerful storms in the early twentieth century. In response, homes built during the early part of the century generally took these hazards into consideration because of custom and general knowledge of local builders and later because of official building standards and codes. However, beginning in the later part of the century, with the housing boom in Miami and national building firms moving into the area, the building code changed as newer building styles and materials were introduced. The result was a weakening of the building code, which, coupled with low enforcement, results in tragic consequences. Galveston, on the other hand, has had a long history of diverse building customs on the island. From interviews with planners and building officials it appears that building practices were generally good during the early part of the century but became weaker, particularly during the midcentury, when much of the slab-on-grade construction was allowed.[6] More recently, Galveston has had some of the strongest building standards and codes in Texas (figure 5.5).

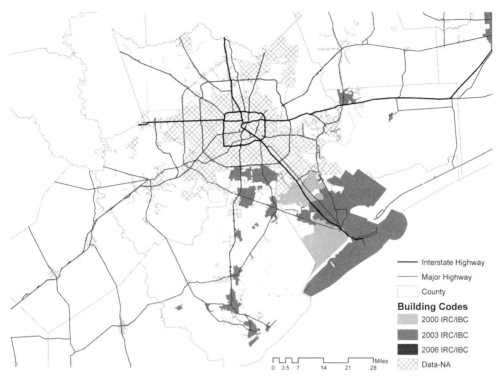

Figure 5.5. This map shows the spatial variation of building codes along the coast in the Houston area. You can see the patchwork nature of building codes in and around Houston, which results in different physical impacts. A higher standard of building codes can reduce a structure's risk of certain hazards. IRC, International Residential Code; IBC, International Building Code.

In our research,[7] we found that many of our expectations about factors related to physical vulnerability were borne out. We found that the seawall performed well as a structural mitigation technique: Homes and businesses that were located behind it were protected from severe damage, whereas those on the bay side of the island sustained much more damage. Structures located in Zone V and Zone A suffered significantly higher levels of damage, net of other factors, than housing not in these zones (see box 4.2 in chapter 4 for flood zone definitions). As expected, housing located in Zone V sustained significantly higher levels of damage than housing in Zone A. Businesses were also affected, and employment centers or work locations should certainly be identified, assessed, and even mapped within hazard zones because they can be a significant factor in recovery (see box 5.2).[8]

Potentially a very useful tool [handwritten margin note]

Box 5.2. Examining the Patterns of Workers' Home and Job Locations Before and After a Major Coastal Hurricane: The Longitudinal Employer–Household Dynamics (LEHD) Database

The LEHD Database is a new publicly available longitudinal dataset. The data provide information about where workers are employed and where they live, via the U.S. Census Bureau's OnTheMap (OTM) interactive Web service. OTM also provides labor characteristics (age, salary, industrial types) and sociodemographic characteristics (race and ethnicity, educational attainment, and sex). The service is based on LEHD Origin–Destination Employment Statistics (LODES) data Version 6.0, which is enumerated by 2010 census blocks. The data are synthetic data that have been "fuzzed," particularly at the lower resolutions (i.e., block group and block levels).

You can use the data on OTM service with GIS to map workers' job and home locations with hazard risk zones from before and after a disaster.[a] This particular example shows the locations of employment in Galveston, Texas, and the surge zones (figure 5.6). This is a rather simple example that a community could easily create with OTM to determine the physical vulnerability of work locations.

a. http://lehd.ces.census.gov/doc/help/onthemap/OnTheMapDataOverview.pdf.

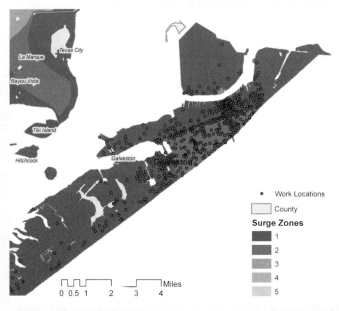

Figure 5.6. The data in this map were taken from OnTheMap, indicating work locations on Galveston Island. You can quickly and easily use this online tool to assess the physical vulnerability of businesses in your area.

The structural characteristics of homes had important consequences for damage from Hurricane Ike. The higher the elevation of the home, the less damage it suffered, with other factors held constant. The age of the home showed perhaps the most interesting relationship in our analysis. We might expect that the older the home, the worse the damage. However, our findings suggest that not only did a cultural tradition of building in less risky areas deteriorate over time, but structural characteristics suited for coastal development did as well, at least until 1958. The decreasing levels of damage during the home age period 1958 to 1911 suggest that this cultural memory of how and where to build appropriately was intact. Increasing levels of damage moving from 2008 to 1958 suggest development patterns resulting from ignorance of appropriate techniques and locations instead of continued construction of resilient housing that can withstand wind, surge, and flooding. The apparent disregard for previously understood construction practices may reflect growth pressures that ultimately placed more households in harm's way. Construction requirements in the form of building codes probably play a role as well.

Critical Infrastructure

Physical vulnerability assessments must also consider infrastructure and critical facilities that represent lifelines, such as bridges, utilities, water, sewer, power, communications, fire and police stations, hospitals, post offices, radio stations, and schools. The presence of these facilities in hazardous areas represents significant vulnerability.[9] Critical facilities are an important component for emergency response and disaster recovery. These essential facilities should not be placed in hazardous areas. To better understand the most physically vulnerable places in your community, overlay the probability of hazard exposure (chapter 4) with critical structures and facilities. Critical infrastructure includes the following:

- Roads
- Bridges
- Dams
- Levees
- Electricity
- Oil and gas, or other energy infrastructure
- Water
- Phone and Internet
- Hospitals
- Schools
- Fire stations
- Police stations
- Nursing homes

- Emergency shelters
- Key commercial and industrial buildings
- Residences

In Galveston, a whole host of critical facilities went down. The city was without power, gas, telecommunications, sewage, and water for more than two weeks, and residents were not allowed to return to their homes for 10 days, causing significant health and safety problems related to mold resulting from wet materials sitting in the late summer heat. The loss of critical infrastructure ultimately increased the level of property damage and loss because the delayed return rendered interiors and contents unsalvageable.

Many communities already have critical facilities and infrastructure in their GIS maps. If you do not have this capability, it can easily be done in Google Maps, Yahoo Maps, or mapping tools such as the Texas Coastal Planning Atlas or tools identified by the American Planning Association (APA).[10] Overlaying these maps, either in a GIS or on hard copy, with hazard maps like those discussed in chapter 4 will identify which critical facilities are located in hazardous areas, along with the probability that they will be affected by a particular type of hazard (figure 5.7).

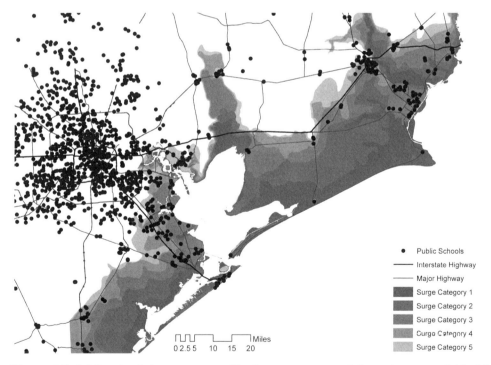

Figure 5.7. Public schools in surge zones. Hurricane surge zones 1–5 are shown overlaid with public schools. You can see the devastating effect of a hurricane along the upper Texas coast if mitigation measures are not taken.

Box 5.3. Protecting Natural Resources

For greater resilience, communities should practice "avoiding riverbanks and riparian areas, and requiring better and more effective storm water management measures for new development" (Beatley, 2000, p. 8). The more impervious surfaces there are in an area, the fewer opportunities for water penetration and storage in the soil. Every square meter of impervious surface in a floodplain results in more than $3,600 in added property damage by floods per year (Brody, Zahran, et al., 2007). A watershed that is less than 10 percent impervious is thought to be "sensitive" (Randolph, 2003). A watershed that is between 10 percent and 25 percent impervious is "impacted," and a watershed that is more than 25 percent impervious is considered to be "non-supporting" (Randolph, 2003). Guiding development away from floodplains is an ecological and economic strategy that will lead to greater resilience.

Tools for identifying natural resources include the following:

LandScope America (www.landscope.org) is an interactive mapping tool developed by NatureServe and the National Geographic Society. This map displays protected areas, conservation priorities, threats, plants and animals, ecosystems, energy, recreation, etc.

NOAA's Coastal Change Analysis Program (C-CAP) (http://www.csc.noaa.gov/ccapat las/) is a Web-based tool that uses multiple datasets and remote-sensed imagery to produce standardized land cover changes. You can view, share, and download developed, forested, and wetland areas, among other land types. Data are available from 1996, 2001, and 2006 so that growth and development can be monitored over time.

Natural Infrastructure

Physical vulnerability also encompasses the natural environment. The protection of the natural environment provides environmental services that, in turn, can reduce physical vulnerability (see box 5.3). For example, wetlands trap floodwaters, remove pollution, and recharge groundwater supplies. They also function as economic drivers in coastal communities because of the natural habitat they provide that attracts fishing, hunting, agriculture, and recreation. Similarly, forests trap carbon from the atmosphere, protect watersheds, help regulate the water cycle and climate, and recycle nutrients, among other things. Biodiversity, the variety of plants and animals in an ecosystem, helps with soil protection, hydrological functions, crop pollination, and pest control, as well as recreation and tourism. Put simply, the natural environment and the functions it serves offers protection from hazards; when we destroy or compromise it, we are increasing our vulnerability.

A resilient community allows natural environmental protective systems to be conserved. Unfortunately, there has been growing debate over the conservation of ecosystems

Box 5.4: Koontz v. St. Johns River Water Management District

Petitioner Coy Koontz applied for a wetland permit to develop 3.7 acres of wetlands on his Florida property. To mitigate environmental impacts, he offered to establish another 11 acres of the property as a conservation easement. St. Johns River Management District denied the permit, stipulating that only 1 acre of wetlands would be permissible for development, or an exaction in the form of payment to improve a separate property miles away would be imposed. The Supreme Court ruled in 2013 that this was a taking of land because the exaction was not a "rational nexus," nor was it "roughly proportional." The court upheld previous rulings that an exaction may be imposed only if it is rationally connected to the needs of the development that creates a burden on the public and is roughly proportional to the burden imposed on the public. In doing so, this case made waves by limiting local government controls on land and placing more authority on private property rights. It certainly begs the question of what governments can do to protect dwindling wetlands and environmentally sensitive areas.

and private property rights in recent years (see box 5.4).[11] "Efforts to constrain natural variability [lead] to self-simplification and so to fragility of the ecosystem," increased ecological vulnerability, and decreased resiliency in the region.[12] Preserving "large, intact patches of native vegetation" or riparian corridors and floodplains should take priority. Conserving environmentally sensitive lands can provide hydrological systems appropriate amounts of land to absorb flood impacts.[13] As new development occurs, in the form of buildings, roads, and bridges, we must assess its impact on ecosystem functions.

One way to decrease the impact of disasters on communities is to formulate policies that discourage growth in disaster-prone areas. Natural physical characteristics that are environmentally sensitive and should be protected include the following:

- Wetlands
- Freshwater sources
- Large stands of trees
- Oyster reefs
- Coral reefs
- Conservation areas
- Dunes and barrier islands

It is important to identify and map the areas in your community that are considered physically vulnerable (figure 5.8). Physical vulnerabilities include structures, critical infrastructure, and natural infrastructure that are key to the proper functioning of the community.

Exercise 4 will walk you through techniques to identify and map physical vulnerabilities.

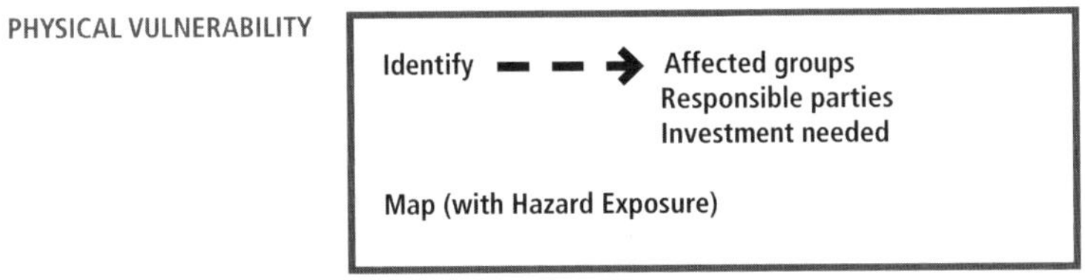

PHYSICAL VULNERABILITY

Identify - - → Affected groups
Responsible parties
Investment needed

Map (with Hazard Exposure)

Figure 5.8. Identify components of physical vulnerability and create a map overlaid with hazard exposures.

Exercise 4. Which Structures Are Vulnerable?

If you were able to create a hazard exposure map, as discussed in chapter 5, use it to overlay the building footprints in your community. It is also useful to overlay land use to determine specifically how many households, businesses, and other structures are expected to be affected. Often, patterns emerge through this process. Are businesses more affected than housing? Are multifamily housing units more affected than single-family homes? Take time to thoroughly analyze the data. Input your assessment into table 5.1.

Table 5.1. Physical Vulnerabilities List: Hurricanes

Structures	Groups Affected	Who's Responsible If Affected?	Need Investment?
Example: Primarily businesses along the coast	Tourism-related industries, port authorities, marina organizations, fisheries businesses	Business owners	Yes. Some are dilapidated.
Critical Infrastructure	Groups Affected	Who's Responsible If Affected?	Need Investment?
Natural Infrastructure	Groups Affected	Who's Responsible If Affected?	Need Investment?

- Identify structures by location and land use type.
- Identify all critical infrastructure in your community.

- Identify all natural infrastructure in your community, including state and national parks, wildlife refuges, and forested areas.

Are there specific groups in these areas that will be more affected? Who is ultimately responsible for the structure if affected? What investment is needed? Add that information to table 5.1.

If you do not have the capability to use mapping software, you can use Web mapping services (e.g., Google, Yahoo) to pinpoint the location of structures in relation to hazards developed in the previous chapter. We have found that even mapping in this way can provide some insight into knowing your community; of course, GIS is preferred. As discussed in chapter 4, some hazard types may not be appropriate to assess spatially. In this case, complete this exercise, thinking holistically about your community. This may take more time because you will complete an inventory of the entire community.

6. Assessing Social Vulnerability

A critical piece, and often the most neglected piece, of resilience to disaster is the identification and mapping of a community's social vulnerabilities. When disaster strikes, its impact is not just a function of its magnitude and where it strikes. Development patterns characterized by sprawl, concentrated poverty, and segregation shape urban environments in ways that isolate vulnerable populations so that poor and rich, white and black, owners and renters, primary residents and vacationers, are separated from one another in clusters and pockets across the community. In many communities, if not most, the social geography interacts with the physical geography to expose vulnerable populations to greater risk. Vulnerable populations are less likely to have access to both information and resources that would allow them to anticipate and respond to a real or perceived threat, yet they are more often than not the groups who most need to attend to warnings to evacuate or seek shelter.

Community vulnerability, in its broadest sense, describes the susceptibility of a community or, importantly, its constituent parts to the harmful impacts of disasters. The foundation of vulnerability analysis, a hazard assessment, generally focuses on a community's exposure to hazard agents such as floods, surge, wave action, or winds.[1] Such assessments identify the potential exposure of populations, businesses, and the built environment (housing, infrastructure, critical facilities, and so on). Also important are the physical characteristics of the built environment, as described in chapter 5, such as wind design features of buildings and the height of structures relative to potential floods, as well as natural and engineered environmental features such as wetlands, dams, levees or seawalls, because they can modify vulnerabilities and concomitant risk. As disaster and hazard researchers critically examine the nature and distribution of disaster impacts and the factors shaping the variability in exposure and access to technology that can mitigate impacts (e.g., shutters, impact-resistant glazing), it has become clear that more than just hazard exposure and the built and natural environment shape vulnerability. A new perspective began to emerge suggesting that social structures and processes also shape vulnerability, hence the term *social vulnerability* (SV).[2]

Variation in existing vulnerabilities influences the exposure of households, businesses, and communities to effects from natural hazards and the capacity and resources available to respond to and recover from disasters. In other words, disasters are not equal-opportunity events; they affect different groups in different ways. Whereas some can easily anticipate and respond to hazard threats, others find it more difficult, if not impossible, even if they know about them and want to respond. As a result, in the aftermath recovery can be highly uneven, with some parts of a community recovering quickly while others lag behind. The uneven nature of recovery can jeopardize the overall vitality and resiliency of a community and bring into question its future.

Here we focus on how social factors influence the ability of communities and their populations (individuals and households) to anticipate, respond, resist, and recover from disasters. Undertaking a spatial analysis of social vulnerability should be a critical element in emergency management, hazard mitigation, and disaster recovery planning, helping communities reduce losses, enhance response and recovery, and thereby strengthen community resilience.

Social vulnerability is defined as "the characteristics of a person or group in terms of their capacity to anticipate, cope with, resist and recover from the impacts of a natural hazard."[3] A social vulnerability perspective focuses attention on the characteristics and diversity of populations in terms of broader social, cultural, and economic factors that shape abilities to anticipate future events, respond to warnings, and cope with and recover from disaster impacts. While the social vulnerability literature continues to grow, it has identified a number of individual and household characteristics that influence one's ability to act at every stage of disaster. Very often, these factors are present in combinations, which can exacerbate vulnerability.[4] These factors may include the following:

- Race and ethnicity (see box 6.1)
- Gender
- Household composition
- Education

- Poverty (see box 6.1)
- Age
- Housing tenure

Box 6.1. The Everyday Disasters of Low-Income and Racial Minority Groups

The following regularly affect low-income and minority groups and are magnified in times of disaster:

- Housing markets systematically fail when it comes to providing low-income housing, which disproportionately affects racial and ethnic minorities.[a]
- Racial and ethnic minorities: tend to have poorer quality of housing, and that housing is often segregated into low-valued neighborhoods, creating "communities of fate."[b]
- The United States still has major problems with discrimination against minorities in buying, selling, and renting housing in the form of racial steering, redlining, attitudes, and lender discrimination.[c]
- Blacks experience higher mortgage rejection rates, pay higher interest rates (including subprime mortgages), are more likely to be subject to predatory lending practices, and, after buying a home, experience lower appreciation rates.[d]
- Minorities, particularly blacks, also have major problems procuring insurance, particularly high-quality insurance.[e]

a. Lake, R. W., "Racial Transition and Black Homeownership in American Suburbs," on *America's Housing*, edited by G. Sternlieb and J. W. Hughes, 419–38, New Brunswick, NJ: Center for Urban Policy Research, 1980; Bratt, R., C. Hartman, and A. Meyerson, *Critical Perspectives on Housing*, Philadelphia: Temple University Press, 1986; Horton, H. D., "Race and Wealth: A Demographic Analysis of Black Homeownership," *Sociological Inquiry* , 1992: 480–89; Alba, Richard D., and John R. Logan, "Analyzing Locational Attainments: Constructing Individual-Level Regression Models Using Aggregate Data," *Sociological Methods and Research* (Sociological Methods and Research) 20 (1992): 367–97; Gyourko, J., and P. Linneman, "The Affordability of the American Dream: An Examination of the Last 30 Years," *Journal of Housing Research* 4, no. 1 (1993): 39–72.

b. Logan, J. R., and H. Molotch, *Urban Fortunes: The Political Economy of Place.* Berkeley: University of California Press, 1987; South, S. J., and K. D. Crowder, "Escaping Distressed Neighborhoods: Individual, Community, and Metropolitan Influences," *American Journal of Sociology* 102 (1997): 1040–84.

c. Guy, R .F., L. G. Pol, and R. Ryker, "Discrimination in Mortgage Lending: The Mortgage Disclosure Act," *Population Research and Policy Review*, 1982: 283–96; Sagalyn, Lynne B., "Mortgage Lending in Older Urban Neighborhoods: Lessons from Past Experience," *Annals of the American Academy of Political and Social Science* 465 (1983): 98–108; Horton, "Race and Wealth"; Feagin, J. R., and M. P. Sikes, *Living with Racism: The Black Middle Class Experience*, Boston: Beacon, 1994; Oliver, M., and T. Shapiro; *Black Wealth/White Wealth: A New Perspective on Racial Inequality*, New York: Routledge, 1997; Holloway, Steven R., and Elvin K. Wyly, "'The Color of Money' Expanded: Geographically Contingent Mortgage Lending in Atlanta," *Journal of Housing Research* 12, no. 1

(2001): 55–90; Shapiro, T. M., *The Hidden Cost of Being African American: How Wealth Perpetuates Inequality*, Oxford, England: Oxford University Press, 2004; Squires, Gregory D., and Sunwoong Kim, "'Does Anybody Who Works Here Look Like Me?' Mortgage Lending, Race, and Lender Employment," *Social Science Quarterly* 76, no. 4 (1995): 821–38.

d. Oliver and T. Shapiro, *Black Wealth/White Wealth*; Flippen, Chenoa, "Unequal Returns to Housing Investments? A Study of Real Housing Appreciation among Black, White, and Hispanic Households," *Social Forces* (University of North Carolina Press) 82, no. 4 (June 2004): 1523–51.

e. Squires, G. D., and W. Velez, "Insurance Redlining and the Transformation of an Urban Metropolis," *Urban Affairs Quarterly*, 1987: 63–83; Squires, G. D., "Why an Insurance Regulation for Prohibit Redlining?," *John Marshall Law Review*, 1998: 489–511; Squires, G. D., S. O'Connor, and J. Silver, "The Unavailability of Information on Insurance Unavailability: Insurance Redlining and the Absence of Geocoded Disclosure Data," *Housing Policy Debate*, 2001: 347–72.

Policies and practices related to disaster response often assume that all residents of an area have the same information and the same resources and ability to act on that information. Furthermore, they assume that all residents will react in the same way. However, vulnerability factors can influence access to and knowledge of resources (physical, financial, and social), control of these resources, and perceived or real power in the larger community or society. They may also influence the capacity of the individual or household to act (figure 6.1). For example, African Americans often rely on social connections rather than media or government to obtain information about threats or hazards.[5] Even if a resident has the same information, he or she may not have the capacity (a car, for example) to evacuate in a timely manner. Renters are typically more mobile or transient and may not have local family connections to facilitate evacuation or sheltering, whereas owners are more likely to have such resources. As a result of these differences, responses to disasters may be quite disparate.

People and households vary in their capacity to anticipate, cope with, respond to, and recover from disasters. Furthermore, they are not randomly distributed in space but rather are concentrated in fairly predictable spatial patterns based on household characteristics. As a consequence, we can develop mapping tools to identify areas with higher concentrations of socially vulnerable populations (see box 6.2).

Understanding these patterns helps us identify areas where resources and information may need to be targeted, depending on the social vulnerability factor. Table 6.1 identifies the most common social vulnerability factors, along with a description of how the factor makes a household vulnerable.

Our approach to social vulnerability mapping is intended to be conducive to community-based planning. We use readily available data from secondary sources such as the

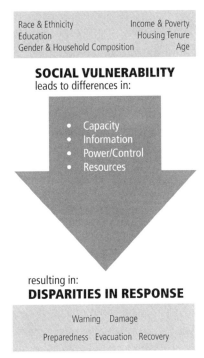

Figure 6.1. Social vulnerability characteristics, such as race and ethnicity, education, gender and household composition, income and poverty, housing tenure, and age, all lead to differences in capacity, information, power and control, and resources. Ultimately, this results in disparities in response to warning, damage, preparedness, evacuation, and recovery. Because of these relationships, we must address social vulnerability in planning and the disproportionality that exists.

U.S. Census to allow broad application of the technique to all communities while providing sufficiently fine resolution to allow planners and emergency managers to easily identify more or less homogeneous pockets of socially vulnerable populations. The logical census units that might be applied to parts of a community are census blocks, block groups, or tracts. Although tracts offer rich social and economic data to measure dimensions of social vulnerability, they also tend to be quite large, often encompassing multiple neighborhoods that can be quite heterogeneous. Although blocks are quite small and homogeneous, the data available are far too limited to capture many social vulnerability dimensions. Block groups are a viable compromise between data availability and spatial scale.

Figure 6.2 displays the seventeen indicators (far left) used to identify socially vulnerable populations. These indicators are considered first-order indicators and include a range of factors related to household structure, age, transportation, housing characteristics, minority status, poverty, educational status, employment status, and language skills. We transformed each of these indicators into a proportion (ranging from 0 to 1) by dividing

Box 6.2. Tools for Identifying Socially Vulnerable Populations

The National Oceanic and Atmospheric Administration (NOAA) has developed an interactive map that models sea level rise against a number of factors. The Web tool displays socioeconomic vulnerability: http://www.csc.noaa.gov/slr/viewer/.

Digital Coast, NOAA Coastal Services, http://csc.noaa.gov/digitalcoast/dataregistry /#/, displays hundreds of maps on hazard vulnerability, natural vulnerability, and social vulnerability.

NOAA's State of the Coast displays population data for coastal counties in the United States. It also provides important information on coastal communities, economies, ecosystems, climate, and more: http://stateofthecoast.noaa.gov/population/welcome.html.

The U.S. Census Bureau Center for Economic Studies has developed a Web mapping tool for communities to better understand their economies. OnTheMap (http://onthemap .ces.census.gov/) lets you evaluate the primary industries and the inflow and outflow of your community, among other things.

The Texas Planning Atlas, as discussed in chapter 4, provides social vulnerability indicators as described in this chapter. Currently, the atlas covers only coastal counties, but we anticipate "lighting up" the whole state in the near future: http://texasatlas.arch .tamu.edu/.

by an appropriate base to facilitate their comparability across census block groups, and in each case, the closer to 1 a block group's proportion, the higher the concentration of vulnerable groups displaying the characteristic of interest in that block group. The advantage of having individual social vulnerability dimensions or measures available to map at the local level is that planners can easily identify and perhaps focus on particular types of vulnerabilities given specific hazard risks.

The real benefit of being able to identify areas that are physically and socially vulnerable for planning purposes is being able to overlap these data so that areas can be identified as being critically vulnerable and hence the focus of emergency management and mitigation activities. For example, figure 6.3a displays areas with high concentrations of minorities (nonwhite). Figure 6.3b shows the concentrations of populations that are also subject to Category 1 and 2 storm surge. In light of the literature that suggest that these populations are less trusting of authorities when it comes to heeding warnings and are more dependent on social networks, local emergency management and planning officials might develop special relationships with churches and civic organizations in these areas to ensure that when official warnings are released, these organizations can reinforce the warnings through informal networks, increasing timely compliance.

Table 6.1. Common Social Vulnerability Factors

Household structure	Larger families, particularly those with a high number of dependents relative to income earners, are more vulnerable, as are single-parent, particularly female-headed households.
Socioeconomic status	A higher level of wealth, income, prestige, and political power increases the ability to prepare for, mitigate against, and cope with physical impacts. Higher-income households are more likely to have insurance and savings with which to initiate and complete recovery.
Gender	Women have a more difficult time in recovery because of limited employment opportunities and lower wages; they often must take primary responsibility for child care and household activities.
Race and ethnicity	Language, culture, and discrimination influence social vulnerability.
Age (older adults and children)	Both young and old are at higher risk because of their reduced mobility, economic constraints, and legal constraints. Households with these higher-risk groups can be limited by time and resource constraints.
Tenure	Renters are more transient, with fewer resources and less control, and are more dependent on property owners for improvements, repairs, and mitigation.
Urban or rural	Rural residents are more vulnerable because of their isolation, tend to have fewer employment opportunities, and are poorer.
Special needs populations	These include the sick, infirm, and disabled.
Employment status	Those who are unemployed or underemployed have fewer resources to draw on.

Figure 6.4 displays another example of layering hazard exposure with social vulnerability characteristics. By taking one first-order indicator, "households without vehicles," we can begin to understand which resources are needed in times of emergency. When this social vulnerability indicator is overlaid by hurricane risk zones, it's not difficult to understand the devastating impact Hurricane Ike had on Galveston and surrounding areas.

These basic first-order indicators can be combined to form second-order social

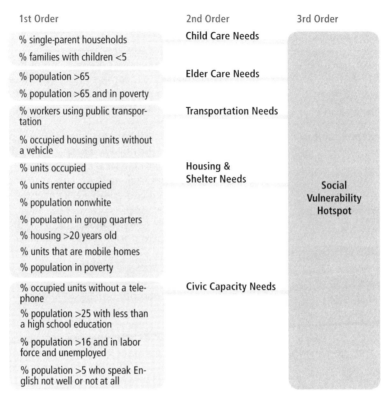

Figure 6.2. This figure displays the seventeen social vulnerability indicators, or first-order indicators. Each of these indicators is included in the second-order indicators: child care needs, elder care needs, transportation needs, housing and shelter needs, and civic capacity needs. When all five second-order indicators exist in a geographic area, it is a hotspot of social vulnerability and will probably experience many of the disparities described.

vulnerability measures indicating special needs that might be relevant during emergency response or disaster recovery (figure 6.2). For example, we develop second-order measures to identify areas with higher potential for child care needs, elder needs, transportation needs, temporary shelter and housing recovery needs, and civic capacity. Any number of second-order social vulnerability measures might be created, depending on the particular focus or emergency functions of interest. Figure 6.5 combines the percentage of workers who use public transportation and the percentage of occupied housing units without vehicles to create the second-order indicator "transportation needs." Imagine this analysis performed on areas affected by Hurricane Sandy in the northeastern United States. In this case, where a significant portion of the population may be considered as having "transportation needs," there may be other indicators yet to be collected by the Census Bureau that can be used to capture the more fine-grained detail needed in that local context. Figure 6.6

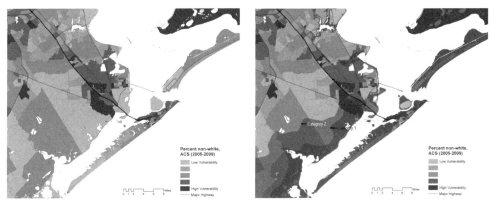

Figure 6.3. *(a)* Spatial distribution of nonwhite population. *(b)* Spatial distribution of the nonwhite population intersected with hurricane surge zones for Category 1 and Category 2 storms. We can see how populations become more vulnerable to this hazard exposure, which can help in decision making and prioritization of resources.

displays surge zones 1 and 2 with the second-order indicator "housing and shelter needs," which combines seven of the first-order indicators in figure 6.2: percentage of occupied units, renter-occupied units, nonwhite population, population living in group quarters, housing more than 20 years old, units that are mobile homes, and population in poverty. Again, we can see the areas that will need significant resources and assistance.

Finally, by simply adding all seventeen indicators, we can create a combined or composite social vulnerability score, pointing to high levels or hotspot concentrations of social vulnerability within and across block groups in a community. Of course, it is possible for a block group to have a very high proportion of socially vulnerable populations (e.g., more than 80 percent who are minorities and are also older adults living in poverty) but very few people living in the block group. To correct for this discrepancy, a weighted social vulnerability measure can be calculated in which the score is weighted by the population density of the block group. In this way, a block group that has a high social vulnerability score and is densely populated will score higher than one that has a similar social vulnerability score but is sparsely populated.

Figure 6.7 displays the weighted social vulnerability composite measure overlaid with Category 1 and 2 surge zones. The weighted social vulnerability measure is particularly useful for quickly identifying areas that have the highest concentrations of socially vulnerable populations. These areas might be useful for urban search and rescue as well as emergency health officials in order to quickly visit and focus attention after a disaster to determine whether there are stranded people or those needing special medical attention.

Because of our research in Galveston after Hurricane Ike, we were able to ground-truth

Figure 6.4. *(a)* Category 1–5 hurricane risk zones. *(b)* Households without vehicles (first-order social vulnerability indicator). *(c)* Intersection of households without vehicles *(a)* and Category 1 and 2 hurricane risk zones. *(d)* Intersection of households without vehicles *(a)* and Category 1–5 hurricane risk zones *(b)*. The darkest areas have high rates of households without vehicles or are in hurricane risk areas and have high rates of households without vehicles. These areas are hotspots of evacuation and response efforts. You can see the greater exposure *(c, d)* to large geographic areas and significant social vulnerability hotspots as the hurricane risk marches inland.

many of the theories in the literature. Figure 6.8 displays the severity of damage sustained on Galveston Island and Bolivar Peninsula after the storm.

The urban core of Galveston, behind the historic seawall (A in figure 6.8), consists of many lower-quality homes that are elevated only a foot or less off the ground, if at all. Poorly constructed homes slid off foundations, or structural systems just collapsed (figure 6.9a). In figure 6.9d, we can see that this area has the highest social vulnerability on the island. In contrast, the West End of Galveston Island (B in figure 6.8), which consists primarily of vacation homes, experienced less damage, with many structures elevated well above surge levels (figure 6.9b). Bolivar Peninsula (C in figure 6.8) received widespread damage and devastation from surge waters. Many homes were wiped clean away

Figure 6.5. Second-order social vulnerability indicator "transportation needs" is overlaid with hurricane zones for Category 1 and 2 storms. We can see large geographic areas in Galveston and the Houston metropolitan area with high transportation needs. You can see how the transportation needs change from figure 6.4, which displays only one of the two indicators that make up the second-order transportation needs indicator.

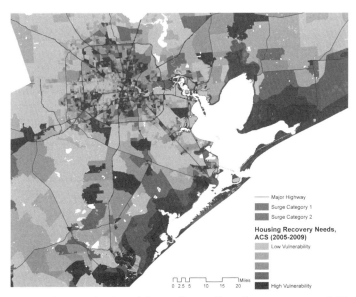

Figure 6.6. Second-order social vulnerability indicator "housing recovery needs" is overlaid with surge zones for Category 1 and 2 storms. We can see large geographic areas that are high in housing needs and those that intersect surge zones. Communities should prioritize these areas by developing assistance programs and guide new development away from these vulnerable areas.

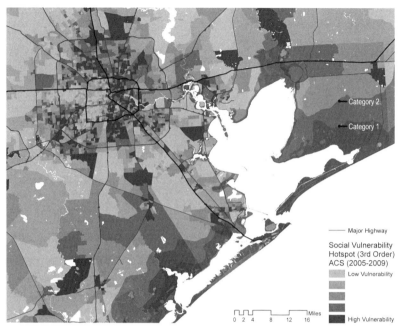

Figure 6.7. The third-order social vulnerability indicator, the total of all seventeen first-order indicators.

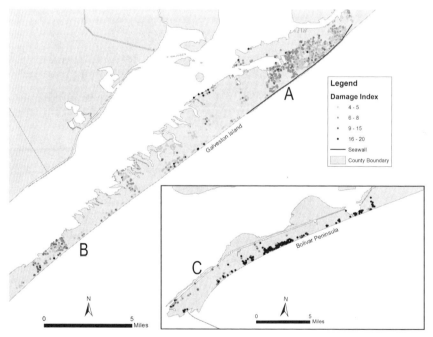

Figure 6.8. Damage index of Hurricane Ike. The map displays the severity of damage on Galveston Island and Bolivar Peninsula after the storm. (Map created by Wesley E. Highfield.)

Figure 6.9. *(a)* In the urban core of Galveston, many lower-quality homes are elevated only a foot or less off the ground, if at all. Here, a poorly constructed home has slid off its foundation, and the other structural systems have also collapsed. (Credit: Shannon Van Zandt, 2008.) *(b)* In contrast, a West End vacation home sits well above the surge level. A block off the Gulf Coast, these high-quality homes sustained only wind damage, which, as seen here, was minimal. (Credit: Shannon Van Zandt, *West End*, 2008.) *(c)* Bolivar Peninsula sustained widespread damage and devastation due to surge waters. Many homes were wiped clean away because they were not built above FEMA base flood elevations. This home is left standing in a neighborhood destroyed by Hurricane Ike. (Credit: Jocelyn Augustino, FEMA, 2008.) *(d)* Compare the social vulnerability with the damage index in figure 6.8. You can see that many of the least socially vulnerable areas suffered the least amount of damage. The urban core and downtown *(a)* are particularly socially vulnerable, and so the impacts in this area will be longer lasting, with slow recovery rates.

because they were not built above FEMA base flood elevations (figure 6.9c). Today, many of the homes on Bolivar Peninsula have been rebuilt, whereas homes in the urban core of Galveston (A in figure 6.8) are still struggling to recover. Although Bolivar Peninsula sustained a majority of the damage in Hurricane Ike, the disparities in recovery are apparent as you drive along the island today and on the social vulnerability map in figure 6.9d.

Conclusion

Resilience implies the ability to resist or absorb impacts and rapidly bounce back from those impacts. In the case of natural disasters and social systems, this implies the ability to prepare, respond, withstand the disaster impacts without major damage, and, most importantly, bounce back from the impact sustained. But when addressing communities, the picture is often far more complex because communities are composed of networks of businesses, government organizations, and, most importantly, households and families living in areas that make up a complex mosaic of socially defined neighborhoods. These neighborhoods are not the same, nor are they equal-opportunity venues. They can be as different as night and day in terms of their socioeconomic composition, the quality and types of housing, and their access and ability to mobilize resources when bad things happen. In a very real sense, social vulnerability mapping reveals disparities that make a difference when it comes to the capacity of residents and households to respond, mobilize resources, and bounce back from natural or other types of disasters.

A social vulnerability mapping approach is a method of identifying target areas likely to experience particular response and recovery needs (figures 6.10 and 6.11). Using social vulnerability mapping in conjunction with hazard maps and physical vulnerability maps, communities can greatly facilitate planning for disaster response, recovery, and mitigation. With this approach we can better plan for and monitor our community vulnerabilities and thereby develop more comprehensive planning approaches that can increase long-term community resiliency.

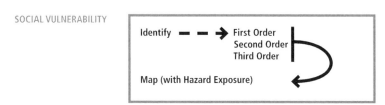

Figure 6.10. Identify first-order, second-order, and third-order social vulnerability characteristics and then map them to understand patterns in your community.

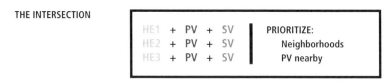

Figure 6.11. The intersection. Overlay hazard exposures (HE), physical vulnerability (PV), and social vulnerability (SV) in a map. From there, you can begin to prioritize neighborhoods and physically vulnerability elements nearby.

Exercise 5. Collecting First-Order Data

Begin by collecting data from the American Fact Finder developed by the U.S. Census Bureau (http://factfinder2.census.gov/faces/nav/jsf/pages/index.xhtml). Each of the first-order indicators can be gathered on this website and through census data sources (figure 6.2). Gather these data at the block group level and transform them into proportions by dividing by the population, number of housing units, or number of occupied units, as appropriate. Once you obtain this information for your community, you should compare the percentages with the county or state values. Comparing community figures with more regional trends will allow you to determine whether your community has greater needs in one or more areas. You should also compare the block groups with one another, to see where you have high levels of social vulnerability indicators. Often the block groups will be clustered in particular areas, and very often they will be in physically vulnerable areas such as in floodplains and surge zones or near locally unwanted land uses such as oil refineries, manufacturing plants, or other technological hazards. The easiest way to understand these vulnerabilities is to map them. It is not necessary to map them for the information to be useful, but we highly recommend doing so, because patterns often emerge through the process.

Exercise 6. Forming Second-Order Data

The second-order indicators may be the most useful information for assessing social needs (figure 6.2). Once you have identified and mapped all the first-order data, we recommend combining indicators to form the second-order indicators.

These second-order indices can help you understand how these household and individual characteristics might translate into specific needs or concerns before, during, and after a disaster. For example, by simply adding proportions of single-parent households with children to the population of children age five or below, we can start to get an idea of which households are likely to have special sheltering needs and child care needs for single parents who must get back to work quickly after a disaster.

Adding the proportion of workers using public transportation to the proportion of occupied housing units without a vehicle reveals a critical need related to evacuation but may also have important implications for prioritizing the restoration of transit lines and other transportation infrastructure, for example. If you are able to map these second-order indices, you are likely to find that households that have these kinds of vulnerabilities are spatially clustered.

We can target useful services to these areas to better meet their needs. Mapping transportation needs may help identify possible evacuation pickup locations and points of distribution for recovery resources after a disaster.

The second-order indices are our recommended suggestions. Many other indices could be developed, which may require additional data from the census or other sources. The technique is what's important, though. Are there specific needs that your community has that are not part of the first- or second-order needs? Make a list of needs you think your community has and determine possible first-order indicators that may be collected to form a new second-order indicator. Every community is different, and we encourage you to think outside the box in ways that best suit your community.

Exercise 7. Forming Third-Order Data

Now you will determine whether there are highly vulnerable hotspots in your community. You can add all the indicators and then map the values, or you can overlay all the second-order maps, each with a similar percentage of transparency. Through this process, which can be done in mapping software or even in Photoshop or PowerPoint if you are in a bind, you will discover the intersection of needs and the pockets of the community that need particular attention. These hotspots are likely to be in areas that are already known to be high poverty, but our research has shown that the nature of the disadvantage in these areas leads to specific responses and outcomes based on the characteristics of the households. For example, in our research in Galveston we found that households living in social vulnerability hotspots were less likely to apply for federal assistance, sustained much higher levels of damage, and were also more likely to experience short-term and long-term displacement.

Overlay all three community characteristics from chapters 4, 5, and 6: hazard exposures (HE), physical vulnerabilities (PV), and social vulnerabilities (SV). Once these maps are overlaid, you can pinpoint the intersection of all three.

PART III.
Planning Strategies

In part II, we explored how to better understand community disaster risk by analyzing hazard exposure, physical vulnerabilities, and social vulnerabilities. Establishing a foundation of facts for a community's disaster risks is critical to inform community-based planning. Whether we are dealing with comprehensive planning or more specific plans such as emergency, response, or recovery planning, strategies are best recommended when based on evidence. We contend that in order to enhance disaster resiliency, hazard mitigation must be consistently addressed in all types of planning activities. A variety of mitigation and planning strategies increase community resistance and robustness in the face of a pending disaster. Through sound hazard mitigation planning and policy implementation before a disaster, we can significantly reduce disaster losses. And afterward, drawing from our disaster experience, we can increase a community's resiliency by interjecting mitigation planning and policy implementation throughout the recovery process. If we fail in doing this, we run the risk of building back the same vulnerabilities our communities exhibited before the disaster. The net effect is that we lose the window of opportunity to learn from and adapt to disaster experiences.

The chapters in part III describe specific planning strategies many communities already are aware of but have not used to increase resilience to disasters. First we describe how to create better hazard mitigation plans. Then we provide a set of tools city and regional planners can use to support mitigation. Finally, we explain ways to create consistency across multiple plans in your community.

Before we move on, let's describe Step 4 to inclusively plan for disasters.

Step 4: Envision

The fourth step to inclusively plan for disasters involves interactively engaging the public in setting goals to mitigate hazards. Visioning and goal setting are typically the most interactive element in engaging the public. The vision should be a short statement that sets the desire of the community to be sustainable or a hazard- or disaster-resilient community. It should be holistic. It could be broad, such as building a sustainable and resilient community in the case of preparation of a comprehensive plan, or more focused, such as improving the urban aesthetics of the main street in the case of an urban design plan.

Generally speaking, goal setting in a disaster planning context requires members of a community to articulate the conditions necessary for the community to be more resilient in the future, along with a set of quantifiable benchmarks. More specifically, the hazard mitigation plan evaluation criteria in chapter 7 suggest that communities concentrate on a set of goals that speak to the need to reduce losses, protect property, or minimize the fiscal impacts of hazards while using available capacity wisely and distributing the cost of hazard mitigation equitably. Start with identification of specific issues that the planning process is being undertaken to address. Often, such issues evolve through consultations and discussion between elected officials, professional staff, local stakeholders, and community members.

Once goals for the community have been established, specific objectives should be developed. Objectives can use many of the strategies identified in part III and should be quantified. This is so communities can measure their own progress over time to determine whether their goals are indeed meaningful to achieving resilience. Some examples include "reduce total damage of hazard impacts by 10 percent in 2010 U.S. dollars," "preserve 80 percent of all floodplains as open space or recreational areas," "maintain good water quality in all streams and water bodies," and "protect 75 percent of all wetlands and forests." Most importantly, goals and objectives should promote increasing the extent to which citizens, especially the most vulnerable members of society, are able to prepare for, survive, and recover from the impacts of hazards. Goals should specify how the population will be safe from hazards and will promote hazard awareness, use available resources efficiently, improve preparedness and response, and promote partnerships with other agencies. Begin this process with your community by completing exercise 8.

Exercise 8. Document Vision and Goals

Organize the taskforce and hold a half-day meeting to begin the envisioning process. Present the results found in part II—the assessment of hazard exposures, physical vulnerability, and social vulnerability—to the community.

Once the factual basis has been established, engage the taskforce in a visioning exercise. Knowing where the community is now, ask them where they would like to be. How do members of the taskforce foresee their community handling a disaster? The vision should be a short, holistic statement. There are a number of online resources that explore strategies for the visioning process. Think about whether the vision developed is in line with other community plans and initiatives.

Then brainstorm potential community goals. Write down everything participants say. Remember that goals should be broad at this point. You may notice that many are similar and can be combined. At this point it is helpful to receive comments from the public. Provide multiple opportunities for input using different media (e.g., social media, open house meetings).

Conduct a follow-up meeting for the taskforce to incorporate community comments and refine the goals. The involvement of the community in developing measurable and achievable goals is an important step in the process.

7. An Assessment of Hazard Mitigation Plans

This chapter introduces and discusses hazard mitigation planning and plans as a critical step in mobilizing a community to increase disaster resiliency. Hazard mitigation plans are in many respects a recent policy tool. Introduced by the federal government, hazard mitigation plans are an approach to help communities better understand their disaster vulnerability, identify strategies and actions the community can use to help lessen their vulnerabilities, and develop priorities for funding these mitigation actions and projects. The Disaster Mitigation Act of 2000 began the process of encouraging local jurisdictions to develop local hazard mitigation plans if the local jurisdiction wanted to gain federal funding to help implement mitigation projects and actions. By mid-2007 approximately 14,000 of these plans had been approved by the Federal Emergency Management Agency (FEMA) throughout the United States. As of 2011, there were more than 26,000 approved plans.[1]

According to FEMA, mitigation planning is recognized as a process for states and communities to identify their resources, policies, and tools to implement mitigation activities.[2] FEMA has identified four major goals in the hazard mitigation planning process:

- Organizing resources
- Assessing risks
- Developing a mitigation plan
- Implementing the plan and monitoring progress

The mitigation plan itself should include information about resources, risk and vulnerability, mitigation policies, and implementation and monitoring. To facilitate the planning process, FEMA has offered guidance to states and local jurisdictions to develop mitigation plans through *State Multi-Hazard Mitigation Planning Guidance* under the Disaster Mitigation Act of 2000, also called the "Blue Book," and through various how-to guides.[3] The Blue Book provides information on the minimum criteria that plans must contain in order to obtain approval from FEMA and guidelines for developing an "enhanced" plan and important information and methods for undertaking the process.

Table 7.1 summarizes the basic elements of a local mitigation plan as specified by FEMA's Blue Book. The first column displays the four major planning components of a plan: planning process, risk assessment, mitigation strategy, and plan maintenance.[4] The second column identifies the key planning subcomponents associated with each component, and the final column specifies the critical planning elements that should be addressed in a plan.

The planning process component, for example, focuses on how the mitigation planning process itself was carried out by identifying public involvement, how the plan was prepared, its incorporation of existing plans, technical information and studies, and how it was reviewed. The risk assessment component should address the basic factual risk information critical for a hazard mitigation plan by identifying and profiling a jurisdiction's hazard risks and spelling out its current trends with respect to vulnerability. In this case *vulnerability* refers to physical vulnerability, such as structures, infrastructure, and critical facilities. It does not address social vulnerability issues, an oft-missed component critical to understanding communities. The mitigation strategy component should describe the goals, mitigation actions, and priorities established on the basis of the risk assessments. The final component, plan maintenance, addresses not only the scheduling and methods for monitoring, evaluating, and updating the plan but also how the plan will be incorporated into other planning efforts and continued public involvement. In addition to the plan requirements outlined in table 7.1, the Blue Book also includes recommendations on how to develop "improved" or "enhanced" plans. For example, FEMA encourages developing mitigation plans for natural *and* human-made or technological hazards even though FEMA requires communities to address only natural hazards. In addition, other recommendations include the identification of special populations at risk, such as older adults, those with disabilities, or other populations with special needs. Mapping, drafting goals and objectives, and developing a cost–benefit analysis are also recommended. If local jurisdictions developed mitigation plans that contain these FEMA-encouraged special considerations, the plan would clearly go beyond the minimum requirements.[5]

The Blue Book also includes a plan review "crosswalk" that outlines the basic requirements and criteria by which reviewers at FEMA evaluate or assess a mitigation action plan to determine whether it meets their basic requirements. In essence, the crosswalk

Table 7.1. Components of Local Mitigation Plans According to FEMA Guidelines: Elements and Critical Issues

	Element	Critical Issues
Planning process	Planning process	Open public involvement process (neighboring communities, business, and other interested parties). A plan should include the document about planning processes, how the plans were prepared, who was involved in the process, and how the public was involved. Review and incorporation of existing plans, studies, and technical information.
Risk assessment	Identifying hazards	Description of all natural hazards that can influence the jurisdiction.
	Profiling hazards	Location or geographic areas of all hazards. Extent of all natural hazards. Probability, likelihood, or frequency that the hazard events would occur. Past history of hazard events (e.g., damage, severity, duration, and date of occurrence).
	Assessing vulnerability: overview	Summary of the community's vulnerability assessment.
	Assessing vulnerability: identifying structures	Description of vulnerable structures in terms of the types and numbers of existing and future buildings, infrastructure, and critical facilities.
	Assessing vulnerability: estimating potential losses	Estimation of the extent of a hazard's impact on the structures in terms of dollar value or percentages of damage. Description of the methods used to estimate impact.
	Assessing vulnerability: analyzing development trends	General description of land uses and development trends.
	Multijurisdictional risk assessment	In multijurisdictional plans, the risk assessment must consider the entire planning area.
Mitigation strategy	Local hazard mitigation goals	Description of mitigation goals that can guide the development and implementation of mitigation actions. Description of how the goals are developed.
	Identification and analysis of mitigation actions	Identification of mitigation actions to achieve the aforementioned goals.
	Implementation of mitigation actions	Description of how the actions are prioritized, implemented, and administered by local governments.
	Multijurisdictional mitigation actions	List of each jurisdiction's actions in multijurisdictional plan.

Table 7.1. continued

	Element	Critical Issues
Plan maintenance process	Monitoring, evaluating, and updating the plan	Description of the schedules and methods of monitoring, evaluating, and updating the plans.
	Incorporating into existing planning mechanisms	Indication of how mitigation plans will be incorporated into other existing plans such as comprehensive plans, capital improvement plans, and zoning and building codes.
	Continued public involvement	Description of how governments will continue public involvement in the plan maintenance process.

Federal Emergency Management Agency (FEMA). *State Multi-Hazard Mitigation Planning Guidance* (Mitigation Planning "Blue Book"). Washington, DC: Author, January 2008.

represents a plan evaluation or assessment protocol. Table 7.2 displays the crosswalk used to review each plan for approval.

As can be seen by comparing tables 7.1 and 7.2, the crosswalk includes the four goals: planning process, risk assessments, mitigation strategy, and plan maintenance. The first column displays fifteen subcomponents. The second column displays a list of thirty-two specific questions associated with each subcomponent. These questions address specific planning elements that should be discussed by each plan. The third column displays the scoring options. Examining these questions in conjunction with the sections in table 7.1 can help you better understand what kinds of issues should be included in a community's hazard mitigation plan. For example, the risk assessment section in table 7.1 suggests identifying and profiling the types of hazards a community is potentially exposed to. In table 7.2, the questions related to hazard identification and profiling provide a more complete understanding of what kinds of information should be included in these sections in order to develop a satisfactory hazard mitigation plan.

In addition to the mitigation plan components, table 7.2 includes a prerequisite section. The prerequisite section assesses whether the mitigation plan has been officially adopted by the local governing body or bodies, in the case of a multijurisdictional plan. The scoring system for the prerequisite section is simply whether the plan has or has not met the requirement of adoption.

For the thirty-two planning element questions, the scoring system is simply a determination by the reviewer as to whether a particular planning element satisfactorily meets the basic plan requirements or whether it needs improvement.

Recall that a mitigation action plan is a requirement to qualify for FEMA mitigation

Table 7.2. Review of Local Hazard Mitigation Plans: The Plan Review Crosswalk

Topic	Element-Related Questions	Scoring System
Prerequisite		
Adoption by the local governing body	Has the local governing body adopted the plan? Is supporting documentation, such as a resolution, included?	Not met or met
Multijurisdictional plan adoption	Does the plan indicate the specific jurisdictions represented in the plan? For each jurisdiction, has the local governing body adopted the plan? Is supporting documentation, such as a resolution, included for each participating jurisdiction?	Not met or met
Multijurisdictional planning participation	Does the plan describe how each jurisdiction participated in the plan's development?	Not met or met
Planning Process		
Documentation of the planning process	Does the plan provide a narrative description of how the plan was prepared? Does the plan indicate who was involved in the current planning process? Does the plan indicate how the public was involved? Was there an opportunity for neighboring communities, agencies, businesses, academia, nonprofits, and other interested parties to be involved in the planning process? Does the planning process describe the review and incorporation, if appropriate, of existing plans, studies, reports, and technical information?	Need improvement or satisfactory
Risk Assessment		
Identifying hazards	Does the plan provide a description of the type of all natural hazards that can affect the jurisdiction?	Need improvement or satisfactory
Profiling hazards	Does the risk assessment identify the location of each natural hazard addressed in the plan? Does the risk assessment identify the extent of each hazard addressed in the plan? Does the plan provide information on previous occurrences of each hazard addressed in the plan? Does the plan include the provability of future events for each hazard addressed in the plan?	Need improvement or satisfactory

Table 7.2. continued

Topic	Element-Related Questions	Scoring System
Risk Assessment, continued		
Assessing vulnerability	Does the plan include an overall summary description of the jurisdiction's vulnerability to each hazard? Does the plan address the impact of each hazard on the jurisdiction?	Need improvement or satisfactory
Assessing vulnerability by identifying structures	Does the plan describe vulnerability in terms of the types and numbers of existing buildings, infrastructure, and critical facilities located in the identified hazard areas? Does the plan describe vulnerability in terms of the types and numbers of future buildings, infrastructure, and critical facilities located in the identified hazard areas?	Need improvement or satisfactory
Assessing vulnerability by estimating potential losses	Does the plan present an overview and analysis of the potential losses to the identified vulnerable structures? Does the plan describe the method used to prepare the estimate?	Need improvement or satisfactory
Assessing vulnerability by analyzing development trends	Does the plan describe land uses and development trends?	Need improvement or satisfactory
Multijurisdictional risk assessment	Does the plan include a risk assessment for each participating jurisdiction as needed to reflect unique or varied risks?	Need improvement or satisfactory
Mitigation Strategy		
Local hazard mitigation goals	Does the plan provide a description of mitigation goals to reduce or avoid long-term vulnerabilities to the identified hazards?	Need improvement or satisfactory
Identification and analysis of mitigation actions	Does the plan identify and analyze a comprehensive range of specific mitigation actions and projects for each hazard? Do the identified actions and projects address reducing the effects of hazards on new buildings and infrastructure? Do the identified actions and projects address reducing the effects of hazards on existing buildings and infrastructure?	Need improvement or satisfactory

Table 7.2. continued

Topic	Element-Related Questions	Scoring System
Mitigation Strategy, continued		
Implementation of mitigation actions	Does the mitigation strategy include how the actions are prioritized? Does the mitigation strategy address how the actions will be implemented and administered? Does the prioritization process include an emphasis on the use of a cost–benefit review to maximize benefits?	Need improvement or satisfactory
Multijurisdictional mitigation actions	Does the plan include at least one identifiable action item for each jurisdiction requesting FEMA approval of the plan?	Need improvement or satisfactory
Plan Maintenance Process		
Monitoring, evaluating, and updating the plan	Does the plan describe the method and schedule for monitoring the plan? Does the plan describe the method and schedule for evaluating the plan? Does the plan describe the method and schedule for updating the plan?	Need improvement or satisfactory
Incorporation into existing planning mechanisms	Does the plan identify other local planning mechanisms available for incorporating the requirements of the mitigation plan? Does the plan include a process by which the local government will incorporate the requirements in other plans when appropriate?	Need improvement or satisfactory
Continued public involvement	Does the plan explain how continued public participation will be obtained?	Need improvement or satisfactory

Federal Emergency Management Agency (FEMA). *State Multi-Hazard Mitigation Planning Guidance* (Mitigation Planning "Blue Book"). Washington, DC: Author, January 2008.

funding. Therefore, as part of the plan at least one identifiable mitigation action must be specified for each jurisdiction included in the plan. The FEMA guidebook does not dictate specific mitigation actions that local hazard mitigation plans will or must include. Instead, FEMA and other federal and state agencies provide information about possible hazard mitigation strategies that may apply to both natural and technological hazards for communities.[6]

Local Mitigation Plans: Assessing Current Plans and Making Them Stronger

A variety of studies have examined hazard mitigation planning at the state level[7] and local level[8] in the past, and recently researchers have again targeted local hazard mitigation planning activities. A group of researchers, including some of the authors, undertook an evaluation of local hazard mitigation plans along the Texas coast in order to better understand the overall quality of these plans and to compare plan quality between different types of hazard mitigation plans: county, city, and regional hazard mitigation plans.[9] Even more recently, Lyles, Berke, and Smith also evaluated samples of local plans in six states—North Carolina, Georgia, Florida, Texas, California, and Washington—in an attempt to understand whether planning mandates improve the quality of local mitigation plans.[10] These studies provide us with a wealth of additional information about the nature of mitigation plans (see box 7.1).

Our study evaluated twelve FEMA-approved hazard mitigation plans: three municipal plans, four county plans, and five regional (multijurisdictional) plans. In total, these twelve plans covered 18 counties and 112 municipalities along the Texas coast. Because

---

Box 7.1. A Mandate for Local Hazard Mitigation Plans

Although many assume that states address hazard planning issues in the same way, there are significant differences in planning powers and authority as well as mandates on municipalities and counties between states. If we consider the states in the Gulf Coast region, for example, there are vast differences between Florida and Texas in terms of mandates and planning authority. Many U.S. Gulf Coast counties have some capacity for limited planning, but some counties must have comprehensive plans, whereas others do not have that requirement. For example, Florida is the only state in the region to mandate local plans. Also, in Florida, both counties and cities have what is known as the home rule and the authority to plan. Home rule is the power and authority a local government is granted by the state. Generally, the ability to develop, implement, and enforce local plans depends predominantly on home rule power. In contrast, municipalities in Texas have planning and enforcement power, but counties do not have such power. Furthermore, Texas does not mandate local comprehensive planning. Therefore, when considering policy and strategy options it can be important to consider just what forms of planning may be possible, if not mandated, and what types of jurisdictions have home rule and hence the authority to undertake various forms of land use regulation.

Source: Jacob, J. S., and S. Showalter. "The Resilient Coast: Policy Frameworks for Adapting the Built Environment to Climate Change and Growth in Coastal Areas of the U.S. Gulf of Mexico." *Sea Grant*, 2007. http://nsglc.olemiss.edu/TheBuiltEnvironment08-sm_000.pdf (accessed April 2014).

each of these plans had already been approved by FEMA, it would make little sense to simply evaluate them based on FEMA's crosswalk shown in table 7.2. Furthermore, we wanted to obtain a more comprehensive assessment of these plans to better understand what they were and were not addressing. The method used to evaluate these plans followed conventional approaches to plan evaluation[11] that consisted of assessing the degree to which each plan addressed a set of planning elements associated with various planning components.[12] In this case, we developed a very comprehensive planning protocol based on what the planning literature suggests should be included in a thorough hazard mitigation plan. In other words, the protocol was much more rigorous and demanding than the minimal guidelines specified by FEMA.

Table 7.3 presents the details of our protocol. This protocol is divided into seven different planning components assessing each plan in terms of its vision statement, planning process, fact basis, goals and objectives, coordination, polices and actions, and implementation process. Each of these seven planning components is, in turn, broken into a variable number of subcomponents, thirty in all. These subcomponents include a total of 164 very detailed planning elements.

Ultimately, each plan was examined to see how well it addressed each of these very detailed planning elements. For example, the plan's vision statement was assessed in terms of two subcomponents: its problem description and its vision statement. More specifically, in the problem description, we looked for a description of the community and its hazard threats, how these local hazards might affect the state, and the nature of current hazard issues.

The third component assessed is the plan's fact basis, which includes four subcomponents: hazard identification, vulnerability assessment, risk analysis, and emergency management. The vulnerability assessment includes not only physical vulnerability in terms of infrastructure, built environment (property), and infrastructure but also assessments of population vulnerability and social vulnerability.

One final example is the sixth plan component, which assesses each plan in terms of the specific mitigation policies and actions identified. This component is assessed by twelve subcomponents (numbers 17–28) that identify a host of possible mitigation strategies, including regulatory tools, modeling techniques, floodplain regulations, incentive-based tools, structural mitigation tools, public education awareness programs, and a host of other actions. These actions should be used by a local jurisdiction in its mitigation portfolio to address its hazard threats and thereby enhance its mitigation status and ultimately resiliency. The actions will be addressed further in chapter 8.

Clearly this protocol is comprehensive in its examination of local hazard mitigation plans. In a very real sense, this protocol can also be thought of as a very detailed guide

Table 7.3. Hazard Mitigation Action Plan Evaluation Protocol

Component and Subcomponents	Specific Planning Elements Assessed
I. Vision Statement	
1. Problem description	1.1 Description of community and historical hazard threats
	1.2 Description of the local hazard impact on the entire state
	1.3 Current or potential hazard issues
2. Vision	2.1 A statement identifying overall image of sustainable and hazard-resilient community or state
	2.2 General goals and objectives
II. Planning Process	
3. General description	3.1 General description of the process to develop a plan
4. Proposed participation techniques in planning process	4.1 Formal public hearings
	4.2 Open meetings
	4.3 Workshops or forum
	4.4 Call-in hotlines
	4.5 Citizen advisory committees
	4.6 Household survey
	4.7 Interviews with key stakeholders
	4.8 Website, Internet, and e-mail
	4.9 Data acquisition and data management
III. Fact Basis	
5. Hazard identification	5.1 General description of projected growth and population
	5.2 Hazard profile
	5.3 Hazard identification
	5.4 Delineation of natural resource areas
	5.5 Delineation of location of hazard
	5.6 Delineation of magnitude of hazard
	5.7 Historical data on the hazard
6. Vulnerability assessment	6.1 Identifies all hazards to the study area
	6.2 Assessment of hazard exposure (property)
	6.3 Social vulnerability assessment
	6.4 Assessment of hazard exposure (population)
	6.5 Assessment of hazard exposure (public infrastructure such as roadways, water utilities, and communication systems)
	6.6 Assessment of hazard exposure (critical facilities such as shelters and hospitals)
	6.7 Social vulnerability (e.g., special needs population)

Table 7.3. continued

Component and Subcomponents	Specific Planning Elements Assessed
7. Risk analysis	7.1 Probability of experiencing hazard event (various magnitudes where applicable) 7.2 Property loss estimation (various magnitudes where applicable) 7.3 Infrastructure impact estimation (various magnitudes where applicable) 7.4 Population risk (various magnitudes where applicable)
8. Emergency management	8.1 Emergency shelter demand and capacity data 8.2 Evacuation clearance time data 8.3 Location of emergency shelter

IV. Mitigation Goals and Objectives

9. Economic impacts	9.1 Any goal to reduce losses or protect property from loss 9.2 Any goal to minimize fiscal impacts of hazards 9.3 Any goal to distribute hazard mitigation cost equitably
10. Physical and environmental impacts	10.1 Any goal to reduce hazard impacts on and preserve open space and recreation areas 10.2 Any goal to reduce hazard impacts on and maintain good water quality 10.3 Any goal to reduce hazard impacts on and protect wetlands and forests (critical natural areas)
11. Public interest	11.1 Any goal to protect safety of population 11.2 Any goal to promote hazard awareness program or improve information exchange 11.3 Any goal to use available resources efficiently 11.4 Any goal to improve preparedness and response to hazard 11.5 Any goal to promote partnership with other agencies

V. Interorganization Coordination and Capabilities

12. Cooperation	12.1 Identification of other government organizations 12.2 Identification of representatives for each of above 12.3 Identification of other stakeholders 12.4 Identification of representatives for each of above 12.5 Consistency with state plan or state mitigation plan 12.6 Integration with other local comprehensive plan 12.7 Integration with FEMA mitigation programs and initiatives (e.g., Flood Mitigation Fund) 12.8 Integration with other independent governments such as municipal utility districts and independent school districts 12.9 Intergovernmental agreements

Table 7.3. continued

Component and Subcomponents	Specific Planning Elements Assessed
13. Proposed participation techniques in proposed actions	13.1 Formal public hearings 13.2 Open meetings 13.3 Workshops or forums 13.4 Call-in hotlines 13.5 Citizen advisory committees 13.6 Household survey 13.7 Interviews with key stakeholders
14. Information sharing on the planned a ctions	14.1 Brochures or other literature 14.2 Newsletters 14.3 Educational workshops 14.4 TV and radio 14.5 Video 14.6 Internet (website)
15. Capacity development	15.1 Funding sources for citizen participation and cooperation with other organization 15.2 Staffing levels (e.g., full-time employees, part-time staff) 15.3 Joint database 15.4 Technical assistance to other organization or citizen 15.5 Improving communications and institutional capacity through training, workshop, and so on 15.6 Develop and improving technical capabilities (e.g., geographic information system, database)
16. Conflict management	16.1 Specification of conflict management procedures and processes

VI. Specific Mitigation Policies and Actions

Component and Subcomponents	Specific Planning Elements Assessed
17. General policy	17.1 Discourage development in hazardous areas 17.2 Support adoption of new regulatory legislation at local level
18. Regulatory tool	18.1 Permitted land use 18.2 Low-density conservation or other hazard zone 18.3 Overlay zone with reduced density provisions 18.4 Dedication of open space for hazards 18.5 Policy to locate public facilities in zones not subject to hazards 18.6 Transfer of development rights 18.7 Cluster development

Table 7.3. continued

Component and Subcomponents	Specific Planning Elements Assessed
18. Regulatory tool	18.8 Setbacks
	18.9 Site plan review
	18.10 Special study or impact assessment for development in hazard zones
	18.11 Building standards or building code
	18.12 Land and property acquisition
	18.13 Impact fees
	18.14 Retrofitting of private structures
	18.15 Separate hazard mitigation plan
	18.16 Relocation of structures out of hazard zones
	18.17 Drainage ordinance
19. Modeling technique	19.1 Modeling tools for evacuation
	19.2 Modeling tools for flooding
	19.3 Modeling tools for others (e.g., debris)
20. Floodplain regulation	20.1 Floodplain management and development
	20.2 Floodplain ordinance
	20.3 Downzoning floodplains
21. Incentive-based tool	21.1 Tax abatement for using mitigation
	21.2 Density bonus
	21.3 Low-interest loans
	21.4 Participation in National Flood Insurance Program (NFIP)
	21.5 Join Community Rating System (CRS)
22. Structural tool	22.1 Levees
	22.2 Seawalls
	22.3 Riprap
	22.4 Bulkheads
	22.5 Detention ponds
	22.6 Channel maintenance
	22.7 Wetland restoration
	22.8 Slope stabilization
	22.9 Stormwater management
	22.10 Sewage
	22.11 Drainage
	22.12 Maintenance of structures

Table 7.3. continued

Component and Subcomponents	Specific Planning Elements Assessed
23. Awareness and educational tool	23.1 Awareness program for community
	23.2 Education and awareness for staff
	23.3 Education and awareness for private stakeholders (e.g., industry, business, or homeowners)
	23.4 Education and awareness for students
	23.5 Real estate hazard disclosure
	23.6 Disaster warning and response program
	23.7 Posting of signs indicating hazardous areas
	23.8 Technical assistance to developers or property owners for mitigation
	23.9 Maps of areas subject to hazards
	23.10 Inclusion of floodplain boundaries
	23.11 Education and training in several languages
	23.12 Hazard information center
24. Social consideration	24.1 Identification of special needs population and preparedness of assistance
25. Public facilities and infrastructure	25.1 Capital improvement plan based on hazard analysis
	25.2 Retrofitting public structures
	25.3 Retrofitting critical facilities
26. Recovery planning	26.1 Land use change
	26.2 Building design change to meet enhanced safety standards
	26.3 Moratorium
	26.4 Recovery organization
	26.5 Private acquisition
	26.6 Financial recovery
27. Emergency preparedness	27.1 Evacuation
	27.2 Sheltering
	27.3 Contingency plan or preparedness plan
	27.4 Emergency operation center (EOC)
	27.5 Require emergency plans
	27.6 Purchasing rescue materials and other equipment
28. Natural resource protection	28.1 General description of best management practice
	28.2 Forest and vegetation management in riparian areas
	28.3 Sediment and erosion control
	28.4 Stream dumping regulations
	28.5 Urban forestry and landscape

Table 7.3. continued

Component and Subcomponents	Specific Planning Elements Assessed
VII. Implementation	
29. Implementation	29.1 Description of implementation process
	29.2 Identification of process for prioritizing assistance to local governments
	29.3 Clear designation of responsibility for implementation
	29.4 Provision of technical assistance for implementation
	29.5 Identification of costs for implementation
	29.6 Identification of funding sources
	29.7 Provision of sanctions
	29.8 Clear timetable for implementation outlined
	29.9 Enforcement-related issues
30. Evaluating, updating, and monitoring	30.1 Description of evaluation, updating, and monitoring process
	30.2 Identification of participants in the evaluating process
	30.3 Clear designation of responsibility for evaluating, updating, and monitoring process
	30.4 Evaluation of funded mitigation projects

that can be used not only to evaluate an existing plan but also as a guide to help local jurisdictions. In developing a local plan, jurisdictions can use the protocol to stimulate thinking on ways to improve a hazard mitigation plan. A community might consider alternative strategies for addressing hazard risks, increase participation in the planning process, and get the word out to the public about the importance of mitigation planning for community resilience.

Table 7.4 presents the scores earned by each of the twelve plans for each of the seven component areas. Without getting lost in the scoring strategy, suffice it to say that essentially, plans were scored based on the degree to which each of the 164 planning elements associated with each planning subcomponent, and ultimately each component, was addressed. In each case a total score based on a ten-point scale earned for each plan component was generated. The last row, "Mean," presents the average score for each component area across the twelve plans, and the last column presents the plan quality score, which is the average component score, for each of the twelve plans.

The highest plan quality score (see last column) obtained by a plan was 5.3, which was earned by one of the regional plans. That score essentially means that this plan

Table 7.4. Plan Quality Assessments for 12 Texas Coastal Plans (2008)

Plans and Types		Vision	Planning Process	Fact Basis	Goals and Objectives	Interorganization Coordination	Policies and Coordination	Implementation	Plan Quality Score
Regional	1	4.0	6.0	3.7	2.7	5.5	3.2	5.8	4.4
	2	7.0	4.5	4.2	5.5	3.6	2.3	4.6	4.5
	3	4.0	5.0	4.2	4.1	4.0	1.5	4.6	4.0
	4	5.0	6.5	3.7	4.5	2.6	2.7	3.1	4.0
	5	7.0	6.5	3.5	72.3	4.7	4.2	4.2	5.3
County	6	2.0	6.0	4.0	3.2	5.4	3.9	6.5	4.4
	7	5.0	5.5	3.5	6.4	1.9	1.4	5.4	4.2
	8	1.0	5.5	3.1	6.8	7.4	3.2	6.2	4.7
	9	0.0	3.0	3.9	5.9	4.8	3.1	7.3	4.0
City	10	4.0	3.5	2.3	5.9	1.9	1.3	6.9	3.7
	11	4.0	6.0	2.4	1.4	5.2	3.7	4.2	3.8
	12	3.0	4.0	1.6	0.9	3.8	3.3	3.5	2.9
Mean		3.8	5.2	3.4	4.6	4.2	2.8	5.2	4.2

scored an average of 53 percent of total points possible across the seven planning component areas. The lowest score was 2.9, and the overall average plan quality score for these twelve hazard mitigation plans was 4.2, which again means that on average these plans earned less than 42 percent of total points (41.6 out of 100). These results certainly suggest that there is a good deal of room for improvement in the quality of regional and municipal hazard mitigation plans. Most disconcerting were the very low average scores for the fact basis and policies and coordination components of these plans, which were scored at 3.4 and 2.8, respectively (see last row). The fact basis is the critical part of a plan that analyzes the jurisdiction's hazard exposure, physical vulnerability, and social vulnerability, as described in part II. The fact basis should be the foundation on which the plan makes recommendations about what kinds of policies and actions a jurisdiction should undertake to lower its disaster vulnerability and risk. If the fact basis does not do a good job of outlining vulnerabilities and risks, then it can be hard to develop a plan that shapes a jurisdiction's future in a direction that lessens vulnerabilities and hence enhances potential resilience.

The low policy and coordination score of only 2.8 suggests that, on average, these plans scored just 28 out of 100 points. Indeed, several plans scored at 1.3- and 1.5-point levels. These very low scores suggest that the majority of these plans did not consider the full range of possible mitigation solutions for addressing their potential hazard vulnerabilities and risks. In fact, they were so low that we decided to undertake a more detailed analysis of the policies and solutions proposed by these plans for reducing their community vulnerabilities and risks. In total, there were 836 mitigation policies and actions proposed to help lessen the vulnerabilities of the 18 counties and 112 municipalities covered by these twelve plans. Just over 34 percent of these were related to structural mitigation solutions—in other words building some form of public infrastructure solution to lessen hazard exposure such as levees, seawalls, and beach renourishment. Interestingly, just over 24 percent were focused on strengthening the emergency management capabilities of these jurisdictions, not mitigation per se. Nearly 26 percent focused on activities that addressed regulatory and planning initiatives related to policy approaches to steer development out of harm's way or strengthen the nature of development occurring in more exposed areas. An additional 14.4 percent addressed community education and awareness programs. Perhaps somewhat surprisingly, only 1.4 percent of the proposed actions addressed natural resource protection or restoration initiatives. On the whole, this mix of proposed actions suggested that there was still an overreliance on technological fixes to solve hazard problems and a tendency to focus on emergency management solutions, not on broad-based mitigation and adaptation solutions to address resiliency issues.

The more recent assessment that Lyles and his colleagues undertook of 175 local hazard mitigation plans in six states had a somewhat different protocol than the one we used in Texas. They too had seven plan components, but theirs were goals, fact basis, policies and actions, participation, interorganizational coordination, implementation, and monitoring. Essentially their broader components conformed more closely to the FEMA crosswalk, but they still examined many more detailed planning elements, and hence their protocol was as comprehensive and detailed as was the one we used in Texas.[13] Their scoring procedure was similar to the one we presented in this chapter, using a ten-point scale; so the scores are interpreted in a manner similar to that of the Texas data. There results are presented in table 7.5, which displays the average plan scores for each component and the overall average for each state. The last row in this table displays the average score for each of the 175 plans they evaluated.

Although there are some differences in the findings between these two studies, what

Table 7.5. Plan Quality Assessments for 175 Local Plans in Six States (2010–2011)

	Goals	Fact Basis	Policies and Actions	Participation	Interorganization Coordination	Implementation	Monitoring	Plan Quality Score
California	5.5	3.0	2.3	5.0	1.7	5.1	3.5	3.7
Florida	5.4	4.0	2.1	4.6	2.5	6.8	3.6	4.1
Georgia	5.5	2.7	3.6	4.3	1.4	3.6	3.5	3.5
North Carolina	5.4	4.5	3.5	4.4	2.3	5.8	3.5	4.2
Texas	4.7	4.0	2.4	5.5	1.2	7.3	3.5	4.1
Washington State	5.3	3.4	2.6	5.6	1.8	6.2	3.6	4.1
Mean	5.0	3.6	2.7	4.9	1.8	5.9	3.5	4.0

is particularly interesting are the commonalities despite the fact that Lyles and colleagues undertook their analysis of updated hazard mitigation plans in Texas and a much broader multistate sample.[14] Focusing on a comparison between the average component scores in both studies (the final rows in each table), the most obvious similarity is that the overall plan quality scores for both studies were 4.2 in our study and 4.0 in the multistate study. Overall, these two scores are quite comparable, suggesting that plans are scoring only about 40 percent, suggesting much room for improvement. The most obvious difference between the two is the much lower score on interorganizational coordination for the multistate study (table 7.5), where the score was only 1.8, compared with the Texas study (table 7.4), where the score was 4.2. This difference probably resulted from the fact that the multistate study was much more rigorous in examining the extent to which each plan actually was linked to or mentioned in other planning efforts by other organizations. For instance, the Texas study focused on interorganizational memoranda of understanding and cross-jurisdictional agreements. Both studies found the policies and actions component to be very low, 2.7 in the multistate study and 2.8 in the Texas study. These scores suggest that in both cases plans considered only a very limited range of planning strategies, implying a failure to consider multiple options or a fuller portfolio of strategies and programs for addressing mitigation across plans. Similarly, both studies also found that the fact basis tends to be quite limited if not weak in hazard mitigation plans. Specifically, the fact basis was scored at 3.5 in the Texas study and 3.4 in the multistate study. These values suggest that the fact basis considers only about 35 percent of possible information-related sources and products when undertaking the assessment of jurisdictional hazard exposure, risk, and various dimensions of vulnerability.

In another publication coming out of their multistate study, Berke, Lyles, and Smith examined further the types of mitigation strategies proposed by plans in North Carolina and Florida.[15] Again, their analysis was somewhat different from what we undertook with the Texas data, but the findings are not that dissimilar. Specifically, they noted that emergency management strategies were by far the most frequently cited as solutions for mitigation, with more than 50 percent of the plans calling for increased funding related to these issues. In our Texas study, the numbers were not quite as high but still substantial at 24 percent, as noted earlier. They found structural protection for infrastructure and private property to be quite high at more than 30 percent each, whereas in Texas, structural protection, in the form of community works such as dams and levees, was the highest at 34 percent. Down much lower on the list were land use polices. The multistate study found that only 12.4 percent of plans mentioned land use policies as strategies that should be undertaken for mitigation. In the Texas study, as noted earlier, our percentage was higher at 26 percent, but we included a variety of policy-related strategies, including both land use and incentive-based programs, such as the National Flood Insurance Program's Community Rating System (CRS) and density bonuses.

On the whole, the findings from the recent literature that has examined recent hazard mitigation plans clearly suggest a number of areas for improvement. Most obvious is the observation that the very low standards associated with FEMA's Blue Book approach and the crosswalk can be improved. It is hard for FEMA to ratchet up the standards for hazard mitigation plans, particularly because these standards must cover a host of different types of jurisdictions, from small communities to state government, to various forms of school systems and tribal areas. The fact that many jurisdictions have very limited legal capacities to undertake many forms of planning, land use policies, and other mitigation strategies such as tax incentives and impact fees is a concern. An online resource was recently created out of the finding associated with the multistate study to help jurisdictions take their hazard mitigation planning activities beyond the minimum requirements associated with the crosswalk. That website can be accessed at http://mitigationguide.org/. The next section describes how Galveston addressed hazard mitigation planning after the hurricane.

Hazard Mitigation Planning in Galveston

Although Galveston participated in a countywide hazard mitigation plan, unique characteristics of the island were not addressed. This point reiterates the importance of more contextualized, local knowledge in community planning. Because of the lack of fine-grained detail, the city decided to update its portion of the county hazard mitigation plan. The city applied for and was awarded a FEMA hazard mitigation grant to fund the majority of the cost of the plan that focused on island-specific issues, primarily coastal and historical resources. In-kind services (e.g., city staff time and resources) were used for the 25 percent match required by the grant.

Because of the more chaotic recovery after the storm, the city felt it necessary to expedite plan development. A consultant was retained by the city to provide the expertise necessary to facilitate the process and create the plan. In developing the hazard mitigation plan, the city asked two basic questions:

- What hazards present the greatest risk to the City of Galveston?
- What are the most effective ways to reduce or eliminate those risks?

The planning process developed a fact basis and evaluated hazards where the city was most vulnerable, including both natural and human-made disasters. A detailed risk assessment was undertaken to elucidate the city's risk to coastal erosion, flooding, extreme wind events, wildfire and urban fires, and hazardous material incidents (fixed site and through transport). The city gave particular consideration to critical facilities, historic structures, and beach and shore issues.

There were several issues in planning for hazard mitigation in a historical community. Many coastal cities were among the first places inhabited in North America and contain significant archaeological and architectural resources. Therefore, it is critical to integrate historic preservation into the local mitigation strategy. The city identified the most significant resources and areas on the island and then prioritized them in terms of vulnerability to disaster and feasibility of mitigation options. The plan investigated improving the ability of historic resources to withstand the impact of a disaster and explored funding sources for preservation-related mitigation.

The hazard mitigation plan also identified the vulnerability of the island's coastline to changing conditions such as rising sea level, increasing storm intensity, and loss of sediment transport. Action items included the city's support for an aggressive beach nourishment program to address critical erosion areas and to restore dune systems that were destroyed to decrease or mitigate damage to public and private property. The city recognized the need to further address the challenges of the coastal environment and included the development of an erosion response plan in the large-scale recovery project, Progress Galveston.

Lessons Learned

In the studies described, the fact bases in most plans were quite low, suggesting the need to bring in much more data and information on which to base hazard mitigation plans, which we addressed in part II. Fortunately, after the storm Galveston made a point to develop an in-depth assessment of current community conditions and hazard risks. Developing a thorough fact basis in hazard mitigation plans is not always easy for smaller communities with limited capacity. State governments and agencies can be critical in helping local communities acquire the necessary data and information either directly or indirectly through grant programs. In addition, universities can be critical partners in gathering and producing data to help in this process. Furthermore, universities can help provide the necessary analytical and GIS skills to transform these data into useful maps to help in planning processes. Local governments, often working together or through regional planning agencies, can combine efforts to obtain the technical expertise to help in these processes. The fact basis for hazard mitigation planning should be the same kinds of data and information used in general or comprehensive planning, as well as transportation, development, and other planning activities. It makes little or no sense to plan a development strategy that will focus on stimulating development in a floodplain while the hazard mitigation plan suggests diverting development elsewhere.

It is also critical that mitigation planning not be left up to emergency management alone. Rather, it should be much more inclusive, joining together personnel from all planning, zoning, and even local economic development agencies. In this way, hazard mitigation strategies in the form of land use planning tools and policies may be incorporated into hazard mitigation plans. Because this particular component was weak in all the studies mentioned, we will take the time to explore planning tools that are appropriate to fold into hazard mitigation plans in the next chapter. Chapter 8 describes the broader range of strategies that might be considered.

Exercise 9: Evaluate Your Plan

The core team should use the hazard mitigation plan evaluation criteria in table 7.3 to evaluate your community's hazard mitigation plan. This will take some time to do, but do not overlook this step. By going through this process, you will better understand the areas you can improve.

Conduct a meeting with the taskforce and present the findings from the hazard mitigation plan evaluation criteria. How does this information affect the goals developed previously? Use this information to refine the goals. Make sure goals are measurable.

8. Planner's Toolbox

Our findings with respect to hazard mitigation planning were somewhat discouraging but not completely unexpected given the literature. The basic patterns we saw in Texas were similar to those found in the variety of states examined by Lyles, Berke, and Smith.[1] Hazard mitigation plans are complying with Federal Emergency Management Agency (FEMA) guidelines but are often quite weak when it comes to actually assessing community vulnerabilities and risks, and the proposed policies and actions tend to be limited in scope, focusing on structural mitigation solutions and more traditional emergency management approaches. These findings led us to consider whether the narrow scope of mitigation actions, particularly the nonstructural policies and strategies, proffered by these plans was perhaps a function of an already narrow repertoire of planning polices and strategies actually being used by jurisdictions in the first place.

The planning literature is replete with discussions and examples of a host of policies and strategies, particularly land use and development polices. Such policies offer comprehensive approaches for addressing mitigation and adaptation without introducing major public infrastructure projects that themselves can promote development in risky areas and often have negative consequences for the natural environment. Moreover, nonstructural approaches can be less costly and provide solutions for avoiding more risky areas[2] and reducing losses from natural disasters.[3] Conceptually, these strategies generally focus on adjusting and adapting human activities, particularly developmental activities, by encouraging development out of harm's way, appropriate development that explicitly addresses the natural hazard exposure and risks associated with an area, and preservation of environmental resources, particularly those in sensitive areas, and thereby enhances the natural environmental services that can reduce natural hazard impact.

The planning literature has offered a host of ways to classify nonstructural strategies.[4] Table 8.1 provides a detailed classification scheme, adopted from the literature, of various types of strategies. Our goal here is not to definitively categorize tools but rather to provide a convenient framework for identifying different strategies and tools. In total, ten strategies are identified, including development regulations and land use management tools, building standards, natural resource protection, public information and awareness tools, local and federal incentive tools, property acquisition tools, financial tools, public and private facilities policies, and private–public sector initiatives. For each strategy, the table lists the primary goal of the strategy and then offers examples of various planning tools—actually policies and strategies—that have been introduced or proposed to reach these goals. In total, thirty-six nonstructural mitigation tools are considered here.

Despite the fact that much has been written about these strategies and tools for potentially addressing mitigation and adaptation, very little is known about how widely these policies have been adopted. Indeed, the last study that examined the issue was published

Table 8.1. Nonstructural Hazard Mitigation and Adaptation Strategies and Policies

Strategy	Goals	Tools
1. Development regulation and land use management	Restrict occupancy in hazardous zones (location). Regulate density. Discourage development in environmentally sensitive or hazardous areas.	Residential subdivision ordinances Planned unit development Special overlay districts Agricultural or open space zoning Performance-based zoning Hazard setback ordinances Stormwater retention requirements
2. Building standards	Design regulations (type and category) that reduce loss and damage.	Building codes Wind hazard resistance standards Flood hazard resistance for new homes Retrofit for existing buildings Special utility codes
3. Natural resource protection	Preserve ecologically sensitive areas.	Wetland protection Habitat protection and restoration Protected areas

Table 8.1. continued

Strategy	Goals	Tools
4. Public information and awareness	Disseminate information and advise individuals, groups, and the community about hazards, hazardous areas, and mitigation techniques and goals.	Public education for hazard mitigation Citizen involvement in hazard mitigation planning Seminars or workshops on hazard mitigation practices for developers and builders Hazard disclosure Hazard zone signs
5. Incentive tools	Encourage landowners and developers to avoid development of environmentally sensitive and hazardous areas. Disperse and reduce risk.	Transfer of development rights Density bonuses Clustered development Participation in the National Flood Insurance Program (NFIP) Participation in the FEMA Community Rating System (CRS)
6. Property acquisition programs	Acquire and hold property for public benefit and use. Remove at-risk property from the private market.	Fees for simple purchases of undeveloped lands Acquisition of developments and easements Relocation of existing structures out of hazardous areas
7. Financial tools	More fairly distribute the public costs of private development.	Lower tax rates Special tax assessments Impact fees or special assessments
8. Critical public and private facilities policies	Direct the location of infrastructure away from hazardous areas.	Requirements for locating public facilities and infrastructure Requirements for locating critical private facilities and infrastructure Using municipal service areas to limit development
9. Private–public sector initiatives	Work with other private entities to mitigate hazard impacts.	Land trusts Public–private partnerships

in 1989 by Godschalk and colleagues.[5] To better understand the portfolio of mitigation strategies and policies that are actually being adopted and used by local jurisdictions, we undertook a study of jurisdictions in the coastal region of Texas. The study's targeted population was the 267 jurisdictions (41 counties and 226 municipalities) in what the

National Oceanic and Atmospheric Administration (NOAA) defines as the coastal zone, which extends well inland from the coast itself. The final sample data collected for this study include data on 124 jurisdictions (26 counties and 98 municipalities) in this region, which can clearly be seen in figure 8.1. For each of these jurisdictions, data were collected from a key informant, usually a jurisdictional planner or development official, on each of the strategies identified in table 8.1. Specifically, they were asked whether each policy or tool was being used and, if so, how extensively. For a more detailed discussion of this study, see Peacock and Husein's work.[6]

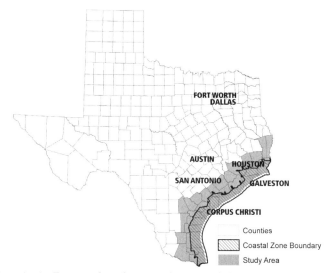

Figure 8.1. Counties in Texas within the coastal zone and the jurisdictions that were evaluated in our research.

The following sections offer a brief discussion of our findings with respect to each of the mitigation strategy and policy groupings mentioned in table 8.1.

Development Regulation and Land Use Management

The literature suggests that development regulations and land use management tools can be significant for promoting hazard mitigation. Gilbert White and other scholars[7] have argued that the impacts of natural disasters in terms of loss of life and property can be minimized through development regulation and land use management. A key reason they can reduce losses is that these policies can be effective at steering development away from hazard areas, thereby reducing exposure.[8] Land use management and development regulations include tools such as zoning and subdivision ordinances[9] and are considered traditional planning approaches.[10]

The land use and development regulations we considered included seven different policy tools: residential subdivision ordinances, planned unit development, performance zoning, special overlay districts and zoning, agricultural or open space zoning, hazard setback ordinances, and stormwater retention requirements. As implied by the name, residential subdivision ordinances focus on the division of property into smaller units such as parcels or lots for subsequent development or sale. Through subdivision regulations, jurisdictions with legal authority can regulate how property can be subdivided for development or resale and can specify public infrastructure; amenities such as public spaces, parks, and green spaces; clustering; and street layouts and designs. Planned unit developments are generally regarded as a form of zoning whereby larger areas of land can be developed in a more flexible way. Developers often provide a master plan for the land that includes, for example, mixed-use commercial and residential areas with variable densities. To achieve this flexibility, the developer can be required to leave open spaces or public amenities to compensate for greater impacts on the property than would otherwise be allowed by local zoning requirements. Performance-based zoning establishes a set of performance standards that developments must conform to in order to limit the impacts of development on natural resources and other surrounding parcels. These standards might include assessments of imperviousness, open spaces, wetland protection, and transportation impacts. Overlay zoning is a technique whereby a new district or zone is superimposed on existing zoning to add additional land use requirements. Overlay zoning has been used to preserve natural resources or even to promote redevelopment and revitalization through special incentives. Each of these four tools—subdivision ordinances, planned unit development, overlay zoning, and performance-based zoning—has the potential to address hazard-related mitigation standards or provisions that can attempt to minimize the impacts of development for generating vulnerabilities in terms of the development itself, surrounding areas, and the overall community.

The remaining are much more direct in their application for mitigation. Agricultural or open space zoning ordinances can be used to preserve forest habitats, hilltops, slopes, and so on in order to limit development in areas that are likely to experience hazards ranging from floods to landslides and to prevent erosion and protect wetlands. Similarly, hazard setbacks require development to be undertaken beyond some distance from either a natural resource, such as dunes or vegetation, or simply a high-hazard area. Finally, stormwater retention requirements can reduce downstream flooding by ensuring that runoff is curtailed as part of the development itself.

Figure 8.2 presents the findings for the set of development and land use regulations. This figure, and the ones that follow, uses horizontal bar graphs to show the percentage of jurisdictions using each of the development and land use policies. Each bar displays the extent to which jurisdictions are using each policy or strategy. In each case, the lighter the bar, the more extensively the policy or strategy is being used; the darker the bar, the less extensively the policy is being used, with black indicating it is not being used at all. In figure 8.2, the policies are arranged in order of prevalence; in this case, higher percentages of jurisdictions have adopted and use residential subdivision ordinances to at least a small extent, followed by stormwater retention, hazard setbacks, planned unit developments, overlay districts, agricultural and open space zoning, and lastly performance-based zoning.

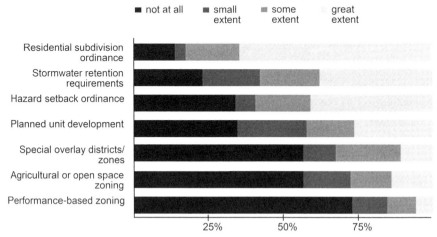

Figure 8.2. Percentages of jurisdictions that use residential subdivision ordinances, stormwater retention requirements, hazard setback ordinances, planned unit developments, special overlay districts, agricultural or open space zoning, and performance-based zoning.

As noted earlier, the data suggest that residential subdivision ordinances are the most extensively used by local jurisdictions, with more than 75 percent of jurisdictions using them to at least some extent and nearly 65 percent using them to a great extent. Stormwater retention requirements are also quite prevalent, with more than 75 percent of jurisdictions using them to at least some extent. With respect to hazard setback ordinances, nearly 60 percent of local jurisdictions are using them at least to some extent. Fewer than 50 percent of jurisdictions are using special overlay districts, and fewer than 43 percent are using agricultural and open space zoning. Nearly 14 percent are making extensive use of agricultural open space zoning, and approximately 10 percent are making extensive use of the overlay zoning. More recent forms of zoning, such as performance-based zoning, are rarely used, with more than 75 percent not using them at all.

The findings with respect to land use and development regulations show that local jurisdictions are generally more focused on trying to shape development via residential subdivision ordinances and to mitigate through stormwater retention requirements and hazard setbacks, with some limited introduction of more incentive-based and flexible approaches such as planned unit developments. These findings are somewhat similar to those of previous studies which suggested that subdivisions and hazard setback ordinances are often used in land use planning.[11] However, the findings from some studies that there is extensive use of zoning ordinances[12] clearly do not hold among our sample of Texas jurisdictions, although there is some use of overlay and open space or agricultural zoning.

Building Standards

Building standards and codes that minimize the loss and damage to structures from natural hazards can be crucial strategies for hazard mitigation (see box 8.1). These strategies are sometimes needed because local governments often display little or no willingness to limit development in high-hazard regions. The inability to control development is a function of many factors, including land development rights, the attachment of residents to their lands, limited choices that can result in purchasing more affordable property in environmentally sensitive or hazardous areas, and pressure from the development community. It is also difficult to control development when people build in high-hazard areas—along the coast, in landslide-prone areas, and along rivers—because of the attractiveness and recreational or economic opportunities. As Beatley notes,[13] the complete avoidance of hazard areas is often not possible. As a consequence, buildings and homes in many high-hazard areas can be subject to high winds, floodwaters, surge, and earthquakes. Therefore, building standards and code requirements should be essential aspects of building and developing in some areas and can be quite effective for reducing damage. Klee, for example, states that "coastal hazards can be reduced through prudent design and construction of structures."[14] He also mentions that designs which allow the passage of wind and water around the structure have been found to be the most effective at reducing damage. A broad-based package of building standards may include traditional building codes, floodproofing requirements, retrofit requirements for existing buildings,[15] and wind hazard resistance technology for new and existing homes.[16]

The building regulation standard and code data we collected were related to five policy areas—the current building code adopted by local jurisdictions, flood hazard standards for new homes, wind hazard resistance standards for new homes, retrofitting for existing buildings, and special utility codes—and are presented in figure 8.3. The data have been sorted as in order of prevalence, and for the most part these standards and regulations were coded as discussed earlier. Flood standards for new home construction have been extensively adopted in these jurisdictions. Indeed, all but 12 percent of the sampled jurisdictions are making use of these requirements, with nearly 80 percent making extensive

Box 8.1. Building Codes

In general, there are two building codes that states and local jurisdictions often adopt: the International Building Code (IBC) for commercial and multifamily structures and the International Residential Code (IRC) for single- and two-family structures.[a] These building codes are generally updated every three years, and they include wind and flood elements. States vary as to whether they have adopted a statewide building code and the extent to which they mandate whether local jurisdictions must or even can adopt a building code. Florida and very recently Louisiana have mandated state building codes, both based on the IBC and IRC. Alabama and Mississippi have state codes that apply to state buildings only, although building codes were developed for coastal areas in Mississippi after Hurricane Katrina, and some coastal counties did adopt these measures. Texas has an official statewide building code, which is a modification of the IBC and IRC, and local municipalities are expected to adopt the statewide code, although they are not required to. More specifically, through its department of insurance, Texas has developed its own version of the IBC and IRC, but local communities, not counties, are free to adopt or not to adopt the codes. Interestingly, until recently counties could not officially adopt a building code. However, now counties can adopt and enforce the building code adopted in their county seat.

a. Jacob, J. S., and S. Showalter. "The Resilient Coast: Policy Frameworks for Adapting the Built Environment to Climate Change and Growth in Coastal Areas of the US Gulf Coast Areas." 2007. http://nsglc.olemiss.edu/TheBuiltEnvironment08-sm_000.pdf (accessed August 28, 2014).

or some use of these requirements. The extensive use of these requirements results from the fact that most jurisdictions are involved with the National Flood Insurance Program.

Building code data used a slightly different coding scheme; the categories and therefore colors convey the nature of the code adopted, with the most recent building code given the lightest gray color and older codes given darker shades of gray. If no building code was adopted, they were coded black. More specifically, if local jurisdictions adopted the most current building code standards available at the time of data collection, the 2009 IRB/IBC codes, they were given the lightest gray. If the local jurisdiction adopted the 2006 or 2003 IRC/IBC codes they were coded with the medium gray, communities using the 2000 IRC/IBC or the even older southern building codes were coded dark gray, and if no building code was adopted, the jurisdiction was coded black. Just less than a quarter of jurisdictions report having adopted the most current 2009 IRC/IBC building code with about double that percentage having adopted either the 2006 or the 2003 IRC/IBC. Overall then, about 70 percent of these jurisdictions report adopting one of the 2003, 2006, or 2009 forms of the IBC/IRC recommended by the Texas Department of Insurance.

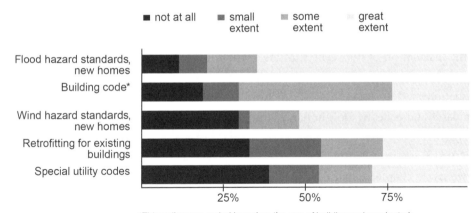

Figure 8.3. Extent to which jurisdictions use flood hazard standards for new homes, building codes, wind hazard standards for new homes, retrofitting for existing buildings, and special utility codes.

Unfortunately, just over 10 percent were still using the oldest version (2000) of the IRC/ IBC or even older southern building code (SBC). Even more disconcerting is the finding that approximately 20 percent of jurisdictions (or 26) have adopted no building code. Most of these jurisdictions are counties, which until recently could not adopt and enforce a building code in Texas; however, a number were also cities.

The implementation of wind hazard regulations for new homes was moderately high, with just over half of the jurisdictions using them extensively and an additional 20 percent using them to at least a small extent. However, just over 30 percent have not adopted wind hazard policies at all. Retrofitting regulations and special utility codes are not extensively used among these jurisdictions. Just over a quarter of these jurisdictions use retrofitting standards extensively, with an additional 40 percent using them to at least a small extent and about a third having no such policies for existing buildings and structures. Similarly, just over 40 percent have adopted no special utility codes, with about 60 percent using them to at least a small extent and half of them using them extensively.

The fact that nearly 70 percent of our sampled jurisdictions have adopted new building codes and are extensively requiring flood standards for new construction is a positive finding. However, as Burby suggests,[17] building codes and flood and wind standards may be effective in reducing losses for new construction and development but have little or no impact on losses to existing development in hazard zones. Of course, this assumes that more recently adopted codes are stronger.[18] Newer codes will have effects when homes are renovated or damaged, assuming that renovations or repairs amount to more than 50 percent of a structure's value. Also, in the case of less substantial improvements such as the installation of hurricane shutters or roofs, retrofitting programs can substantially improve mitigation with new code adoption. On the whole, when compared with other regulations, it does appear that jurisdictions are making more extensive usage of building standards and codes as tools in hazard mitigation.

Natural Resource Protection

As we saw in chapter 7, natural resource protection was not often proposed as part of mitigation plans. However, the idea of preserving and protecting natural resources for coastal hazard mitigation has been discussed by many scholars. Often, development results not only in the settlement of hazardous areas but also in the destruction of ecosystems, such as wetlands or dune areas, that can provide protection from natural perils such as surge and flooding.[19] In addition, the lack of natural barriers such as wetlands, barrier islands, estuaries, dunes, and forests has been linked to greater risk from many types of hazards, such as flooding, hurricanes, subsidence, storm surge, and coastal erosion.[20]

Some researchers suggest mitigation strategies should focus on ecosystem management in order to maintain the protective features of natural environments, such as the use of vegetation for reducing wave action, current energy, and erosion and for trapping sediment that is urgently needed.[21] Other mitigation strategies include enhancing coral reefs, preserving and enhancing dune formation and sand bars, and protecting and planting forests. Brody and colleagues have shown a strong and direct relationship between wetland loss and flood-related damage and loss of life. Specifically, they have examined the development of wetlands, which essentially means filling in and otherwise altering wetlands, which results in higher subsequent flood damage, with cumulative effects. The inescapable conclusion of this research is that the preservation of wetlands, and consequently the ecosystem services they provide, can be a strong tool for mitigation and resiliency.[22]

Figure 8.4 displays the data on natural resource protection tools, which include wetland protection, protected area preservation, and habitat protection and restoration. The results clearly suggest that these approaches are rarely used by local jurisdictions. On the whole, these regulations are not extensively used, with more than 50 percent of jurisdictions not adopting actions. However, at least with wetland protection, just over 20 percent do use this policy extensively, with another 15 percent using it to some extent. Only 10 percent use habitat protection or restoration policies extensively, and 66 percent do not use these policies at all. Similarly, 62 percent do not use protected area policies to protect natural resources at all, and only 12 percent use these policies extensively.

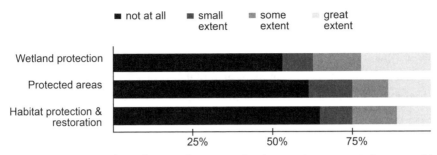

Figure 8.4. Percentages of jurisdictions that use wetland protection, protected areas, and habitat protection and restoration.

In light of the findings from both the Texas study and the multistate study of hazard mitigation plans and actions, natural resource protections were rarely considered as part of proposed hazard mitigation actions, and more often than not, they are not considered at all. These findings certainly suggest that natural resource protection as a potential hazard mitigation strategy is underused. Perhaps in part this is because such protection is underrecognized as an effective tool, even though the research has clearly shown that natural areas can be important elements of a comprehensive mitigation strategy.

Public Information and Awareness

Hazard awareness strategies can be an important step for community success in implementing a broad-based hazard mitigation program. For example, Hyndman and Hyndman state that public awareness can promote the adoption of mitigation actions to reduce disaster impacts by influencing households and individuals to "modify their behaviour or their property to minimize such impacts."[23] Beatley also suggests that hazard disclosure and hazard zone signs forewarn property owners, developers, and local officials of the real hazard exposure and potential for future disasters.[24] Importantly, given the high mobility of our population, these policies can help newcomers better understand the potential danger of natural hazards and promote mitigation.[25] Educational programs can increase community commitment to mitigation policies.[26] Hazard information and awareness programs also can be thought of as a mechanism through which land use practices and patterns might be altered voluntarily. The hope is that, as residents, builders, developers, and others gain a better understanding of their hazard exposure and risk, they will make adjustments that will improve the mitigation status of an area. For example, homeowners might consider installing impact-resistant windows or even storm shutters on their homes, even though such mitigation requirements were not in effect when their homes were built. Unfortunately, some stakeholders in local communities oppose these kinds of programs because they consider them bad for business and cast a negative light on the community. For example, signage that notes the locations of fault lines or floodplains can be quite informative for local populations, and yet many oppose this strategy because it dissuades people from buying homes near such signs.

There are a host of these programs that might be considered. For this research, we focused on five different strategies often mentioned in the literature[27]: public education for hazard mitigation, citizen involvement in hazard mitigation planning, seminars on hazard mitigation practices for developers and builders, hazard disclosure statements as part of real estate and other transitions, and the use of hazard zone signage. Figure 8.5 displays the various responses for each strategy.

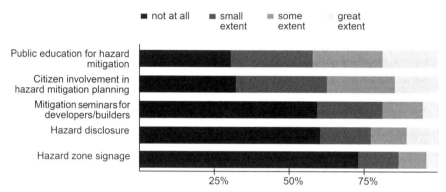

Figure 8.5. Percentages of jurisdictions that use public education for hazard mitigation, citizen involvement in hazard mitigation planning, mitigation seminars for develops and builders, hazard disclosures, and hazard zone signage.

Public education programs focusing on hazard mitigation are by far the most extensively used strategy among our sample jurisdictions. Although almost 30 percent do not use these programs at all, nearly 70 percent are making use of them, with nearly 20 percent using them to a great extent. Similarly, promoting citizen involvement in hazard mitigation planning has been adopted in nearly 70 percent of all jurisdictions, with nearly 14 percent of local jurisdictions promoting this extensively. Unfortunately, more than 60 percent of jurisdictions are not offering mitigation seminars to builders and developers, nor are they using hazard disclosure statements. Also, nearly 75 percent of jurisdictions have not adopted any kind of hazard signage to identify areas that are at higher risk. On the other hand, it is not insignificant to note that nearly 40 percent of jurisdictions are offering training classes to builders and developers and requiring hazard disclosure statements at least to a small extent. Similarly, at least 25 percent are using hazard signage to some extent in their jurisdictions to help inform the public of high-hazard areas in their community.

Although information dissemination and awareness tools are inexpensive and have the potential to promote voluntary mitigation, these programs are not being used by local jurisdictions. Our findings suggest that there is strong adoption of public education programs and citizen involvement in hazard mitigation planning, but we must be cautious in interpreting how effectively these education programs are reaching the public and how many citizens are actually involved in mitigation planning efforts. The fact that nearly 40 percent of these communities are offering some form of education programs to builders and developers is promising, particularly because these two constituencies play such prominent roles in development activities. On the other hand, the fact that disclosure statements and signage programs are not widely adopted is a clear area for improvement.

Incentive Tools

Incentive tools are a strategy to encourage builders, developers, or property owners to engage in practices consistent with hazard mitigation or adaptation.[28] These strategies may be undertaken by a local community to shape the nature of development in their community, whereas others are undertaken by the federal government to shape the behavior of individuals, households, or even local jurisdictions and state governments. The latter can certainly be seen with respect to hazard mitigation planning and flood-related mitigation.

Local incentive programs are focused primarily on shaping the behaviors of local developers and landowners by promoting development patterns consistent with community development goals, such as preserving natural environmental resources and promoting hazard mitigation. For example, developers may be allowed to exceed density or height limits if they also undertake actions that might enhance mitigation in some manner, such as avoiding building in high-hazard areas, modifying building designs to enhance mitigation, or clustering development in areas away from wetlands. Density bonuses are another example whereby a developer might build structures conforming to higher wind or flood standards in return for the community allowing higher densities within a development than normally would have been permitted. A somewhat more complex approach is transfer of development rights (TDRs). Communities can transfer the right to develop land from one area, perhaps an environmentally sensitive or high-hazard area, to a less environmentally sensitive or less hazardous area.[29] Under this strategy, a community designates both conservation "sending zones," such as an open space directly along a waterway or a natural wetland where development is not permitted or is to be discouraged, and "receiving zones," where additional development density is permitted if the developer transfers development rights to the original property.[30]

The National Flood Insurance Program (NFIP), which provides flood insurance to homeowners in flood hazard areas, has elements of an incentive program.[31] The NFIP requires that certain standards in building and land preparation be followed for home-owners in a municipality or county to qualify for coverage.[32] In a similar manner, many state-supported wind insurance programs demand higher building standards and inspections to qualify for coverage in state-managed wind pools. FEMA's Community Rating System (CRS) can also be thought of as a community-wide incentive program.[33] This program allows communities to earn flood insurance premium discounts if the community undertakes flood mitigation actions that exceed the NFIP minimum requirements.[34] The CRS classes are based on eighteen activities, which are grouped into the following four main categories: public information, mapping and regulation, flood damage reduction, and flood preparedness.[35] Research has shown that communities in both Texas and Florida not only can reduce premiums by being involved in this program but, most importantly, can substantially reduce flooding losses.[36] In other words, research has shown that this program clearly reduces losses.

Figure 8.6 presents the results for participation in federal flood-related programs or use of local incentive programs. Specifically, federal programs include the NFIP and the CRS. Local incentives include the transfer of development rights from environmentally sensitive and hazardous areas, density bonuses, and cluster development away from environmentally sensitive and hazardous areas. By and large, participation in the federal programs is much higher than implementation of local programs. A remarkably high percentage, nearly 64 percent, of local jurisdictions participated in NFIP to a great extent, with substantial percentages also claiming participation to a lesser extent. Generally speaking, a community is either in or out of the NFIP. Most jurisdictions indicating "small extent" or "some extent" were listed on the FEMA or NFIP websites as participants, and these smaller levels simply reflect smaller floodplains and thus lower participation rates. For all intents and purposes, nearly 89 percent of jurisdictions participate in the NFIP, which guarantees some compliance with general flood standards. Participation in CRS is more moderate yet still substantial. Indeed, just over 70 percent of jurisdictions participate in the CRS program, with more than half of these participating extensively, denoting the substantial investment in commitments and implementation of flood-related mitigation efforts.

Unfortunately, a very different pattern emerges when we consider local incentive programs. Density bonuses, cluster development, and transfer of development rights are rarely implemented. Indeed, almost across the board, nearly 90 percent of jurisdictions have not adopted these policy options at all. It is possible, as suggested by Schwab and colleagues, that these programs are simply difficult for many local jurisdictions to implement and manage without substantial capacities.[37] The findings with respect to local incentive programs appear to be in contrast to a number of studies that suggest the

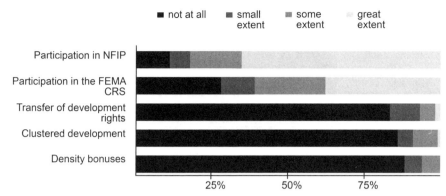

Figure 8.6. Percentages of jurisdictions that use the National Flood Insurance Program (NFIP), the NFIP's Community Rating System (CRS), transfer of development rights, cluster developments, and density bonuses.

adoption of these programs, particularly in California, at somewhat higher rates.[38] Even with respect to earlier studies, the percentages were generally only twice our participation rates, which suggests overall low adoption and implementation.

Overall, the findings clearly suggest that the two federal programs have very high adoption and implementation rates, particularly when compared with local incentive programs and policies. The incentives they provide, in terms of access to flood insurance and discounts, are attractive enough to local governments and their citizens to ensure more extensive participation, particularly when compared with local incentive programs.

Property Acquisition Programs

Property acquisitions, through fee simple purchases or purchase of the development rights to properties, are very direct methods of preventing development from spreading to hazardous or environmentally sensitive areas. Furthermore, relocating structures out of hazardous areas can have the same effect, after structures are threatened. Figure 8.7 displays findings related to property acquisition programs, including fee simple purchases, acquisition of development rights or easements, and relocation of existing structures. As should be readily evident, these programs were not widely used by local jurisdictions; indeed, more than three quarters of the jurisdictions never made use of these kinds of programs, and if they were practiced, it was only on rare occasions.

Although they are direct and highly effective at keeping development out of high-hazard areas, local governments are slow to adopt these programs for a variety of reasons. As Beatley has noted, these programs can be very expensive.[39] For a community to buy up what is often seen as prime property along the coast or waterway can be highly expensive, and it reduces tax revenues. In the aftermath of a disaster, local communities

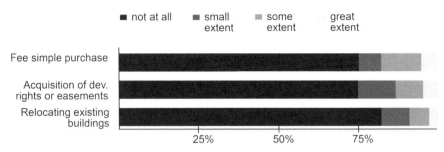

Figure 8.7. Percentages of jurisdictions that use fee simple purchases, acquisition of development rights or easements, and relocating existing buildings.

can combine their resources with those of state and federal governments to buy out "repetitive loss properties" or properties that are subject to new or modified hazard setback demands. Local communities often hesitate to do so, either because other private landowners near these properties do not want "public" property near their properties or because local governments lose tax revenue while also assuming maintenance and other associated liabilities. Although these properties can become community amenities in the form of parks and recreational areas, local jurisdictions often are loath to adopt property acquisition programs. These results are not surprising given previous research that has also noted how few communities propose land and property acquisition programs as part of their planning efforts.[40]

Financial Tools

Because many local jurisdictions have the capacity to levy taxes and impose impact fees or special assessments, these can be powerful tools as either incentives or disincentives to develop in certain places or to use particular design and building features or techniques. Examples of these kinds of financial tools include lower tax rates for preserving natural resources or preserving open space and limiting development intensity, special tax assessments for specific coastal, hazardous, or natural resource areas, and impact fees or special assessments for the development of environmentally sensitive or hazardous areas. Figure 8.8 displays the use of financial tools and policies.

These policies are by far the most unpopular compared with the others examined. Very few jurisdictions use these types of policies, with more than 90 percent of jurisdictions not adopting any of these strategies. Less than 10 percent are using lower taxes as an incentive for not developing in high-hazard or environmentally sensitive areas, 9 percent have at least minimally used impact fees or special assessments, and just over 7 percent at least to a small extent are levying special tax assessments for developing in environmentally sensitive or high-risk areas. These results are consistent with previous

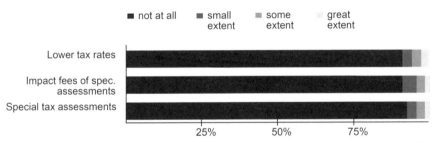

Figure 8.8. Percentages of jurisdictions that use lower tax rates, impact fees of special assessments, and special tax assessments.

studies which suggest that these more market-based mechanisms, whether as incentives or disincentives, were rarely included or were rarely used.[41] However, a number of states, such as Florida, have made impact fees an important mechanism not only for financing mitigation activities but also for funding a great variety of programs to help local communities plan for and undertake mitigation activities.

Critical Public and Private Facilities Policies

Policies related to the placement of public facilities, public or private critical facilities, and municipal service areas can keep buildings and infrastructure out of hazardous and sensitive environmental areas and shift future development into safer areas. Of course, keeping critical facilities, whether private or public, also helps ensure that critical facilities and agencies, such as fire, police, and emergency medical services, can respond in the event of a disaster. Figure 8.9 displays the survey results for these policies.

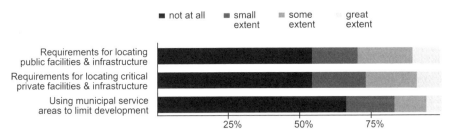

Figure 8.9. Percentages of jurisdictions that use requirements for locating public facilities and infrastructure, requirements for locating critical private facilities and infrastructure, and the use of municipal service areas to limit development.

Even a cursory examination suggests that the percentages of local jurisdictions using these policies are also low but not nearly as bad as we saw previously. It is disappointing to see that just under 55 percent of jurisdictions made no special requirements for locating public and private facilities and infrastructure out of harm's way or at least in less risky locations. On the other hand, that does not necessarily mean that these facilities *are* located in high-hazard areas within these jurisdictions. Furthermore, at least 45 percent of sampled jurisdictions explicitly have policy requirements, at least to some extent, that critical and public facilities and infrastructure must not be located in high-hazard or risky areas. Unfortunately, the least common of these tools is the use of municipal service areas to limit development. More than 66 percent of jurisdictions do not use municipal service areas to limit or steer development away from high-hazard or environmentally sensitive areas. Only 5 percent make extensive use of this kind of policy, with the remaining 29 percent using such policies on only a limited basis.

These findings are somewhat surprising. Although there can certainly be problems in using municipal service areas to limit development—particularly without a comprehensive plan guiding such decisions—ensuring that critical facilities are located outside high-hazard areas seems to be a basic public safety requirement. This finding is not consistent with some studies which found that policies requiring critical public and private facilities to be sited out of hazardous and sensitive areas are common.[42]

Private–Public Sector Initiatives

As noted earlier, local jurisdictions often have limited resources to devote to mitigation planning and implementation. In these situations, involving and partnering with the private sector in the mitigation process can be significant. These partnerships might be as simple as supplementing public education programs, as when local hardware and building stores offer training and how-to programs for putting up hurricane shutters or roofs. These programs may involve much more elaborate initiatives, including facilitating the establishment of land trusts and public–private partnerships for obtaining development rights. As can be seen in figure 8.10, these kinds of programs are not often used among our sample jurisdictions. Essentially 80 percent of jurisdictions have not made use of any form of public–private partnerships for broad-based hazard mitigation activities, although 20 percent are using them at least to a limited extent. Still fewer jurisdictions

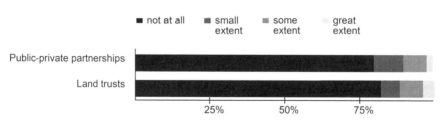

Figure 8.10. Percentages of jurisdictions that use public–private partnerships and land trusts.

are making use of land trusts as a way of ensuring that some areas are not developed in their communities, although here again, at least 17 percent are making at least limited use of them. Of course, this figure does not provide details about how extensive or critical the land areas are that are being protected by these programs. So it is possible that, although these strategies are not often used, the areas that are protected are nevertheless critical for mitigation or preservation.

Pulling the Pieces Together

In order to get an overall picture of how and what kinds of nonstructural mitigation policies and strategies are being used, figure 8.11 presents all thirty-six planning tools, ranked on a scale from 0 to 3 in terms of their average adoption or implementation rating. The higher the rating, the more extensively the policy or strategy is being used across jurisdictions; conversely, the lower the rating, the more unlikely it is to be adopted. The top three tools are the only ones to have averages greater than 2: participation in the NFIP, subdivision ordinances, and requiring flood standards for new construction. The latter is highly related to and probably a function of the requirements for participation in the NFIP.

The next five policies or strategies are similar in that they have averages above 1.5, suggesting not only adoption but at least some spread in implementation. These strategies are wind standards for new construction, stormwater retention for new developments, building codes, participation in the CRS, and hazard setback ordinances. Of the top eight strategies, most are focused on flooding or wind hazards, addressing building standards, or addressing overall jurisdictional vulnerabilities by participating in the NFIP or CRS, as well as using hazard setbacks. Interestingly, the only general development land use control strategy that is widely used is subdivision ordinances. This is the principal land use strategy used.

Retrofitting standards for existing structures, planned unit developments, special utility standards, public education programs, citizen involvement in hazard mitigation planning, and wetland protection are the six other strategies or policies that have an average rating above 1. This implies that they are being widely adopted among jurisdictions, but their implementation is limited. Nevertheless, it is important that existing structures are being addressed and equally important that there have been attempts to educate communities in terms of their hazard risks and vulnerabilities. It is also significant that wetland protection, as an element of environmental sustainability and mitigation, is being adopted by some jurisdictions.

On the whole, it appears that a limited number of mitigation policies and strategies are being adopted by jurisdictions in our sample. Indeed, only fourteen of the thirty-six tools we considered are being adopted by jurisdictions. The ones that are being adopted

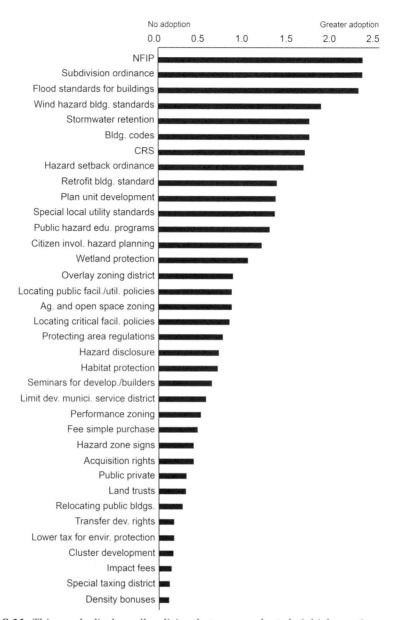

Figure 8.11. This graph displays all policies that were evaluated. A higher rating means that more jurisdictions adopt such policies. We can see that a significant number of jurisdictions are not using the full breadth of strategies available.

do appear to be targeting the highest hazards that these jurisdictions are currently facing: flooding and wind-related hazards. It is also evident that the portfolio is narrowly focusing on these issues and, for the most part, tackling them in terms of building codes and standards, which focus primarily on new construction, and in terms of setbacks, which provide some limitations to development. However, many tools that would address preserving and keeping development out of high-hazard and environmentally sensitive areas are not being used. In fact, the picture that emerges is one of a very limited portfolio of mitigation strategies and policies being used. Comprehensive mitigation to address broad-based mitigation is likely to require a more robust portfolio of strategies that will include a variety of mechanisms to bring about mitigation.

How do these results compare with those by Godschalk, Brower, and Beatley back in the late 1980s?[43] Unfortunately, the two instruments and kinds of policies that were included in these two surveys were somewhat different, in part because we considered so many new and additional approaches proposed today. Fortunately, a number were sufficiently close that we felt comfortable directly comparing them. One additional difference between the two surveys was that they simply asked whether the policy was adopted. To better ensure comparability, we collapsed ours to "adopted" or "not adopted." The results are presented in figure 8.12.

It is interesting to note the similarities and differences between our more recent sample in Texas and their sample from the Atlantic coast. To facilitate comparisons, the strategies have been rank ordered from low levels of adoption to high, based on the Godschalk and colleagues findings. Although preferential tax assessments are quite comparable between

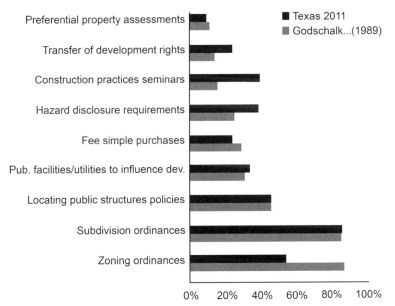

Figure 8.12. The last time a study of this nature was done was in 1989. This graph compares the adoption of nine strategies in 2011 with those evaluated in 1989.

the two samples, it is clear that transfer of development rights, seminars for builders, and hazard disclosures are actually much more widely adopted and practiced among current Texas jurisdictions than they were in 1989. Interestingly, fee simple purchases of private land, seeking to limit development using utility districts, requiring public facilities to be built in nonhazardous areas, and the use of subdivision ordinances are all quite comparable between their earlier Atlantic sample and our more recent Texas sample. Finally, and perhaps not surprisingly, the use of zoning was clearly much more prevalent and widespread in their sample than we find in Texas. Although the finding of limited use of zoning is not surprising in Texas, it is interesting to note that transfer of development rights, special education programs, and hazard disclosures are all much more likely to be used or required.

Despite their limited use for hazard mitigation, the strategies and policies described in this chapter are all regular tools city and regional planners use. This planner's toolbox can be incorporated into hazard mitigation plans and the variety of other plans your community may have. In chapter 9 we will describe the need for consistency across plans as a means to shore up coordination to lead toward disaster-resilient practices.

Here we describe Steps 5 and 6, Prioritize and Implement, to inclusively plan for disasters.

Step 5: Prioritize

This chapter describes a range of policies and actions that can be incorporated into disaster management and plans. In addition, the most effective disaster plans reinforce other adopted plans and their policies. Planners should use this step in the process to engage the public in a conversation about which strategies are most appropriate for addressing community issues. Again, there are many ways to approach this task and dozens of guidance documents available in the public domain. In general, planners should find ways to help citizens come up with unique and innovative solutions for community issues by connecting them to experts in the field, presenting case studies of promising practices, or even arranging field trips to exemplary places. In addition, the best strategies emerge from a careful look at the political, systemic, economic, and personal realities at play in institutions and communities.[44] Finally, taskforce members should consider the cost of strategy implementation, which performance measures are most useful for measuring progress, and where the resources will come from to sustain the work.

Step 6: Implement

This step of the process requires groups to define who will do what, and when, with regard to the execution of disaster management plans. In other words, it is time to identify manageable tasks and responsible parties. Hopefully, the experience of participating in the process from beginning to end will foster more commitment and accountability from taskforce members and others with a stake in the outcome of the implementation of planning strategies. At this stage planners can help participants break strategies down into manageable tasks, effectively converting vision into action. Furthermore, implementation plans should strive to maximize the deployment of community capacity by spreading accountability across multiple community stakeholders. Finally, the selected strategies are administered through appropriate implementation mechanisms.

Exercise 10. Prioritizing Objectives and Actions

How do the findings in this chapter compare with your community? Do you see similar patterns in your community? Is your community making use of a full range of strategies and policies, or are they as narrowly focused as we saw in Texas?

We are going to walk through a process of prioritizing the data collected in part II as a way of determining which strategies and tools to use. Look back at the maps and

Table 8.2. Putting the Pieces Together: Prioritizing Method

Hazard type:
Example: Hurricane (mapping risk and surge zones)

Disaster agent characteristics and potential impacts:
Example: Flooding and surge waters, high winds, loss of electricity increases risk of high temperatures, tornadoes, reduced mobility limits access to resources, high demand and low staff in hospitals, access to clean drinking water

Map Hotspot Key	Neighborhood or Area	Social Vulnerability Indicators	Social Vulnerability Consequences	Physically Vulnerable Structure Within or Near?
Example 1	Downtown	Transportation needs Child care needs	Evacuation rate decreased; children with limited access to resources disproportionately affected; psychological and mental health impacts; increased likelihood of death	Yes, Fire Station 1

information you developed in part II. Which areas in your community are social vulnerability hotspots? What are the needs of these areas, and what are the potential consequences if these needs are not addressed? Are these areas in or near physically vulnerable structures or infrastructure? Think about the potential impacts of this highly vulnerable hotspot. What are some possible strategies discussed in this chapter that might be used to mitigate these areas? Input your community's information into table 8.2.

Potential Impacts of This Hotspot	Possible Actions, Strategies, Programs
Limited access to first responders and medical help and supplies; immobility and reduced evacuation rate will result in more people with limited access to first responders; psychological and mental health impacts on residents, esp. children; high temperatures, limited access to food, and limited mobility will increase likelihood of death	Public–private partnerships Develop business recovery program with the council of government Stronger building codes Stronger code enforcement

Exercise 10 continues on next page

The areas that are both socially vulnerable and physically vulnerable should be priority areas. Which priority areas align with the goals developed? Write a list of all priority areas and possible goals that would help support these areas. Now think about what objectives are needed to achieve each goal as it relates to priority areas. With the taskforce, develop a list of measurable and achievable objectives. Brainstorm which policies and strategies described in this chapter might be used to support priority areas. Form a taskforce meeting to discuss which possibilities are feasible. Directly incorporate agreed-upon strategies as action items. An example action item chart is seen in table 8.3. You will see funding sources and responsible parties. The action item chart will directly help the implementation of strategies and move the community to achieving goals. Incorporate the goals, objectives, action items, and implementation chart into the plan.

Table 8.3. Goal 1: Reduce total damage to all structures affected by flooding by 20% over 10 years in 2010 USD

Objective 1.1: Preserve 80% of all floodplains as open space or recreational areas within 10 years

Objective 1.2: Protect 80% of all wetlands within 5 years

Objective 1.3: Prioritize structural mitigation capital improvement projects to areas that are considered socially vulnerable within 2 years

Objective 1.4: Develop ordinances that prohibit new development to occur in the 100-year floodplain as of the 2010 FEMA maps within 2 years

	Action	Responsible Party with Contact Person	Anticipated Action Accomplished Date	Funding Source	Key: Which Priority Area Does the Goal Support?
Example: Action 1.1.1	Amend wetland permitting process	City council, planning staff George Ramirez, 512-000-9999	Within 1 year	N/A	1
Action 1.1.2	Develop a prioritized list of all wetlands, property owners, and uses				
Action 1.1.3	Set up a transfer of development rights program				

Table 8.3. continued

	Action	Responsible Party with Contact Person	Anticipated Action Accomplished Date	Funding Source	Key: Which Priority Area Does the Goal Support?
Action 1.2.1	Prioritize structural mitigation capital improvement projects to areas that are considered socially vulnerable within 2 years				
Action 1.2.2	Hire a consultant to conduct a drainage study to assess priority areas				
Action 1.2.3	Apply for grants that support hazard mitigation, drainage, and infrastructure improvements				
Action 1.3.1	Amend ordinance to prohibit new development in 100-year floodplain				
Action 1.3.2	Rezone land				

9. Striving for Consistency

Consistency, in a person, is defined as "the quality or fact of staying the same at different times."[1] This implies that various dimensions of a person such as thought, behavior, feelings, reason, and will are consistent with one another over time. This does not necessarily guarantee consistent outcomes, but it is compatible with opinions and values of the person.[2] When consistency is applied to human groups, communities, organizations, and companies, researchers identify two important aspects: one that stands together as a whole and a reasonable or logical harmony between parts.[3]

Urban planning literature repeatedly emphasizes the importance of consistency in local approaches for delivery and implementation of sustainable development and hazard mitigation policies.[4] Not only do plans need to be generated in a community to promote mitigation, preparedness, response, and recovery, but they need to be consistent with each other and with all other plans in the community. Figure 9.1 displays the roles the disaster phases play over time, as seen in chapter 3. You will note the addition of "consistency" arrows to the left of the model. As reiterated throughout the book, comprehensive planning, emergency and preparedness planning, mitigation planning, and recovery planning should all occur before a disaster. Not only should these activities occur before disaster strikes, but a logical harmony between the various plans is needed. Most communities prepare a variety of local plans to guide future growth and development (e.g., land use, transportation, and urban design plans). Each of these local plans focuses on the exclusive viewpoints of the individual planners and plan-making agencies. Rarely do

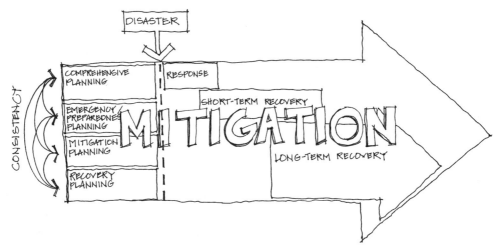

Figure 9.1. Consistency of plans that address the disaster phases must align with all other plans in a community (e.g., comprehensive plans, land use management plans).

these plans connect with each other or even coordinate policy implementation. This lack of consistency between the local plans limits the ability of local government to effectively implement sustainable development decisions. Moreover, it can lead to arbitrary or capricious decisions that advance selected interests.

With respect to hazard mitigation, we are concerned with the lack of consistency of policies among various local plans. Therefore, we adopt a definition similar to that in the macroeconomic literature wherein a decision is to be considered inconsistent if it brings about a change in decision rules that makes it possible for contradictory or inappropriate decisions to be made in the future.[5] The principle of consistency as applied to local planning for disaster mitigation implies that a local policy is to be considered inconsistent if it increases community exposure to risk from known natural hazards. For example, local development policies that encourage development along the coastline and riverine systems should be considered inconsistent with the local hazard mitigation policies, because they result in increased exposure of citizens and property to known hazards. Plans may not only be inconsistent, they may also prescribe contradictory actions. For example, a hazard mitigation plan may recommend steering development out of areas that are increasingly vulnerable to flooding, while the same jurisdiction's comprehensive plan may seek to intensify new development in existing urban corridors that happen to be near the edge of existing floodplains. This may be done under the guise of "smart growth" but may not be so smart at all.[6]

The principle of consistency is not new to local planners. Most planners are familiar with the consistency doctrine as applied to zoning and comprehensive plans.[7] Adherence to the consistency doctrine requires local jurisdictions to enact zoning policies and regulations to carry out, implement, or effectuate comprehensive plans. However, the degree of consistency has been open to interpretation, both in local policy making and in legal opinion, resulting in high variation across the country.[8] Judicial interpretations of state statutes and planning laws have created a wide variety of frameworks for local planning, but numerous studies have shown significant sustainability benefits as a result of the application of the consistency doctrine.

Although the consistency doctrine is entrenched in local land use planning and zoning, it is yet to be established in local planning for effective implementation of hazard mitigation policies. Given the growing need to limit local exposure to known hazards and the increasing threat of climatic changes, it is imperative that planners adopt the consistency principle across all local plans and development policies to minimize community exposure to natural hazards.

Consistency matters because future growth and development cannot proceed unless we minimize our impact on the environment. Unsustainable and insensitive patterns of growth will only result in increasing costs to the economy, environment, and public health. Adoption of the consistency principle will ensure successful implementation of hazard mitigation goals and policies that the public rightfully expects from the local government.

Adoption of consistency principles as a legitimate policy mandate offers numerous advantages. Most hazard mitigation actions and environmental issues such as climate change require that planners take a long-term view that spans multiple electoral periods. Consistency provides a political cover for local decision makers who are likely to face difficulty in implementing unpopular long-term decisions. This will also provide a greater sense of security for the general public, property owners, and developers who desire predictability and stability in local development policies. Furthermore, this approach provides a rational and reasonable framework for decision making across all local planning regimes to minimize losses from existing and anticipated hazards.

Typically, local planning is a continuous cyclical process consisting of seven key steps (as described in chapter 1). These planning steps follow a logical sequence, and there is an expectation of community participation at each stage.

Although the sequential steps of the planning process are important and ensure logical consistency of the process, it is also important to recognize the iterative nature of plan making. Interrelationships exist between the seven planning stages. Information gained at a later stage can result in adjustment of the outcomes of the earlier stage through feedback linkages. Often, data analysis (Assess) can provide insights into local issues that may not have been considered at the initiation of the planning process. These data, along with local knowledge, should inform the goals, objectives, and priorities established (Envision and Prioritize). By monitoring, evaluating, and updating goals, objectives, and prioritized actions, planners should identify new issues and move through the process again.

Most communities carry out a parallel process of multihazard mitigation planning, as described in the earlier chapters of the book. As we discussed earlier, lack of connection between hazard mitigation planning and other local planning processes results in development patterns that increase probability of higher losses in case of hazard impacts. Therefore, it is imperative to identity opportunities for integrating hazard mitigation planning processes in the local plan-making framework. Figure 9.2 illustrates such an integrated framework for plan making. It is important to consider hazard mitigation at the start of the planning process during the assessment of the community (Assess) and the formulation of the goals, objectives, and priorities (Envision and Prioritize). In the subsequent planning steps, plan makers can purposefully incorporate programs that are

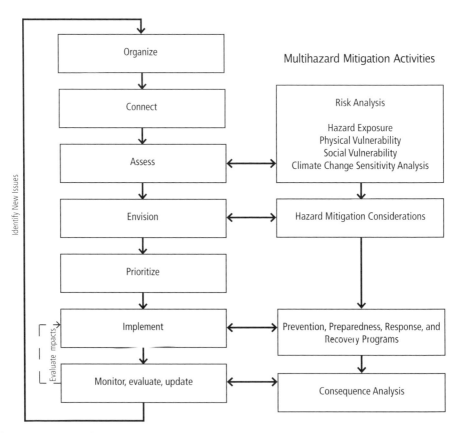

Figure 9.2. Hazard mitigation strategies can be integrated into the established inclusive planning process.

likely to contribute to prevention, preparedness, response, and recovery. Similarly, consideration of risk consequences as a part of evaluation (Monitor, Evaluate, Update) will ensure that the resultant plans are sustainable and resilient. Attention to hazard mitigation at the outset ensures that the subsequent steps of the planning process are sensitive to the hazard risks faced by the community.

Hazard Mitigation Elements in Local Plans

It is envisaged that integration of hazard mitigation consideration in local planning will result in plans that recognize threats from natural hazards and climate change and will recommend policies that limit community exposure to risk from extreme events. Such an integrated planning process could be easily integrated with the comprehensive plan-making process that many communities undertake. A comprehensive plan is the official vision of growth and development adopted by a local government. It outlines the overall direction and nature of development based on an assessment of the existing conditions and future demands of the community. With a long time frame (usually 20–30 years), this plan provides information and guidance to the public and private stakeholders about how future decisions are likely to be made about the existing and future built environment in a community. At a minimum, a comprehensive plan includes an assessment of issues and opportunities the community faces, an analysis of existing conditions and characteristics of the community, the built environment and the natural environment, analysis of trends and future growth trajectories, and connectivity between other elements (e.g., land use, transportation, housing) of the plans.

Not all communities prepare such comprehensive plans. A number of communities undertake specific planning initiatives in lieu of the comprehensive plan or even to complement the comprehensive plan. In each of these planning initiatives, there exist opportunities to incorporate hazard mitigation considerations in the plan-making process. In the following subsection we focus on some of the common local plans that describe opportunities to ensure consistency with hazard mitigation goals.

Land Use Plans

The land use plans (or the land use elements of a comprehensive plan) present the distribution of existing and future land uses. Often these are in the form of color-coded maps that display the location and distribution of various land uses. Ideally, the process preparing a land use plan involves three important steps. First, site surveys are conducted to identify existing distribution of land uses within the community. Second, based on the future growth projections, demand (quantity as well as location) for various land uses is estimated for the plan year. Third, a future land use plan is prepared that highlights the desired distribution of land uses in the plan year based on a suitability analysis (both social and environmental) (see box 9.1). A land use plan is expected to estimate all land use needs until the chosen plan year and provide policies to ensure that these needs are met in accordance with the overall development vision of the community. Most communities today use sophisticated mapping techniques and geographic information systems (GISs) for analyzing existing environmental and landscape constraints in development of a sustainable land use plan. In the last few decades, a number of advanced community participation tools such as crowdsourcing, participatory workshops, and envisioning dialogues have also been adopted by communities to assess existing needs and identify future development demands.

Box 9.1. Scenario Planning

City planning is based on forecasting: the ability to look forward into the future and predict what is likely to occur. Forecasting accurately is notoriously difficult, and many planners have given it over entirely to more technically accurate projections done by demographers and others. However, projections are limited by the expectation that current trends will be extended into the future. Planners need to consider the question that planning scholar Andy Isserman posed: "How can change change?"[a] In other words, if our projected path takes us somewhere we don't want to go, what can we do to change it?

In a rational planning model, all possible alternatives are supposedly considered. Given the unfeasibility of considering essentially an infinite number of possibilities for the number of parameters being considered, the development of likely scenarios makes planning more accessible to residents and also helps them choose the most desirable outcomes from the array of scenarios presented. Scenario planning is a tool used by planners and others to package possible futures in stories that can be understood and responded to. They can also provide guidance on the types of actions and policies that can help the community get where it wants to go.

Scenarios set up stories for what is likely to happen under selected conditions. Of course, the development of scenarios is in itself placing limits on (and potentially biasing) the alternatives considered. Scenarios must be based on an accurate assessment of current conditions—a sound fact basis, as we like to call it, that relies on assessments of demographic, economic, physical, and environmental conditions. A poor fact basis is destined to produce inaccurate or inappropriate forecasts. Scenarios should also identify key drivers of change in a community and assess the likelihood of certain events occurring. As scenarios are developed, care should be taken to provide a well-balanced range of options that is responsive to the local community political and cultural context and the data on social, economic, physical, and environmental change that is expected in the future.

Typically, scenarios include a "current trends" scenario, which answers the question, "What will happen if we continue down our current path?" This scenario is usually set up as a straw man, designed to illustrate to residents and stakeholders how current trends such as suburban sprawl or low-density residential development will lead to unsustainable or undesirable outcomes related to land consumption, traffic congestion, encroachment into high-hazard areas, or devastation of existing natural resources. Alternative scenarios provide snapshots of how different community priorities may influence future consequences. Indicators are chosen (as part of a participatory process) to gauge community progress on important variables related to community health, quality of life, or prosperity, and their values are projected into the future given the conditions prescribed by the scenario. They may include, for example, changes in measures of air or water quality, changes in measures of the affordability of housing, changes in measures of traffic congestion, changes in measures of social vulnerability, and so on.

Then, alternative scenarios are compared with each other in terms of how well they perform on these indicators, which are often numerous but are organized into categories. An alternative scenario that prioritizes public health, for example, might emphasize measures related to providing sidewalks, reducing air pollution, and maintaining water quality. An alternative scenario that prioritized economic development might emphasize an increase in the number of information sector jobs or the extension of data infrastructure. An alternative scenario that prioritized resilience might emphasize the preservation of wetlands, the reduction of poor residents living in the floodplain, or capital investment in infrastructure related to evacuation, just to name a few. By comparing alternative scenarios along a range of indicators, residents and policymakers can better understand the trade-offs that may be necessary to achieve stated community goals.

For more information about scenario planning and how to do it, see the Oregon Sustainable Transportation Initiative (OSTI) at http://www.oregon.gov/ODOT/TD/OSTI/pages /scenarios.aspx.

a. Isserman, Andrew M. "Projection, Forecast, and Plan on the Future of Population Forecasting." *Journal of the American Planning Association* 50, no. 2 (1984): 208–21.

Hazard mitigation can be integrated into the land use planning process by providing technical analysis and facilitating community participation that will enable community members to make wise choices from among alternative strategies for future development (table 9.1).[9] During the data collection phase of land use plan preparation, efforts should be made to map risk areas for all known hazards. This hazard assessment informs the

Table 9.1. Opportunities for Hazard Mitigation and Climate Change Considerations in Local Plans

Types of Plans	General Purpose	Hazard Mitigation and Climate Change Considerations
Land use plans	Identify areas (zones) for different types of development (e.g., housing, commercial, industrial). Provide long-term policy direction on land use and development, transportation, and overall community development.	Identify local hazard areas (e.g., earthquake zones, flooding areas, steep slopes, floodplains). Designate low-development and no-development zones. Establish a framework for frequent evaluation of local development and growth patterns.
Transportation plans	Improve connectivity through road, pedestrian, transit, and bicycle infrastructure. Plan for long-term and short-term transportation issues.	Identify and improve weak transportation links. Identify and coordinate emergency transportation networks. Identify at-risk assets.
Economic development plans	Identify and prioritize economic opportunities.	Identify and address local economic capacity and exposure issues. Identify and create opportunities for socially and economically vulnerable populations. Promote green development opportunities.
Public health plans	Promote policies to improve quality of life. Prevent diseases and make public safety improvements.	Incorporate risk assessments (socioeconomic and health impacts). Prioritize health risks associated with climate change and other natural hazards (e.g., heatwaves, airborne diseases). Facilitate and expedite local strategies that are likely to minimize the adverse impacts.
Physical infrastructure development plans	Improve management of water, stormwater drainage, wastewater, and solid waste.	Avoid locating facilities in high-risk areas. Incorporate resistance and redundancy. Identify and prioritize at risk assets (climate and hazard proofing). Analyze impacts on local supply, demand, and infrastructure networks.

community about the type and location of relevant hazard risks. This knowledge helps citizens identify alternative development strategies and build consensus to adopt policies that limit development in such risk areas (see box 9.1).[10] Such zones can be designated as no-development or limited-use zones wherein the only permitted uses are those that are unlikely to significantly increase loss of life and property in case of an extreme event.

Because anticipated climatic changes are likely to increase the footprint of the risk zones, a greater margin of safety should be considered for designating development zones in a community. For example, a larger buffer may be considered beyond the FEMA-designated 100-year floodplain to ensure that a likely increase in flooding caused by climate change does not result in increased losses. Also, it is important to recognize that the local forecasts of climate change impacts will evolve over the next decade or so. As the quality and reliability of the future climate change models improve, communities need to be prepared for frequent updates to the local hazard risk maps. Plans should incorporate a system of frequent updates in the land use planning framework.

Transportation Plans

Transportation plans are typically prepared to address connectivity issues in the community. Transportation plans play a key role in realizing a community's vision of growth and development.[11] A local transportation plan assesses existing transportation needs, analyzes traffic demands, and examines the relationship between different modes of transportation. It includes long-range and short-range programs that have a combination of capital improvement projects and operational strategies for transportation infrastructure. Transportation policies also focus on monitoring existing conditions, forecasting future connectivity corridors based on anticipated population and employment distribution, addressing current and projected transportation problems and needs, and analyzing transportation improvement strategies.

Within disaster preparedness, transportation planning addresses primarily evacuation planning. Transportation evacuation plans identify critical evacuation routes and the location and condition of those with special transportation needs, assess the type of transportation necessary, and coordinate with local and regional agencies to ensure quick evacuation. Although it is desirable to include this assessment in local transportation plans, many times it is handled exclusively through an emergency response plan. Inclusion of such analysis in local transportation plans can provide numerous hazard mitigation benefits while ensuring an efficient evacuation response. Additionally, transportation plans can undertake a number of other hazard mitigation actions that will result in sustainable and more resilient transportation infrastructure. These actions include identifying and addressing the weak links, avoiding siting of critical infrastructure facilities in known risk areas, and creating a framework for interagency cooperation (see table 9.1).

Transportation planning should include climate change considerations because the transport sector is highly vulnerable to climate change.[12] Transport infrastructure is sensitive to extreme weather (e.g., flooding of transportation routes, threats to passenger safety during heatwaves, and delays due to storms) and long-term climatic changes (e.g., permafrost melting under roads in the Arctic, concrete degradation). Along the northern Gulf Coast, an estimated 2,400 miles of major roadway and 246 miles of freight rail lines are at risk of permanent flooding within this decade as relative sea level is expected to rise by about 4 feet.[13] Furthermore, the ability of the transport sector to respond rapidly to climate change is constrained by its reliance on long-lasting infrastructure (e.g., bridges, tunnels, railway lines, roads, airports, seaports).[14] Therefore, anticipatory action is imperative for the transportation sector.

Economic Development Plans

An economic development plan guides local efforts to stimulate economic growth and preserve the existing employment base. Such plans may also include strategies to ensure the increase in real wages, stabilization of the local tax base, and economic diversification to insulate the local economy from a downturn in specific sectors. A typical economic development plan includes a series of background studies conducted to identify the strengths and weaknesses of the community or the region and assess the need for economic growth and diversification. Often, these plans also include an assessment of the regional and state economic context with advanced analytical tools to analyze local economic performance in the larger context.

Although many communities undertake economic development planning initiatives after a disaster to jump-start recovery, there is an evident lack of hazard mitigation consideration in predisaster economic development planning. Risk analysis of local economic activities considered in hazard mitigation planning can serve as a policy guide to develop strategies that minimize risk to businesses and other economic activities from extreme weather events. Economic development plans should identify the location and distribution of vulnerable population groups within the community. These social vulnerability assessments are critical in determining appropriate economic development policies to ensure that these groups are considered in economic development strategies (see table 9.1).

Attention to vulnerable groups in economic policy development plans will also contribute toward building local adaptive capacity to climate change. Stability and quality of livelihoods influence individual vulnerability, well-being, and self-protection. Research has suggested that businesses that engage in predisaster planning see fewer losses and more rapid recovery when disasters occur.[15] At the same time, the pattern of livelihood access across different social groups is related to the local governance and economic development policies. Consideration of these issues in economic development plans will help avoid negative impacts of climate change on asset and income distribution and probably lead to greater success of the livelihood strategies for different population groups within the community.

Public Health Plans

Recently, a number of local governments have begun to appreciate the links between local development and public health priorities. These concerns are either embodied as a standalone component of the local comprehensive plan or included in other local planning initiatives related to land use, transportation, recreation, emergency response, and open space elements. Ideally such plans should be based on public health data analysis to identify priority issues and develop appropriate responses to ensure public welfare. A detailed assessment of local public health infrastructure, including short-term and long-term care facilities and emergency response infrastructure, is often included in the development of public health plans. Some communities include these plans in the overall process of community health assessment and improvement planning.

Incorporating local hazard risk considerations in public health plans provides an ongoing implementation framework for development and continued support of critical emergency response infrastructure. Consideration of local risks is critical in siting decisions for critical facilities within the community. Analysis of the nature and distribution of existing hazard risks within the community can help local planning officials design strategies to provide public health facilities that are resilient and can continue to support disaster response services during an extreme hazard event (see table 9.1).

Climatic changes in the coming decades are likely to have a significant impact on human health by changing the existing weather conditions to which people are accustomed. Warmer average temperatures can lead to hotter days and more frequent and longer heatwaves. An increase in the number of heat-related illnesses and deaths is likely. Moreover, increased risks of flooding, high winds, and declining air quality will pose direct threats to people. Predicted changes in temperature, precipitation patterns, and extreme events could increase the spread of some diseases, posing new challenges for public health agencies. Proactive planning for climate change will help address a number of factors that determine local public health outcomes. Particularly, policies that improve the effectiveness of a community's public health and safety systems to address and prepare for the risk and the behavior, age, gender, and economic status of people likely to be affected will help mitigate the negative impacts of climate change.

Physical Infrastructure Development Plans

To effectively manage local development and ensure a good quality of life for citizens, municipal authorities historically have had the responsibility to plan for, coordinate, provide, or otherwise ensure the basic infrastructure facilities such as water supply, wastewater, stormwater, and solid waste management services. As part of the local planning process, local governments undertake detailed assessments of demand, supply, and distribution networks for these infrastructure facilities. Individual emergency response plans are also prepared by agencies responsible for development and maintenance of these infrastructure systems in a community.

The process of establishing infrastructure development plans must consider existing hazard risks and avoid locating critical infrastructure facilities in high-risk zones. Threats to sources and distribution networks from known hazards also must be assessed and addressed in local infrastructure plans. For example, if a community depends largely on surface water supply sources, alternative sources or water management strategies must be considered for prolonged periods of drought. Local infrastructure planning should include two key attributes of resilient infrastructure: resistance and redundancy. Infrastructure systems should be designed to withstand the impacts of at least the known likely extreme events. This capacity includes the ability to absorb such disruptions and the additional ability to cope with disruptions larger than anticipated. Critical components of the infrastructure should have layers of redundancy wherein failure of a key component does not cripple the whole system. Adding redundancy to the system provides greater flexibility and tolerance to the system. This will ensure continued optimal performance, even during extreme events (see table 9.1).

Climate change is likely to exacerbate the existing threats to the local physical infrastructure. Consideration of local impacts of climate change in local infrastructure plans will ensure that resistance and redundancy design parameters take into account predicted changes in the local conditions. For example, water supply plans should analyze the impact of changing weather conditions and precipitation on the local availability of water sources, changes in water demand, and impacts on distribution networks. Similarly, all infrastructure development plans should analyze the specific impacts of climate change on supply, demand, and distribution components of the systems.

Land use plans, transportation plans, public health plans, economic development plans, and physical infrastructure development plans are all examples of possible community plans that can incorporate hazard mitigation. Making a point to ensure logical harmony and consistency between these plans will yield more focused, strategic community initiatives and decision making. Inconsistency is typically not intentional, but when a community emphasizes this value, the weight and impact of the plans as a whole and individually are sustained.

Progress Galveston

After Hurricane Ike, the City of Galveston reinitiated its comprehensive planning process and is a great example of how planning efforts can and should be integrated to achieve consistency, which leads to resiliency. Progress Galveston was an ambitious planning project designed, according to the 2011 Galveston Comprehensive Plan, "to ensure public and private actions aligned to improve Galveston's livability, sustainability, and competitiveness" after Hurricane Ike.[16] Funding for the development of the Progress Galveston project was provided through Community Development Block Grant Disaster Recovery monies. Progress Galveston began in January 2011 and was divided into three major sections: the comprehensive plan update, six specialized plans, and revisions to the zoning code as new land development regulations.

The comprehensive plan portion of the project was an update to the 2001 plan. As mentioned previously, a thirty-member citizen-based steering committee had been working on the update before Hurricane Ike and was prepared to take a draft forward for adoption when the storm hit the island. After their participation in the Long-Term Community Recovery Plan process, the steering committee members created a new vision statement and specifically addressed issues that were identified for further review by the recovery plan in the new infrastructure, disaster planning, transportation, and human elements. Other innovative approaches were to set long-range policy for conservation and development, help decision makers resolve issues and leverage assets, provide clarity for residents and business owners, and provide a foundation for decisions to be made in the following areas:

- Land use, zoning, and subdivision approvals
- Hazard mitigation
- Neighborhood revitalization
- Transportation and infrastructure
- Economic development
- Natural resource conservation

The comprehensive plan was adopted by the Galveston City Council on October 27, 2011.

The specialized plans were developed in two phases. The first phase included plans for parks and recreation, historic preservation, and coastal management and erosion response; the second phase focused on mobility and thoroughfare, disaster recovery, and community sustainability. The parks and recreation plan, historic preservation plan, erosion response plan, and thoroughfare plan were adopted throughout 2011 and 2012. The disaster recovery plan and community sustainability plan were completed as internal policy documents and did not need adoption by the city council. The plans are intended to implement the comprehensive plan, comply with state and federal requirements, and provide access to funding and assistance programs that may not otherwise be available. The erosion response plan was one of the most controversial aspects of the Progress Galveston project but also one of the most critical for the island.

The beach erosion experienced in Hurricane Ike was equivalent to approximately 30 years of the annual rate of erosion in a single event. The dramatic change in the landscape encouraged the City of Galveston to develop an erosion response plan. Furthermore, Title 31 of the Texas Administrative Code, §15.17 states that "local governments must develop plans for reducing public expenditures for erosion and storm damage losses to public and private property, including public beaches." Galveston's erosion response plan focuses primarily on dune restoration. Dunes are considered a structural mitigation technique, which can protect existing investments. Healthy dunes, in combination with nourishment efforts, provide the following benefits:

- Reduce expenditures for erosion and storm damage losses
- Absorb the force of high waves
- Prevent or delay inland flooding
- Provide a sediment source for natural recovery

Some of the strategies in the plan include developing a dune conservation area to protect areas appropriate for dune restoration projects, creating an enhanced construction zone to minimize the impact of construction in eroding areas, and clarifying and simplifying the local review processes for beachfront construction. Construction standards that were put into place include the following:

- No paving or altering of a site seaward of 25 feet from north toe of dune
- Payment of a fee-in-lieu if a dune system doesn't exist and a dune restoration project is infeasible
- Driveway limitations requiring that a minimum of 15 percent of the front yard remain unimproved
- Fibrous reinforced concrete standard applied to projects in the dune conservation area
- Impervious surface limit for large-scale construction

Additionally, the erosion response plan also required an engineer's certifications for beachfront construction, plat notation or affidavit on applicability of beachfront construction rules for properties, and financial assurance requirements for large-scale structures to fund relocation, demolition, or removal of the structure. The erosion response plan was adopted by the Galveston City Council on April 12, 2012.

Finally, Progress Galveston also included the creation of a unified development ordinance. The Land development regulations (LDRs) were intended to consolidate all development-related regulations so that the public could more easily understand the process for approvals and city staff would be able to more easily administer the code. The scope of the LDRs included development standards for infrastructure; subdivision regulations, including wetland and land conservation protection; and a fully developed a future land use map for the city. The stated goals of the LDR portion of the Progress Galveston projects were as follows:

- Support economic development and revitalization
- Improve preparedness for future disaster scenarios
- Update standards and incorporate best practices
- Deal with unique areas (urban core, historic neighborhoods, the West End and East Ends of the island, and the Gateway corridor)
- Keep Galveston eclectic

Several articles of the LDRs were adopted in 2011 and 2012. However, the LDRs are still being discussed and developed at the time of this printing.

Cities must take advantage of the opportunities for change and improvement after a disaster event to avoid similar challenges in the future. Great lessons may also be learned through the successes, and failures, of communities that have experienced events that are risk factors for your own area. Although disaster recovery is always difficult, planners must take the time to assess the vulnerabilities and ensure that actions are taken to mitigate these risks and provide a more resilient future for coming generations.

Here we describe the final step to inclusively plan for disasters.

Step 7: Monitor, Evaluate, and Update

The seventh step to inclusively plan for disasters is the continual process of monitoring, evaluating, and updating plans. This is an opportunity to create feedback loops as a way to adapt to changing conditions. Comprehensive and other community planning products should be considered living documents. Subsequent outcomes of plan implementation should be measured with respect to desired performance parameters and used to inform successive plan-making initiatives. Ongoing monitoring and regular evaluation of plan implementation are important activities for groups interested in making the timely adjustments necessary to keep the work on course. Many communities rely on action plans to implement short-term, medium-term, and long-term actions, and strong plans will include performance targets that allow communities to assess whether they are making progress toward their goals. Regular evaluation through annual reports or other reporting mechanisms can also provide valuable feedback for groups wanting to show other community stakeholders and investors evidence of success.[17] Fortunately, many state and federally mandated disaster management plans require updates every 5 years. In addition, if the local disaster plans are aligned with the comprehensive plan or other community plans and regulations, it may be necessary to update the plan whenever changes to other plans are made. However, because the work of community engagement takes a lot of time and patience, a community's fact basis may take some time. In reality, this process will be ongoing. Nevertheless, being aware of these changes and updates will allow you to effectively update the hazard mitigation plan.

Exercise 11. Monitoring Plans

Establish a schedule to regularly review or audit actions, objectives, and goals. Predetermine meetings with the core team and taskforce to achieve actions items, objectives, and goals. Incorporate this schedule into the plan and stick to it. Monitor changes to the assessment of the community about every 10 years (at each decennial census).

10. Conclusion

Decades of disaster research have clearly established that comprehensive proactive planning is the best way to minimize and avoid hazard losses. In his seminal work, Dennis Mileti states that a disaster is a symptom of broad and basic problems of unsustainable growth and development.[1] We can reduce vulnerabilities and increase resilience by incorporating urban planning into the hazard planning process, through land use management practices and public engagement techniques.

Community resilience is built on a foundation of evidence-based decision making. In this book we have given you tools to (1) help communities assess their own vulnerability to natural disasters, which are increasing in both frequency and severity; (2) identify ways to mitigate both social and physical vulnerability through effective land use planning; and (3) engage communities in building capacity at the local level to address identified issues. Throughout, we have provided both a theoretical understanding of issues and practical suggestions, with examples for how to implement them in your own community.

We hope that you have learned the following:

- Increasing disaster losses are consequences of complex interactions between a variety of factors, including chronic social problems, unsustainable development patterns, and policy mechanisms that discount hazard risks.
- The ability to adapt to community changes can be achieved through the collaborative planning process.
- Understanding community characteristics, specifically hazard exposures, physical

vulnerabilities, and social vulnerabilities, is also essential for foundational knowledge in decision making.

- There are specific strategies for creating a high-quality hazard mitigation plan, employing land use management tools and policies, and promoting consistency across all plans in a community.

We intend this book to be used by community planners and citizens first to take a critical look at their own vulnerability, and then to use the techniques described herein to initiate a community-based effort to start to address it. We believe that the most successful community-based planning will engage a broad swath of community interests. We know that open discussion between equal citizens in planning and decision making can transform a community.[2] Together, all parties should use their experience and expertise to develop solutions.[3] Public participation should involve listening to and respecting all values. By doing this, we promote community engagement, solve problems, and create a better future. Solutions that involve citizens are inherently messy, but it is the very complexity of this planning process that makes it so crucial. For communities to increase their resilience, they must overcome weak spots in the ties that bind them. Community capacity—the relationships between community members and organizations, and the array of resources available to them—must be exercised and maintained. These resources cannot be left unattended and then be expected to perform at a critical moment. An engaged and informed community will provide support, both emotional and physical, for planning activities that mitigate future disasters. They will support a robust and ongoing data collection and planning effort that, properly executed, can reduce vulnerability and increase resilience.

Is Galveston resilient? The memorial to the 1900 storm that devastated the island, seen in figure 10.1, reminds us that cities do recover, adapt, and survive. Whether Galveston has become more resilient after 2008's Hurricane Ike is still an unanswered question. The jury is still out, as is always the case for all communities, which are ever changing and adapting to new economic, political, social, and environmental realities. As a community, let's be mindful of who we are and where we want to be, ever hopeful, reaching for and aspiring to a community that can face the challenges set before us.

Cities must take advantage of the opportunities for change and improvement that follow a disaster event to avoid similar challenges in the future. Hope is the driving factor that can push a community toward resilience.

Figure 10.1. This is the memorial to the 1900 storm in Galveston, Texas, located along the sea-wall. It is a monument to those who have lost their lives and to the spirit of the people of Galveston. (Credit: Dustin Henry, *Hope and Resilience*, 2014.)

Appendix

Federally Authorized Programs

- Federal Grants: Find and apply for federal grants (www.grants.gov/).
- Federal Grants Wire: A free resource for federal grants, government grants, and loans (www.federalgrantswire.gov).
- Government Loans: Search for disaster relief loan programs (www.govloans.gov/loans /type/4).
  - Business Physical Disaster Loans: The U.S. Small Business Administration (SBA) provides loans for small businesses up to $2 million to repair or replace business assets.
  - Economic Injury Disaster Loans: The SBA provides loans for small businesses up to $2 million to meet working capital needs.
  - Emergency Farm Loans: The U.S. Department of Agriculture (USDA) Farm Service Agency (FSA) provides emergency loans to help farmers and ranchers.
  - Home and Property Disaster Loans: The SBA provides homeowners loans of up to $200,000 to repair or replace their primary residence to its predisaster condition.
  - Military Reservist Economic Injury Disaster Loan Program: This provides funds to eligible small businesses to compensate for a military reservist being called up during a disaster.
  - Army Corps of Engineers: With specific authorization from Congress, the Corps can design and construct large-scale projects. Smaller projects can be built through the Corps Continuing Authorities program (http://www.usace.army.mil /Locations.aspx).
- Grant Search: A website that allows you to search for all types of government, non-profit organization, and private sector grants (www.federalgrants.com).
- Institute for Water Resources (http://www.iwr.usace.army.mil/):
  - Emergency Operations: The U.S. Army Corps of Engineers under the National Response Framework is assigned the primary agency for Emergency Support

Function (ESF) #3, Public Works and Engineering. It also provides support for ESF #9, Search and Rescue. The Corps provides bottled water, critical public facility restoration, debris management, emergency infrastructure assessments, temporary emergency power, temporary housing, temporary roofing, and urban search and rescue (http://www.usace.army.mil/Missions/EmergencyOperations/National ResponseFramework.aspx).

- Emergency Preparedness and Disaster Relief: The U.S. Army Corps of Engineers has authority under PL 84-99, Flood Control and Coastal Emergencies. This bill establishes an emergency fund for preparedness and response, as well as rehabilitation. Rehabilitation includes reconstruction of damaged flood protection systems (http://asacw.hqda.pentagon.mil/disasterrelief.aspx).
- Emergency Streambank and Shoreline Protection: The U.S. Army Corps of Engineers is authorized to construct bank protection for highways or other public works projects (http://www.mvr.usace.army.mil/BusinessWithUs/Outreach CustomerService/FloodRiskManagement/Section14.aspx).

- Bureau of Ocean Energy Management (BOEM): Promotes energy independence, environmental protection, and economic development. It oversees offshore oil and gas exploration (http://www.boem.gov/).
- Bureau of Safety and Environmental Enforcement (BSEE): Develops regulatory standards and provides enforcement for offshore oil and gas exploration (http://www.bsee.gov/).
- Department of Agriculture (http://www.csrees.usda.gov/fo/funding.cfm):
  - USDA Disaster Assistance Programs: Provides various disaster assistance for current programs (http://www.disasterassistance.gov/).
    - Nutrition Assistance: Provides food for those in need after a disaster.
      - USDA Foods for Disaster Assistance: Under the National Response Framework, provides food assistance to disaster relief agencies at mass feeding sites and shelters.
      - D-SNAP: States can request additional benefits for people affected by disasters who wouldn't otherwise qualify.
    - Landowners, Farmers, Ranchers, and Producers Assistance:
      - Conservation programs:
        - Emergency Conservation Program: Provides funding for farmers and ranchers affected by natural disasters.
        - Emergency Watershed Protection (EWP) Program: Provides technical and financial assistance to people and properties threatened by excessive erosion and flooding (http://www.nrcs.usda.gov/wps/portal/nrcs/detail /national/programs/landscape/ewpp/?&cid=nrcs143_008258).
        - Emergency Watershed Protection Program, Floodplain Easements: Provides the purchase of floodplain easements for emergency situations.
      - Crops:
        - Noninsured Crop Disaster Assistance Program: Provides financial assistance to eligible producers affected by natural disasters.

- Tree Assistance Program: Provides partial reimbursement to orchardists and nursery tree growers affected by natural disasters.
- Supplemental Revenue Assistance Payments Program: Covers revenue losses for federally declared disaster areas.
  - Livestock, honeybees, and farm-raised fish:
    - Emergency Assistance for Livestock, Honeybees, and Farm Raised Fish: Provides emergency assistance to producers and covers losses from natural disasters.
    - Livestock Forage Disaster Program: Provides assistance to livestock producers for forage losses due to drought and wildfires.
    - Livestock Indemnity Program: Provides assistance to livestock producers for livestock deaths.
  - Loans:
    - Emergency Loan Program: Provides emergency loans to producers after a natural disaster.
  - Housing assistance:
    - Single-family assistance: Natural disaster loans and grants are available after a federally declared disaster.
    - Multifamily assistance: Residents in rural development apartment complexes can apply for occupancy in USDA-financed apartment complexes in declared disaster areas.
- Watershed and Flood Prevention Operations (WFPO) Program: Provides technical and financial assistance to plan and implement authorized watershed project plans (http://www.nrcs.usda.gov/wps/portal/nrcs/detail/national/programs /landscape/wfpo/?cid=nrcs143_008271).
- Wetlands Reserve Program (WRP): Provides technical and financial support to help landowners protect or restore wetlands (http://www.nrcs.usda.gov/wps /portal/nrcs/main/national/programs/easements/wetlands/).
- Watershed Surveys and Planning: Helps agencies to protect watersheds from damage caused by erosion, flooding, and sediment, and to conserve land and water resources (http://www.nrcs.usda.gov/wps/portal/nrcs/main/national/programs /landscape/wsp/).
- Conservation Innovation Grants: Provides funding opportunities to agriculturalists to spur conservation innovation projects.
- Rural development (www.rurdev.usda.gov):
  - Emergency Community Water Assistance Grants: Grants are designed for rural communities with significant decline in quantity or quality of drinking water (http://www.rurdev.usda.gov/UWP-ecwag.htm).
  - Rural Business Opportunity Grant (RBOG) Program: Promotes sustainable economic development in rural communities (http://www.rurdev.usda.gov/BCP _RBOG.html).
  - Rural Business Enterprise Grant (RBEG) Program: Provides grants for rural projects that finance and facilitate development of small and rural emerging

businesses (http://www.rurdev.usda.gov/BCP_rbeg.html).

- Rural Economic Development Loan and Grant (REDLG): Provides funding to rural projects through local utility organizations (http://www.rurdev.usda.gov/BCP_redlg.html).
- Water and Environmental Programs (WEP): Provide loans and grants for drinking water, sanitary sewer, solid waste, and storm drainage facilities in rural areas and cities and towns of 10,000 people or less.

- Department of Housing and Urban Development (HUD) (http://portal.hud.gov/hudportal/HUD?src=/topics/grants):
  - Community Development Block Grant (CDBG) program: Provides grants to communities to address a large array of needs (http://portal.hud.gov/hudportal/HUD?src=/program_offices/comm_planning/communitydevelopment/programs).
  - CDBG Disaster Recovery Assistance: Provides grants to communities in declared disaster areas (http://portal.hud.gov/hudportal/HUD?src=/program_offices/comm_planning/communitydevelopment/programs/dri).

- Department of Transportation, Federal Highway Administration (http://www.fhwa.dot.gov/discretionary/index.cfm):
  - Emergency Relief (ER) Program: Provides funding for the repair and reconstruction of federal aid highways and roads after a natural disaster (http://www.fhwa.dot.gov/programadmin/erelief.cfm).
  - Pipeline and Hazardous Material Safety Administration (PHMSA) Hazardous Materials Emergency Preparedness (HMEP) Grant Program: Provides emergency preparedness grants, supplemental public sector training, and hazardous material instructor training grants (http://www.phmsa.dot.gov/hazmat/grants).

- Department of Homeland Security (http://www.dhs.gov/dhs-financial-assistance):
  - Grants and Assistance Programs for Governments (http://www.fema.gov/tribal/grants-and-assistance-programs-governments#1):
    - Community Disaster Loan Program: Provides funds to jurisdictions affected by disasters that have lost substantial tax revenue.
    - Fire Management Assistance Grant Program: Provides assistance for the mitigation, management, and control of fires.
    - Hazard Mitigation Grant Program: Provides grants to state or local governments for long-term hazard mitigation after a disaster.
    - Public Assistance Grant Program: Provides assistance after a federally declared disaster.
    - Reimbursement for Firefighting on Federal Property: Provides reimbursements for direct costs and losses.
    - Community Assistance Program, State Support Services Element: Provides funding to states to provide technical assistance to communities that participate in the National Flood Insurance Program (NFIP).
    - Flood Mitigation Assistance Program: Provides funding to states and communities that reduce or eliminate the long-term risk of flooding.

- National Dam Safety Program: Provides funding to states to strengthen their dam safety programs.
- National Earthquake Hazard Reduction Program: Provides assistance to reduce risk of earthquake impact.
- NFIP: Enables property owners to purchase flood insurance.
- Pre-Disaster Mitigation Program: Provides funds for hazard mitigation planning and implementation before a disaster event.
- Repetitive Flood Claims Program: Provides funds to states or communities to reduce long-term risk of floods for structures that have had one or more claims.
- Severe Repetitive Flood Claims Program: Provides funds to states or communities to reduce long-term risk of floods for structures that are considered "severe repetitive loss" structures.
- Superfund Amendments and Reauthorization Act: Provides funding for training in emergency planning, preparedness, mitigation, response, and recovery capabilities associated with hazardous chemicals (http://www.fema.gov/grants-administration/superfund-amendments-and-reauthorization-act-sara-title-iii).

- Federal Emergency Management Agency (FEMA) (http://www.fema.gov/grants):
  - Comprehensive Planning Guide (CPG) 101: To develop and maintain emergency operations plans (http://www.fema.gov/pdf/about/divisions/npd/CPG_101_V2.pdf).
  - Community Emergency Response Teams (CERTS): A program that educates people about disaster preparedness and trains people in basic response skills (http://www.fema.gov/community-emergency-response-teams).
  - Competitive Training Grants Program (CTGP): Provides funds to applicants to develop and provide innovative training on homeland security needs (http://www.fema.gov/competitive-training-grants-program).
  - Cooperating Technical Partners (CTP): Provides funds to applicants who are interested in helping to maintain accurate flood maps (http://www.fema.gov/cooperating-technical-partners-program).
  - COPS Interoperable Communications Technology Program: Provides funding to help communities develop effective interoperable communication systems for public safety and emergency services providers (http://www.cops.usdoj.gov/default.asp?item=1268).
  - Homeland Security Grant Program (HSGP) (FY2012) (http://www.fema.gov/fy-2013-homeland-security-grant-program-hsgp-0):
    - Assistance to Fire Fighter Grants (AFG): Provides grants for fire departments to increase their ability to protect the public (http://www.fema.gov/welcome-assistance-firefighters-grant-program).
    - Emergency Management Performance Grant (EMPG): Provides direction, guidance, coordination, and assistance for the protection of lives and property (http://www.fema.gov/fy-2013-emergency-management-performance-grants-empg-program-0).

- Intercity Passenger Rail (IPR) Security Grant Program: Provides grants for the security of passenger rails (http://www.fema.gov/fy-2013-intercity-passenger-rail-ipr-amtrak-0).

- Nonprofit Security Grant Program (NSGP): Provides grants for target hardening and security enhancements and activities (http://www.fema.gov/preparedness-non-disaster-grants/urban-areas-security-initiative-nonprofit-security-grant-program).

- Port Security Grant Program (PSGP): Provides support for maritime transportation infrastructure security (http://www.fema.gov/fy-2013-port-security-grant-program-psgp-0).

- State Homeland Security Program (SHSP): Provides assistance to address the identified planning, organization, equipment, training, and exercise needs to prevent, protect against, mitigate, respond to, and recover from disasters (http://www.fema.gov/fy-2013-homeland-security-grant-program-hsgp-0#1).

- Transit Security Grant Program (TSGP): Provides grants to support transportation security activities (http://www.fema.gov/fy-2014-transit-security-grant-program-tsgp).

- Tribal Homeland Security Grant Program (THSGP): Provides funds to help strengthen capacity to handle an act of terrorism (http://www.fema.gov/fy-2013-tribal-homeland-security-grant-program-thsgp-0).

- Urban Areas Security Initiative (UASI): Provides grants to urban areas to address the unique needs to preventing acts of terrorism (http://www.fema.gov/fy-2013-homeland-security-grant-program-hsgp-0#2).

  - Preparedness (Non-Disaster) Grant Program: Provides funds for states and local governments to prepare for, respond to, and recover from an event dealing with a weapons of mass destruction or terrorism incident involving chemical, biological, radiological, nuclear, and explosive devices and cyberattacks (http://www.fema.gov/preparedness-non-disaster-grants).

- Buffer Zone Protection Program: Provides funds to help communities surrounding high-priority critical infrastructure and key resource (CIKR) assets (https://www.fema.gov/media-library/assets/documents/20601).

- Chemical Stockpile Emergency Preparedness Program (CSEPP): Provides emergency preparedness assistance and resources to communities surrounding the Army's chemical warfare agent stockpiles (http://www.fema.gov/technological-hazards-division-0/chemical-stockpile-emergency-preparedness-program).

- Disaster Assistance: A Guide to Recovery Programs: Provides descriptions and contact information for federal programs that may be able to provide disaster recovery assistance to eligible applicants (http://www.fema.gov/media-library/assets/documents/6341).

- Emergency Food and Shelter Board Program: Provides assistance immediately after a disaster by providing food, lodging, 1 month's housing payments, 1 month's utility bills, and equipment necessary to feed and shelter people (https://www.efsp.unitedway.org/efsp/website/index.cfm).

- Emergency Operations Center Grant Program (FY2011): Provides funds to improve emergency management and preparedness capabilities by supporting the construction of Emergency Operations Centers (http://www.fema.gov/fy-2011-emergency-operations-center-grant-program).

- Homeland Security Exercise and Evaluation Program: Provides a set of guiding principles to conduct exercise programs (https://www.llis.dhs.gov/hseep/index.php).
- Law Enforcement Terrorism Prevention Programs: Provides funding to support law enforcement terrorism prevention activities.
- Multi-Year Flood Hazard Identification Plan (MHIP): Provides flood hazard data and maps for those at highest risk (http://www.fema.gov/national-flood-insurance-program-0/multi-year-flood-hazard-identification-plan).
- National Incident Management System (NIMS): Provides concepts and principles to methodically plan for emergencies and disasters (http://www.fema.gov/national-incident-management-system).
- National Hurricane Program: Provides state funding for hurricane preparedness and mitigation (http://www.fema.gov/region-iii-mitigation-division/national-hurricane-program).
- Public Assistance Grant Program: Provides assistance so communities can quickly respond to and recover from major disasters or emergencies declared by the president (http://www.fema.gov/public-assistance-local-state-tribal-and-non-profit).
- Radiological Emergency Preparedness (REP) Program: Ensures that citizens are prepared, informed, and educated on nuclear and radiological disaster events (http://www.fema.gov/radiological-emergency-preparedness-program).
- Regional Catastrophic Preparedness Grant program: Supports coordination of regional hazard planning (http://www.fema.gov/preparedness-non-disaster-grants/fy-2011-regional-catastrophic-preparedness-grant-program).
- Section 406 Hazard Mitigation Grant Program: Provides guidance on the appropriate use of hazard mitigation funding (http://www.fema.gov/public-assistance-local-state-tribal-and-non-profit/hazard-mitigation-funding-under-section-406-0).
- Environmental Protection Agency (EPA) (http://www2.epa.gov/home/grants-and-other-funding-opportunities):
  - Drinking Water State Revolving Fund (DWSRF): Provides grants and funding for states to allocate to communities for the installation, upgrade, or replacement of infrastructure (http://water.epa.gov/grants_funding/dwsrf/index.cfm).
  - Gulf of Mexico Project Funding: Provides funding for the restoration and protection of coastal marine resources (http://www.epa.gov/gmpo/pubinfo/pigrants.html).
  - Nonpoint Source Pollution Funding: Provides funding for projects that address water quality issues (http://water.epa.gov/polwaste/nps/funding.cfm).
  - Water Pollution Control Program Grants: Provides funding to states for ongoing water pollution control programs (http://water.epa.gov/grants_funding/cwf/pollutioncontrol.cfm).
  - Water Quality Cooperative Agreements: Provides funding to promote environmentally beneficial activities (http://www.epa.gov/owm/cwfinance/waterquality.htm).

- Watershed Funding: Provides funding to watershed organizations to provide adequate tools and resources (https://ofmpub.epa.gov/apex/watershedfunding /f?p=fedfund:1).
- Wetland Program Development Grants (WPDGs): Provides funding to coordinate research, education, and studies related to water quality (http://water.epa.gov /grants_funding/wetlands/grantguidelines/index.cfm).
- Federal Corporation for National and Community Service: A federal agency that invests in nonprofit organizations that provide needed services (http://www .nationalservice.gov/).
  - AmeriCorps: Creates jobs and provides assistance to young people entering the workforce (http://www.nationalservice.gov/programs/americorps).
  - Senior Corps: Helps meet the needs of communities by working with Americans aged 55 and older to mentor, teach, befriend, and serve people and their communities (http://www.nationalservice.gov/programs/senior-corps).
- National Institute of Justice: The research, development, and evaluation agency for the Department of Justice (http://ojp.gov/funding/funding.htm):
  - Communications Technology, Office of Justice Programs (OJP): Helps law enforcement communicate across agency and jurisdiction boundaries (http://www.nij .gov/topics/technology/communication/pages/welcome.aspx).
- National Oceanic and Atmospheric Administration (NOAA):
  - Coastal Zone Management (CZM) Program (FY2013), Office of Ocean and Coastal Resource Management: A voluntary partnership with coastal and Great Lakes states to address coastal issues in a comprehensive manner and on a national scale (http://coastalmanagement.noaa.gov/funding/welcome.html).
- National Storm Shelter Associations (OJP): Provides tornado- and hurricane-proof shelters (http://www.nssa.cc/).
- SBA (http://www.sba.gov/about-offices-content/1/2462):
  - Disaster Loan Program: Provides low-interest disaster loans to homeowners, renters, and businesses of all sizes (http://www.sba.gov/content/disaster-loan -program).

Education and Training

- American Red Cross: Provides disaster relief in the form of food, shelter, health, and mental health services (http://www.redcross.org/lp/take-a-class).
- Centers for Disease Control and Prevention (CDC) bioterrorism training and education: Provides training on anthrax, botulism, plague, smallpox, viral hemorrhagic fevers, and other bioterrorism concerns (http://www.bt.cdc.gov/bioterrorism/training.asp).
- EPA Watershed Academy Webcast Seminars: Provides webcast training sessions on watershed tools, programs, and opportunities (http://water.epa.gov/learn/training /wacademy/webcasts_index.cfm).
- FEMA Blog: Provides great resources and articles on disasters (www.fema.gov/blog).
- FEMA Center for Domestic Preparedness (CDP): The premier hazard training center in the nation (https://cdp.dhs.gov/).

- FEMA HAZUS Training: Regularly scheduled training sessions at the National Emergency Training Center in Maryland (http://www.fema.gov/hazus-training).
- FEMA Hazardous Materials Emergency Preparedness Training and Planning: Trains local emergency planning committees to evaluate their plans for gaps in hazardous material response and preparedness (http://www.fema.gov/hazus-training).
- FEMA National Preparedness Directorate National Training and Education: Online catalogue of courses provided by FEMA's Center for Domestic Preparedness (CDP), Emergency Management Institute (EMI), and National Training and Education Division (NTED) (http://www.training.fema.gov/).
- MetEd by University Corporation for Atmospheric Research and NOAA's National Weather Service (NWS): Provides education and training on meteorology and weather forecasting (https://www.meted.ucar.edu/training_detail.php).
- NOAA Education Resources: A collection of modules on hurricanes for educators and students (http://www.education.noaa.gov/Weather_and_Atmosphere/Hurricanes.html).
- U.S. Army Corps of Engineers Water Resources Training and Education (http://www.iwr.usace.army.mil/Missions/Training/WaterResourcesTraining.aspx).
- U.S. Department of Health and Human Services (http://www.remm.nlm.gov/training.htm).

Best Practices in Hazard Mitigation

- FEMA's Mitigation Practices: The website contains best practices in hazard mitigation to learn from others' success stories (http://www.fema.gov/mitigation-best-practices-portfolio).
  - Local Multi-hazard Mitigation Planning Guidance (2008): A guidance document that helps local governments meet requirements for implementing FEMA's Local Mitigation Plans (http://www.ksready.gov/AdvHTML_doc_upload/Local_Mitigation_Plan_Guidance_FINALforRelease070108.pdf).
  - Mitigation Planning Toolkit: A Web-based tool that follows planning methods for states and local and tribal communities to illustrate the importance of having hazard mitigation plans and assist in the development process (http://www.fema.gov/media-library-data/20130726-1826-25045-3194/reg4_rm_toolkit.pdf).
- Local mitigation strategies:
  - Alabama state hazard mitigation plan.
  - Colorado best practices in natural hazard planning and mitigation.
  - Disaster-Resistant Communities Group: This website contains a list of projects that have been completed in Florida (http://www.drc-group.com/prr-cp.html).
  - Florida local mitigation strategy (LMS): This website provides documents on local mitigation strategies (http://www.miamidade.gov/fire/mitigation.asp).
  - Florida hazard mitigation best practice guides.
  - Georgia local hazard mitigation plans and success stories: Hazard mitigation success stories from local governments and communities throughout Georgia (http://www.gema.ga.gov/gemaohsv10.nsf/4f697eb5f4cbd51d85257729004931f8/0ddf1951c5770ce8852578c70066acea?OpenDocument).

- ○ Louisiana hazard mitigation plan.
- ○ Mississippi hazard mitigation plan (2012).
- ○ South Carolina hazard mitigation plan (2010).
- ○ Texas hazard mitigation plan (2010–2013).
- ○ Washington state enhanced hazard mitigation plan (2011).
- ○ Wisconsin state and local hazard mitigation planning and success stories: This website contains hazard mitigation success stories that have been implemented in many Wisconsin communities (http://emergencymanagement.wi.gov/mitigation/stories.asp).

- National Governors Association Center for Best Practice: The only research and development firm that caters just to governors creates solutions for the many public policy challenges they face. Topics addressed are economic, human services and workforce, education, environment, energy and transportation, health, homeland security, and public safety (http://www.nga.org/cms/center).

- Public and Private Sector Best Practice Stories for All Hazards, by FEMA: A document that contains best practice stories from all over the United States in both the public and private sectors regarding all types of hazards (file://filer.arch.tamu.edu/Grad/KLB6829/Documents/nps57-081011-01.pdf).

- Texas Local Jurisdictions Best Practices: A search engine for best mitigation practices, divided by regions and states (https://www.llis.dhs.gov/bestpracticeslist).

- U.S. Army Corps of Engineers Planning Guidance Notebook: Focusing on water resource management, this document describes the overall implementation and planning process that the U.S. Army Corps of Engineers uses in their projects (http://planning.usace.army.mil/toolbox/library/ERs/entire.pdf).

- U.S. Army Corps of Engineers Planner's Study Aids: Provides a multitude of documents about coastal storm damage reduction, ecosystem restoration, flood risk management, hydropower, navigation, recreation, water supply and quality, and watersheds (http://www.usace.army.mil/Missions/CivilWorks/ProjectPlanning/Products/StudyAid.aspx).

- U.S. EPA Natural Disaster and Weather Emergency: A website to learn more about the different types of disasters, current disasters, and ways to reduce the risks by being prepared (http://www.epa.gov/naturalevents/).

Best Practices by Hazard Type

- Climate change:
  - ○ EPA Adapting to Climate Change: The impacts and adaptation efforts for climate change are explained by region or sector (http://www.epa.gov/climatechange/impacts-adaptation/).
  - ○ NOAA Climate Prediction Center: Expert assessments on current weather and potential future climate impacts (http://www.cpc.ncep.noaa.gov/products/expert_assessment/).
  - ○ NWS Forecast Model: Provides forecasts and current conditions on weather, water, and climate data (http://www.weather.gov).

○ Natural Resources Conservation Service (NRCS): Provides land managers and owners with different mitigation tools in conservation practices for reducing greenhouse gas emissions (http://www.nrcs.usda.gov/wps/portal/nrcs/main/national/climatechange/mitigation/).

○ NWS Aware and Disaster Preparedness Report: This free publication provides data on different aspects of emergency management (http://www.nws.noaa.gov/os/Aware/index.shtml).

○ U.S. Global Change Research Program: This website displays the impact of present and future climate changes affecting society (http://www.globalchange.gov/about.html).

• Earthquakes:

○ Earthquake Country Alliance: This website is a resource on regional earthquake activity and resiliency efforts in the United States (http://www.earthquakecountry.info/roots/index.html).

○ National Earthquake Hazards Reduction Program (NEHRP): Provides a link to the National Earthquake Hazards Reduction Program Annual Report for fiscal year 2011 (http://www.nehrp.gov/pdf/2012NEHRPAnnualReport.pdf).

○ Network for Engineering Earthquake Simulation (NEES): Webinar series for practitioners and researchers on the losses avoided by earthquake reduction (http://nees.org/education/for-professionals/researchtopracticeseries).

• Floods:

○ Best Practices for Flood Mitigation: This website provides a link to success stories in flood mitigation for a county in Wisconsin along with a link to FEMA's best practices and case studies (https://www.countyofdane.com/emergency/flood/strategy/practice.aspx).

○ EPA Mold Remediation: The site contains information about mold remediation in schools and commercial buildings (http://www.epa.gov/mold/mold_remediation.html).

○ NFIP Community Rating System (CRS) Program: This program is designed to provide incentives for communities to partake in community floodplain management by reducing flood insurance premium rates if the community follows CRS practices (http://www.fema.gov/national-flood-insurance-program-community-rating-system).

○ Kinston, North Carolina (floodplain management): An example of a floodplain management success story (http://www.fema.gov/media-library/assets/documents/3807?id=1790).

○ Mecklenburg County (flood mitigation implementation and stormwater management): These two sites contain multiple links to information about drainage, flooding, and stormwater management for Mecklenburg County (http://charmeck.org/stormwater/DrainageandFlooding/Pages/Default.aspx, http://charmeck.org/stormwater/Projects/Pages/Default.aspx).

○ Mississippi Coastal Mapping Projects: A website that provides various publications and documents produced by FEMA and Mississippi Emergency Management Agency for people involved in mitigation and reconstruction efforts in the Gulf

Coast region of Mississippi (http://www.mscoastalmapping.com/Floodplain Managers.htm#Other).

- ○ NFIP: This program works with communities that have adopted FEMA's requirements to reduce flooding by giving property owners flood insurance that helps protect them against damages (https://www.floodsmart.gov/floodsmart/pages /about/nfip_overview.jsp).
- ○ Service Assessment by NOAA: This is a link to a service assessment that was conducted after record floods hit parts of Tennessee and western Kentucky in May 2010 (http://www.nws.noaa.gov/os/assessments/pdfs/Tenn_Flooding.pdf).
- ○ Shoreline Management: This site contains information and a toolbox that provide guidance to shoreline management (http://coastalmanagement.noaa.gov /shoreline.html).
- ○ Stormwater Best Management Practices: This is a national menu for best practices in stormwater management (http://cfpub.epa.gov/npdes/stormwater/menuofbmps /index.cfm).

- • Heat:
  - ○ CDC Hot Weather Health Emergencies: A prevention guide to help educate people on the dangers of extreme heat (http://www.bt.cdc.gov/disasters/extremeheat /heat_guide.asp#emerg).
  - ○ EPA AIRNow: A website that provides daily information on the air quality index throughout the United States (http://airnow.gov/index.cfm?action=topics.about _airnow).
  - ○ EPA Energy Star: A program that certifies top-performing products that are considered to be energy efficient and rates the energy efficiency of buildings (http://www.energystar.gov/buildings/home?c=business.bus_index).
  - ○ NOAA's NWS Air Quality Forecast: This site provides information on national air quality and the ozone layer (http://www.nws.noaa.gov/ost/air_quality/).
  - ○ National Association of Clean Air Agencies (NACAA): This website provides links to other state and local air quality agencies (http://www.4cleanair.org).

- • Hurricanes:
  - ○ Hurricane Ike: Nature's Force vs. Structural Strength: A study conducted after Hurricane Ike by the Institute for Business & Home Safety to determine how nature's force affected the structural strength of buildings (http://www.disastersafety.org /wp-content/uploads/hurricane_ike.pdf).
  - ○ Hurricane Katrina: A resource of best practices performed after Hurricane Katrina (http://www.fema.gov/mitigation-best-practices-portfolio/mitigation-best practices-portfolio-hurricane-katrina-alabama).
  - ○ Mitigation Assessment Team's Technology Transfer: This site helps with the Mitigation Assessment Team's technology transfer by providing access to documents on different topics produced by FEMA that are needed for the recovery process (http://www.fema.gov/technology-transfer).
  - ○ NWS National Hurricane Center: This website contains information on hurricanes along with preparedness and cyclone information (http://www.nhc.noaa.gov).

- Tornadoes:
  - NOAA Service Assessment: A service assessment that was conducted after the historic tornadoes hit the southeastern United States in April 2011 (http://www.nws.noaa.gov/os/assessments/pdfs/historic_tornadoes.pdf).
  - Public and Community Safe Rooms: This website provides information on how to build public and community safe rooms (http://www.fema.gov/safe-rooms/public-and-community-safe-rooms).
  - The Northeast States Emergency Consortium (NESEC): A website that contains information about emergency management for all hazards in the northeastern states (http://www.nesec.org/about.cfm.html).
- Tsunamis:
  - Geohazard International: A tsunami preparedness guidebook that helps prepare communities in developing countries for tsunamis (http://gcohaz.org/projects/tsunami_guidebook.html).
  - NOAA Center for Tsunami Research: Research on forecasting the speed and accuracy of tsunamis while trying to prepare warnings (http://nctr.pmel.noaa.gov).
  - USGS Pacific Coastal & Marine Science Center: Scientific research through multiple disciplines focused on the Pacific coast and other Pacific Ocean U.S. regions (http://walrus.wr.usgs.gov).
- Wildfires:
  - Bastrop Complex Wildfire, Texas: A website for disaster relief information for Bastrop County, Texas (http://www.co.bastrop.tx.us/bcdisaster/).
  - Fire Dynamics Simulator in Texas: This report was conducted using the Fire Dynamics Simulator (FDS) to determine how wind affects the thermal and fire conditions on single-story residential homes (http://www.nist.gov/customcf/get_pdf.cfm?pub_id=909779).
  - National Database of State and Local Wildfire Hazard Mitigation Programs: This database provides information about current policies and programs that pertain to wildfires (http://www.wildfireprograms.usda.gov).
  - National Interagency Coordination Center (NICC): This website provides information about eleven different regions of the United States for wildfire awareness and mitigation (http://www.nifc.gov/nicc/).
  - Texas Extension Disaster Education Network (EDEN): This website provides resources about wildfires and rangeland fires in Texas (http://texashelp.tamu.edu/004-natural/fires.php).
  - USGS Fire Ecology: This website contains information about different topics in fire ecology (http://www.werc.usgs.gov/ResearchTopicPage.aspx?id=6).
  - USGS Wildfire Hazards: A National Threat: This document provides quick information on the threats associated with wildfires (http://pubs.usgs.gov/fs/2006/3015/2006-3015.pdf).
- Wind:
  - Florida's Foundation: A document on how to protect your home against the damages caused by wind during hurricanes (http://www.floridadisaster.org/mitigation

/Documents/Wind%20Mitigation%20Booklet%20.pdf).

○ New School Building "Hardened" Against the Wind: An article about how a town in Wisconsin rebuilt its schools to help protect against wind damage (http://emergencymanagement.wi.gov/mitigation/stories/hm-oakfield_success.pdf).

○ Texas Department of Insurance (TDI) Windstorm Inspection Program: A program that provides assistance to property owners with the rules and regulations for structures located along the Texas Gulf Coast that are looking to get coverage through the Texas Windstorm Insurance Association (http://www.tdi.texas.gov /wind/index.html).

○ Wind Mitigation Inspection: A course for inspectors and students on how to perform wind mitigation inspections (http://www.nachi.org/wind-mitigation -inspection-course.htm).

Best Practice in Planning, Management, and Administration

• Building codes:

○ American Society of Civil Engineers (ASCE): This webpage provides building codes and standards (http://www.asce.org/ProgramProductLine.aspx?id=6277).

○ Building code resources:

▪ Building codes by FEMA: A list of building code resources and documents for the 2009, 2012, and American Society of Civil Engineers (ASCE) flood resistant provisions (http://www.fema.gov/building-code-resources).

▪ Building codes by states: A free website that provides building codes for each state and jurisdiction (http://www.iccsafe.org/content/pages/freeresources.aspx).

▪ California Code of Regulations (CCR): Information on California's Building Standards Codes and the California Code of Regulations (http://www.bsc.ca .gov/codes.aspx).

▪ Hurricane Andrew Building Codes (video): A video on Florida's building codes, how Hurricane Andrew affected these codes, and the importance of creating a baseline code (http://www.disastersafety.org/video/ibhs-hurricane-andrew -building-codes/).

▪ Building Code Reference Library: This webpage provides detailed information on building codes for all fifty states, major cities, and some counties (http://www.reedconstructiondata.com/building-codes/).

▪ Florida Department of Business & Professional Regulation: This webpage provides information on Florida's building codes (http://www.floridabuilding.org /c/default.aspx).

▪ Institute for Business & Home Safety (IBHS) building code: A resource and blog used for best practices for building in storm surge–prone areas (https://www .disastersafety.org/blog/article-details-best-practices-for-building-in-storm-surge -prone-areas/?articleId=6923).

▪ Disaster Safety Building Codes: Provides some basic information about building codes along with other resources that pertain to building codes; click on each state to see which building codes are currently in effect (https://www .disastersafety.org/building-codes/).

- Rating the States: An assessment of eighteen hurricane-prone states and their residential building codes and enforcement systems for life safety and property protection (http://www.disastersafety.org/wp-content/uploads/ibhs-rating-the -states.pdf).
  - National Institute of Building Sciences Whole-Building Design Guide (WBDG): A website that provides building design guidelines for natural hazards and security (http://www.wbdg.org/design/resist_hazards.php).
- Coastal zone management (CZM):
  - CZM Program by NOAA: A list of all the states and territories that are working on ocean and coastal management; each state has its own link to describe its specific ocean and coastal management program (http://coastalmanagement.noaa.gov /mystate/welcome.html).
  - NOAA Boundary Making: A handbook on best practices for boundary making for marine managed areas (http://www.csc.noaa.gov/digitalcoast/publications /marine-managed-areas).
- Environmental quality:
  - Renewable National Resources Foundation (RNRF): Access to publications and reports based on renewable resources (http://www.rnrf.org/rrj.html).
  - U.S. Department of Energy (DOE) National Environmental Policy Act: This page contains the most current guidelines for appropriate use of mitigation and monitoring as set by the Council on Environmental Quality (http://ceq.hss.doe .gov/current_developments/new_ceq_nepa_guidance.html).
  - U.S. Forest Service (USFS) Healthy Forests Initiative: The page contains information supporting the Healthy Forests Initiative (http://www.fs.fed.us/projects /hfi/tools.shtml).
- Land use planning:
  - American Planning Association (APA): The APA has conducted research on integrating hazard mitigation into local planning and introduced best practices (http://www.planning.org/research/hazards/).
  - Annotated bibliography on integrating hazard mitigation in local planning and best practices: A list of resources for integrating hazard mitigation into local planning that is divided into three sections: publication, case examples, and resources (http://www.planning.org/research/hazards/pdf/hazardsbibliography.pdf).
  - The Bureau of Land Management (BLM): This website provides resource management plans (RMPs) for all public lands in the United States (http://www.blm.gov /wo/st/en/prog/planning/planning_overview.html).
- Recovery planning:
  - American City and County: Coastal towns rethink development patterns; Katrina recovery plans incorporate mixed uses (http://americancityandcounty.com/mag /government_coastal_towns_rethink).
  - NOAA Post-storm Assessments: Provides reports of different hurricane post-storm assessments (http://www.csc.noaa.gov/hes/postStorm.html).
  - U.S. American Society of Civil Engineers (ASCE): Provides a wide range of resources

not only for civil engineers but for professionals and the public to help with building and repairing infrastructure damaged by disasters (http://www.asce.org /Content.aspx?id=2147485253).

Technical Tools and Modeling Tools for Best Practices

- Evacuation modeling:
  - Consequence Assessment Tool Set/Joint Assessment of Catastrophic Events (CATS/ JACE): Software that helps create hazard assessments using a wide variety of data.
  - Evacuation Traffic Information Systems (ETIS): A traffic analysis system created to facilitate analysis across state lines.
  - Recommended practices for hurricane evacuation traffic operations by the Texas Transportation Institute (TTI): A research project providing traffic operation recommendations based on lessons learned from hurricane evacuation (http://tti .tamu.edu/search/?q=hurricane+evacuation).
  - Hurricane Evacuation (HURREVAC): Storm tracking and decision support for government emergency maintenance officials (http://www.hurrevac.com/).
  - Hurricane Evacuation Management Decision Support System (EMDSS): Storm tracking and decision support for government emergency maintenance officials, focusing on when and where to begin evacuation (http://link.springer.com /article/10.1007%2Fs11069-006-9013-1#page-1).
  - Mass Evacuation Transportation Model (MASSVAC): Estimation tool for time it takes to evacuate patients from one healthcare facility to another.
  - Oak Ridge Evacuation Modeling System (OREMS): Evacuation decision support, uses traffic simulation from the Department of Transportation (http://cta.ornl.gov/cta/).
- Flood risk modeling:
  - Hydrologic Engineering Centers River Analysis System (HEC-RAS): Performs one-dimensional hydraulic calculations for different channels, both natural and constructed (http://www.hec.usace.army.mil/software/hec-ras/).
  - NFIP Flooding Costs/Flood Risks: Introduction to flooding, flood analysis models, and explanation of how to use flood maps (https://www.floodsmart.gov /floodsmart/pages/partner/tools_resources.jsp).
  - Sea, Lake, and Overland Surges from Hurricanes (SLOSH): NWS-developed model of wind fields that cause storm surge in hurricanes (http://www.nhc.noaa.gov /surge/slosh.php).
  - Sources of Assistance (Reducing Damage from Localized Flooding: A Guide for Communities): A list of contact information for organizations that have information about flood problems.
- Multihazards:
  - FEMA HAZUS: Site for estimating potential losses from earthquakes, wind, and floods (http://www.fema.gov/hazus).
  - National Institute of Building Sciences (NIBS) Multihazard Risk Assessment/HAZUS: Site for estimating potential building and infrastructure losses from earthquakes, riverine and coastal floods, and hurricane winds (http://www.nibs.org/?page=hazus).

- Spatial Hazard Events and Losses Database for the United States (SHELDUS): Records of county-level hazard dataset for the United States for eighteen different natural hazard event types (http://webra.cas.sc.edu/hvri/products/sheldus.aspx).
- Texas Planning Atlas Mapping Service: Comprehensive online database of Texas (http://texasatlas.tamu.edu/).
- Texas Hazard Mitigation Package (THMP): THMP is an online digital geographic data resource for hazard analysis in Texas (http://thmp.info/).
- Winter weather:
  - National Climate Data Center (NCDC) GIS-Based Map Interface: An online GIS-based interface with several different maps based on information from the NCDC (http://gis.ncdc.noaa.gov/map/viewer/#app=cdo).
  - NCDC NOMADS Ensemble Probability Tool: Gives probabilities for a given set of conditions happening at a given location (http://nomads.ncdc.noaa.gov/EnsProb/).
  - NCDC Weather and Climate Toolkit: Allows exporting and visualization of climate data (http://www.ncdc.noaa.gov/wct/).
  - WunderMap: Online weather mapping application with access to multiple layers of weather data (http://www.wunderground.com/wundermap/?l).
- Wildfires:
  - USGS Fire Danger Forecast: Online mapping application for fire danger forecasting (http://firedanger.cr.usgs.gov/).
  - USGS LANDFIRE Data Distribution Site: Online mapping application for viewing USGS datasets (http://landfire.cr.usgs.gov/viewer/).

Academic Resources on Best Practices (e.g., journal articles, books, reports)

- Mitigation:
  - Samuel D. Brody, Sammy Zahran, Wesley E. Highfield, Sarah Bernhardt, and Arnold Vedlitz. "Policy Learning for Flood Mitigation: A Longitudinal Assessment of the Community Rating System in Florida." *Risk Analysis* 29, no. 6 (2009): 912–29.
  - Deyle, R. E., Chapin, T. S., and Baker, E. J. "The Proof of the Planning Is in the Platting: An Evaluation of Florida's Hurricane Exposure Mitigation Planning Mandate." *Journal of the American Planning Association* 74, no. 3 (2008): 349–70.
  - Gladwin, H., Lazo J., Morrow, B. H., Peacock, W. G., and Willoughby, H. E. "Social Science Research Needs for the Hurricane Forecast and Warning Systems." *Natural Hazards Review* 8, no. 3 (2007): 87–95.
  - Godschalk, D. R. "Avoiding Coastal Hazard Areas: Best State Mitigation Practices." *Environmental Geosciences* 7, no. 1 (2000): 13–22.
  - Nelson, A. C., and French, S. P. "Plan Quality and Mitigating Damage from Natural Disasters: Case Study of the Northridge Earthquake with Planning Policy Consideration." *Journal of the American Planning Association* 68, no. 2 (2002): 194–207.
  - Peacock, W. G. "Hurricane Mitigation Status and Factors Influencing Mitigation Status among Florida's Single-Family Homeowners." *Natural Hazards Review* 4, no. 3 (2003): 1–10.
  - Peacock, W. G., and Prater, C. "Social Protection and Disaster Risk Reduction."

Chapter 56 in Ben Wisner, J. C. Gillard, and Ilan Kelman, eds., *Handbook of Hazards, Disaster Risk Reduction and Management*. London: Routledge, 2012.

○ Peacock, W. G., Brody, S. D., Prater, C., Wunneburger, D., Ndubisi, F., Martin, J., Grover, H., Kang, J. E., Husein, R., Burns, G., and Kennedy, T. *Status and Trends of Coastal Vulnerability to Natural Hazards Project*. Annual Report for Phase 1, 2008.

○ Peacock, W. G., Brody, S. D., Prater, C., Wunneburger, D., Ndubisi, D., Martin, J., Grover, H., Kang, J. E., Husein, R., Burns, G. R., and Kennedy, T. *Status and Trends of Coastal Vulnerability to Natural Hazards Project*. Annual Report for Phase 2, 2009.

○ Peacock, W. G., Brody, S. D., Grover, H., Wunneburger, D., Kang, J. E., Husein, R., Burns, G. R., Kim, H. J., Ndubisi, F., and Martin, J. *Status and Trends of Coastal Vulnerability to Natural Hazards Project*. Annual Report for Phase 3, 2011.

○ Peacock, W. G., Grover, H., Mayunga, J., Van Zandt, S., Brody, S. D., and Kim, H. J. *The Status and Trends of Population Social Vulnerabilities along the Texas Coast with Special Attention to the Coastal Management Zone and Hurricane Ike: The Coastal Planning Atlas and Social Vulnerability Mapping Tools*, 2011.

○ Peacock, W. G., Husein, R., Burns, G. R., Kennedy, T., Kang, J. E., and Prater, C. *The Elite Report: A Report on the Perception of State, County, and Local Officials Regarding the State of Texas Mitigation Plan, Coastal Management Plan and the Promotion of Mitigation Efforts in the Texas Coastal Management Zone*, 2009.

○ Peacock, W. G., Kang, J. E., Husein, R., Burns, G., Prater, C., Brody, S. D., and Kennedy, T. *An Assessment of Coastal Zone Hazard Mitigation Plans in Texas*, 2009.

○ Peacock, W. G., Kang, J. E., Lin, Y.-S., Grover, H., Husein, R., and Burns, G. R. *Status and Trends of Coastal Hazard Exposure and Mitigation Policies for the Texas Coast: The Mitigation Policy Mosaic of Coastal Texas*. Hazard Reduction and Recovery Center, Texas A&M University , 2009.

○ Prater, C., and Kennedy, T. *Integrating Coastal Zone Management and Hazard Mitigation: Assessing the Potential Compatibilities of the Coastal Management Program and State of Texas Mitigation Plan*. Hazard Reduction and Recovery Center, Texas A&M University, 2009.

○ Schwab, J. C., ed. *Hazard Mitigation: Integrating Best Practices into Planning*. Chicago: American Planning Association, Planning Advisory Service Report Number 560, 2010.

○ Yue, G., Peacock, W. G., and Lindell, M. K. "Florida Households' Expected Response to Hurricane Hazards Mitigation Incentives." *Risk Analysis* 31, no. 10 (2011): 1676–91.

○ Zahran, S., Brody, S. D., Grover, H., and Vedlitz, A. "Climate Change Vulnerability and Policy Support." *Society and Natural Resources* 19 (2006): 771–89.

○ Zahran, S., Brody, S. D., Highfield, W. E., and Vedlitz, A. *Nonlinear Incentives, Plan Design, and Flood Mitigation: The Case of the Federal Emergency Management Agency's Community Rating System*, 2008.

○ Zahran, S., Brody, S. D., Highfield, W. E., and Vedlitz, A. "Non-linear Incentives, Plan Design, and Flood Mitigation: The Case of the Federal Emergency Management Agency's Community Rating System." *Journal of Environmental Planning and Management* 53 no. 2 (2008): 219–39.

- Vulnerability:
  - Boruff, B. J., Emrich, C., and Cutter, S. L. "Erosion Hazard Vulnerability of US Coastal Counties." *Journal of Coastal Research* 21, no. 5 (2005): 932–42.
  - Brody, S. D., Zahran, S., Vedlitz, A., and Grover, H. "Examining the Relationship between Physical Vulnerability and Perceptions of Global Climate Change in the U.S." *Environment and Behavior* 40, no. 1 (2008): 72–95.
  - Cutter, S. L., Boruff, B. J., and Shirley, W. L. "Social Vulnerability to Environmental Hazards." *Social Science Quarterly* 84, no. 1 (2003): 242–61.
  - Peacock, W. G., Kunreuther, H., Hooke, W. H., Cutter, S. L., Chang, S. E., and Berke, P. R. *Toward a Resiliency and Vulnerability Observatory Network: RAVON*, HRCC reports: 08–02R 2008.
  - Simpson, D. M., and Human, R. J. "Large-Scale Vulnerability Assessments for Natural Hazards." *Natural Hazards* 47 (2008): 143–55.
  - Zahran, S., Brody, S. D., Peacock, W. G., Vedlitz, A., and Grover, H. "Social Vulnerability and the Natural and Built Environment: A Model of Flood Casualties in Texas." *Disasters* 32, no. 4 (2008): 537–60.
  - Zhang, Y., Lindell, M. K., and Prater, C. S. "Modeling and Managing Vulnerability of Community Businesses to Environmental Disasters." *Disasters* 33, no. 1 (2009): 38–57.
- Resiliency and sustainability:
  - Brody, S. D., Grover, H., Bernhardt, S., Tang, Z., Whitaker, B., and Spencer, C. "A Multi-Criteria, Spatial Site Suitability Analysis for Oil and Gas Exploration in Texas State Coastal Waters." *Environmental Management* 38, no. 4 (2006): 597–617.
  - Brody, S., Highfield, W., Peacock, W. G., and Gunn, J. "The Influence of Development Intensity on Flood Damage along the Gulf of Mexico: Examining the Erosion of Resiliency." *Journal of Planning Education and Research* 31, no. 4 (2011): 438–48.
  - Brody, S. D., Zahran, S., Highfield, W., Grover, H., and Vedlitz, A. "Identifying the Impact of the Built Environment of Flood Damage in Texas." *Disasters* 32, no. 1 (2008): 1–18.
  - Godschalk, D. R. "Urban Hazard Mitigation: Creating Resilient Cities." *Natural Hazards Review* 4, no. 3 (2003): 136–43.
  - Mileti, D. S. *Disasters by Design: A Reassessment of Natural Hazards in the United States*. Washington, DC: Joseph Henry Press, 1999.
  - Peacock, W. G., Brody, S. D., Seitz, W. A., Merrell, W. J., Vedlitz, A., Zahran, S., Harriss, R. C., and Stickney, R. R. *Advancing the Resilience of Coastal Localities: Developing, Implementing and Sustaining the Use of Coastal Resiliency Indicators: A Final Report*. Hazard Reduction and Recovery Center, Texas A&M University, 2010.
  - Peacock, W. G., Van Zandt, S., Henry, D., Grover, H., and Highfield, W. "Social Vulnerability and Hurricane Ike: Using Social Vulnerability Mapping to Enhance Coastal Community Resiliency in Texas." Chapter 7 in *Severe Storm Prediction, Impact, and Recovery on the Texas Gulf Coast*, edited by Phillip B. Bedient. College Station, TX: Texas A&M Press, 2012.

- Recovery:
  - Al-Nammari, F. M., and Lindell, M. K. "Earthquake Recovery of Historic Buildings: Exploring Cost and Time Needs." *Disasters* 33, no. 3 (2009): 457–81.
  - Deyle, R., Eadie, C., Schwab, J., Smith, R., and Topping, K. *Planning for Post-Disaster Recovery and Reconstruction*, 483–84. Chicago: APA Planning Advisory Committee, 1998.
  - Olshanky, R. B., and Johnson, L. A. *Clear as Mud: Planning for the Rebuilding of New Orleans*. Chicago: American Planning Association Planner's Press, 2010.
  - Peacock, W. G., Morrow, B., and Gladwin, H. *Hurricane Andrew: Ethnicity, Gender and the Sociology of Disasters*. London: Routledge, 1997.
  - Zhang, Y., and Peacock, W. "Planning for Recovery? Lessons Learned from Hurricane Andrew." *Journal of the American Planning Association* 76, no. 1 (2010): 5–24.
- Emergency planning:
  - Chiu, Y.-C., Zheng, H., Villalobos, J. A., Peacock, W. G., and Henk, R. "Evaluating Regional Contra-Flow and Phased Evacuation Strategies for Central Texas Using a Large-Scale Dynamic Traffic Simulation and Assignment Approach." *Journal of Homeland Security and Emergency Management* 5(1), no. 34 (2008): 1–27.
  - Lindell, M. K. "EMBLEM2: An Empirically Based Large-Scale Evacuation Time Estimate Model." *Transportation Research* Part A 42 (2008): 140–54.
  - Lindell, M. K., Prater, C. S., and Peacock, W. G. "Organizational Communication and Decision Making for Hurricane Emergencies." *Natural Hazards Review* 8 (August 2007): 50–60.
  - Lindell, M. K., Prater, C. S., and Perry, R. W. *Introduction to Emergency Management*. Hoboken NJ: Wiley, 2007.
  - Lindell, M. K., Prater, C. S., and Perry, R. W. *Fundamentals of Emergency Management*. Washington, DC: FEMA, 2006.
  - Perry, R. W., and Lindell, M. K. *Emergency Planning*. Hoboken, NJ: Wiley, 2007.
- Natural resource management:
  - Brody, S. D., Highfield, W., Hyung-Cheal, R., and Weber, L. "Examining the Relationship Between Wetland Alteration and Watershed Flooding in Texas and Florida." *Natural Hazards* 40, no. 2 (2007): 413–28.
  - Brody, S. D. *Ecosystem Planning in Florida Solving Regional Problems through Local Decision-Making*. Burlington, VT: Ashgate, 2008.
  - Ndubisi, F. *Ecological Planning: A Historical and Comparative Synthesis*. Baltimore, MD: Johns Hopkins University Press, 2002.
  - Tierney, K. J., Lindell, M. K., and Perry, R. W. *Facing the Unexpected: Disaster Preparedness in the United States*. Washington, DC: Joseph Henry Press, 2001.

Organizations and Associations

- Multihazards:
  - APA Growing Smart: A guidebook of legislation that can be used for planning practice (http://www.planning.org/growingsmart/).
  - American Red Cross: An organization that responds to disasters, focusing on immediate needs.

- FEMA Mitigation: Manages the NFIP and works to mitigate long-term effects of disasters (http://www.fema.gov/what-mitigation).
- Institute for Business and Home Safety (IBHS): Research organization to promote and discover better hazard mitigation practices (https://www.disastersafety.org/).
- International Strategy for Disaster Reduction: United Nations hazard strategy focusing on disaster prevention instead of response (http://www.unisdr.org/).
- National Institute of Building Sciences Multihazard Mitigation Council: A group of experts in different fields that formed to work toward hazard mitigation (http://www.nibs.org/?page=mmc).
- USGS Hazards: Research group focusing on providing policymakers and public with information on hazards (http://www.usgs.gov/natural_hazards/).
- Union of Concerned Scientists: Citizens and scientists for environmental solutions, special resource information for the Gulf Coast: A group dedicated to figuring out solutions to environmental issues (http://www.ucsusa.org/).

- Drought:
  - National Interagency Fire Center: Wildfire fighting center for the nation (http://www.nifc.gov/).
  - U.S. EPA Water Conservation: Site full of information on water conservation (http://www.epa.gov/greeningepa/water/).
  - U.S. Drought Portal: Weekly updated drought map of the United States.

- Earthquakes:
  - Building Seismic Safety Council (BSSC): Organization that provides a forum to learn about earthquake safety (http://www.nibs.org/?page=bssc).
  - Earthquake Engineering Research Institute (EERI): Organization focusing on engineering research to promote earthquake mitigation (https://www.eeri.org/index.php).
  - International Code Council (ICC): Develops codes for safe and resilient building construction (http://www.iccsafe.org/Pages/default.aspx).
  - Ready: Information site about earthquake preparedness (http://www.ready.gov/earthquakes).
  - ShakeOut: A worldwide earthquake drill. The site provides information on how to get involved (http://www.shakeout.org/).

- Fires:
  - The Fire Safe Council: California statewide nonprofit that provides grants and other resources to promote fire safety (http://www.cafiresafecouncil.org/).
  - Firewise Communities: An organization devoted to teaching wildfire mitigation practices to homeowners and other local residents (http://www.firewise.org/?&sso=0).
  - National Fire Protection Association: Government organization doing fire mitigation and prevention research, training, and code development (http://www.nfpa.org/?cookie_test=1).
  - National Institute of Standards and Technology: Government organization for fire mitigation and prevention research.

- ○ National Interagency Fire Center: Wildfire fighting center for the nation (http://www.nifc.gov/).
- Floods:
  - ○ Association of State Floodplain Managers (ASFPM): Works to promote flood safety and protect floodplains through education and policy promotion (http://www.floods.org/).
  - ○ Flood Smart: Site that provides flood information and includes the NFIP, which holds participating houses and communities to standards to minimize flooding damage and impact (https://www.floodsmart.gov/floodsmart/).
  - ○ State Offices and Agencies of Emergency Management: List of contact information for state offices and agencies of emergency management.
- Hurricanes and wind:
  - ○ HazNet: The National Sea Grant Network website provides coastal natural hazard information.
  - ○ Hurricane and Storm Damage Risk Reduction: Army Corps of Engineers program to reduce risk of hurricane damage in New Orleans. Has useful information and links on the website (http://www.mvn.usace.army.mil/Missions/HSDRRS.aspx).
  - ○ NOAA's NWS National Hurricane Center: Useful website with hurricane tracking and other information on hurricanes (http://www.nhc.noaa.gov/).
  - ○ Wind Science and Engineering Research Center, Texas Tech University: Research center at Texas Tech University focusing on wind science and engineering (http://www.depts.ttu.edu/nwi/).
- Research institutes:
  - ○ Disaster Research Center, University of Delaware: Social science hazard research is a focus of this institute (http://www.udel.edu/DRC/).
  - ○ Hazards Center, University of North Carolina at Chapel Hill: Focus on coastal hazards; led by U.S. Department of Homeland Security (http://coastalhazardscenter.org/).
  - ○ Hazard Reduction and Recovery Center, Texas A&M University: Research on all types of hazards, including emergency preparedness and response (http://hrrc.arch.tamu.edu/about/).
  - ○ Hazards & Vulnerability Research Institute, University of South Carolina: Conducts basic research on hazards, trains future researchers, and does educational outreach to communities (http://webra.cas.sc.edu/hvri/).
  - ○ Natural Hazards Center, University of Colorado at Boulder: Collects and shares research with a focus on sustainability (http://www.colorado.edu/hazards/about/).
  - ○ FEMA's Listing of Emergency Management Collegiate Programs: List of college programs with emergency management courses (http://www.training.fema.gov/emiweb/edu/collegelist/).

Notes

Part I

1. Mileti, D. S. *Disasters by Design: A Reassessment of Natural Hazards in the United States*. Washington, DC: Joseph Henry Press, 1999.
2. Timmerman, P. "Vulnerability, Resilience and the Collapse of Society," *Environmental Monograph 1* (Institute for Environmental Studies, University of Toronto), 1981.
3. Mileti, *Disasters by Design*.
4. Bruneau, Michel, Stephanie E. Chang, Ronald T. Eguchi, George C. Lee, Thomas D. O'Rourke, Andrei M. Reinhorn, Masanobu Shinozuka, Kathleen Tierney, William A. Wallace, and Detlof von Winterfeldt. "A Framework to Quantitatively Assess and Enhance the Seismic Resilience of Communities," *Earthquake Spectra* 19, no. 4 (November 2003): 733–52; Tierney, K., and M. Bruneau, "Conceptualizing and Measuring Resilience," *Transportation News* , May–June 2007: 14–17.
5. Berke, P. R., and T. J. Campanella, "Planning for Postdisaster Resiliency," *Annals of the American Academy of Political and Social Science* 604, no. 1 (2006): 192–207; Peacock, W. G., H. Kunreuther, W. H. Hooke, S. L. Cutter, S. E. Chang, and P. R. Berke, *Toward a Resiliency and Vulnerability Observatory Network: RAVON*, HRRC reports: 08-02R, 2008.

Chapter 1

1. Kunreuther, Howard C. and Erwann O Michel-Kerjan. *A War with the Weather: Managing Large-Scale Risks in a New Era of Catastrophes*. Cambridge, MA: MIT Press, 2009.
2. EM-DAT, *The OFDA/CRED International Disaster Database*, 2009, http://www.emdat.be /database (accessed November 2011).
3. Munich Reinsurance Company, *Topics Geo: Natural Catastrophes 2010, Analysis, Assessments, And Positions*, Munich: Author, 2011.
4. Ibid.
5. Poumadre, M., C. Mays, S. Le Mer, and R. Blong, "The 2003 Heat Wave in France: Dangerous Climate Change Here and Now," *Risk Analysis* 2005: 1483–94.
6. Burby, R. J., "Hurricane Katrina and the Paradoxes of Government Disaster Policy: Bringing About Wise Governmental Decisions for Hazardous Areas," *Annals of the*

American Academy of Political and Social Science 604, no. 1 (2006): 171–91.

7. Burby, R. J., "Hurricane Katrina and the Paradoxes of Government Disaster Policy: Bringing About Wise Governmental Decisions for Hazardous Areas," *Annals of the American Academy of Political and Social Science* 604, no. 1 (2006): 171–91.

8. Mileti, D. S., *Disasters by Design: A Reassessment of Natural Hazards in the United States*, Washington, DC: Joseph Henry Press, 1999.

9. National Oceanic and Atmospheric Administration, *NOAA's State of the Coast: National Coastal Population Report, Population Trends from 1970–2020*, March 2013, developed in partnership with the U.S. Census Bureau.

10. Costanza, R., O. Perez-Maqueo, M. L. Martinez, P. Sutton, S. J. Anderson, and K. Mulder, "The Value of Coastal Wetlands for Hurricane Protection," *AMBIO: A Journal of the Human Environment* 37, no. 4 (2008): 241–8.

11. For detailed discussions and analysis of wetland alteration, its consequences, and an extensive focus on the Texas coast, see Brody, S. D., W. E. Highfield, and J. E. Kang, *Rising Waters: The Causes and Consequences of Flooding in the United States*, Cambridge, England: Cambridge University Press, 2011; Brody, S. D., and S. Zahran, "Estimating Flood Damage in Texas Using GIS: Predictors, Consequences, and Policy Implications," in *Geospatial Technologies and Homeland Security: Research Frontiers and Challenges*, edited by D. Sui, New York: Springer, 2008; Brody, S. D., S. E. Davis, W. E. Highfield, and S. P. Bernhardt, "A Spatial–Temporal Analysis of Section 404 Wetland Permitting in Texas and Florida: Thirteen Years of Impact Along the Coast," *Wetlands* 28, no. 1 (2008): 107–16; Brody, S. D., S. Zahran, P. Maghelal, H. Grover, and W. E. Highfield, "The Rising Costs of Floods: Examining the Impact of Planning and Development Decisions in Property Damage in Florida," *Journal of the American Planning Association* 73, no. 1 (2007): 330–45; Brody, S. D., W. E. Highfield, H. C. Ryu, and L. Spanel-Weber, "Examining the Relationship between Wetland Alteration and Watershed Flooding in Texas and Florida," *Natural Hazards* 40, no. 2 (2007): 413–28; and Zahran, S., S. D. Brody, W. G. Peacock, A. Vedlitz, and H. Grover. "Social Vulnerability and the Natural and Built Environment: A Model of Flood Casualties in Texas." *Disasters* 32, no. 4 (2008): 537–60.

12. Brody et al., "The Rising Costs of Floods."

13. U.S. Census Bureau, U.S. Census data, 2010.

14. Brody, S. D., D. R. Godschalk, and R. J. Burby, "Mandating Citizen Participation in Plan Making: Six Strategic Planning Choices," *Journal of the American Planning Association* 69, no. 3 (2003): 245–64.

Chapter 2

1. Klein, R. J. T., R. J. Nicholls, and F. Thomalla, "Resilience to Natural Hazards: How Useful Is This Concept?" *Environmental Hazards* 2003: 35–45; Manyena, S. B., "The Concept of Resilience Revisited," *Disasters* 30, no. 4 (December 2006): 434–50; Norris, F. H., S. P. Stevens, B. Pfefferbaum, K. F. Wyche, and R. L. Pfefferbaum, "Community Resilience as a Metaphor, Theory, Set of Capacities, and Strategy for Disaster Readiness," *American Journal of Community Psychology* 41, no. 1–2 (March 2008): 127–50.

2. Bates, F. L., and W. G. Peacock, *Living Conditions, Disasters, and Development: An Approach to Cross-Cultural Comparisons*, Athens: University of Georgia Press, 2008.

3. Peacock, W. G., H. Kunreuther, W. H. Hooke, S. L. Cutter, S. E. Chang, and P. R. Berke, *Toward a Resiliency and Vulnerability Observatory Network: RAVON*, HRRC reports: 08-02R, 2008.

4. Bruneau, M., et al., "A Framework to Quantitatively Assess and Enhance the Seismic Resilience of Communities," *Earthquake Spectra* 19, no. 4 (November 2003): 733–52.

5. Comfort, L., et al., "Reframing Disaster Policy: The Global Evolution of Vulnerable Communities," *Environmental Hazards* 1, no. 1 (1999): 39–44; Maguire, B., and P. Hagan, "Disasters and Communities: Understanding Social Resilience," *Australian Journal of Emergency Management* 22 (2007): 16–20; Bates and Peacock, *Living Conditions, Disasters, and Development*; Berke, P. R., and T. J. Campanella, "Planning for Postdisaster Resiliency," *Annals of the American Academy of Political and Social Science* 604, no. 1 (2006): 192–207; Smith, G., and D. Wenger, "Sustainable Disaster Recovery: Operationalizing an Existing Agenda," in *Handbook of Disaster Research*, edited by H. Rodriguez, E. Quarantelli, and R. Dynes, New York: Springer, 2006; Wilbanks, T. J., "Enhancing the Resilience of Communities to Natural and Other Hazards: What We Know and What We Can Do," *Natural Hazards Observer* 32 (2008): 10–11; Peacock et al., *Toward a Resiliency and Vulnerability Observatory Network*.

6. Olshansky, R., L. Hopkins, and L. Johnson, "Disaster and Recovery: Processes Compressed in Time," *Natural Hazards Review* 13, no. 3 (2012): 173–78.

7. Innes, J. E., and D. E. Booher, "Reframing Public Participation: Strategies for the 21st Century," *Planning Theory & Practice* 5, no. 4 (2004): 419–36.

8. Burby, R. J., R. E. Deyle, D. R. Godschalk, and R. B. Olshansky, "Creating Hazard Resilient Communities through Land-Use Planning," *Natural Hazards Review*, 2000: 99–106.

9. Innes and Booher, "Reframing Public Participation."

10. Chaskin, R. J., "Defining Community Capacity: A Framework and Implications from a Comprehensive Community Initiative," *Urban Affairs Association Annual Meeting*, Chicago: The Chapin Hall Center for Children at the University of Chicago, 1999.

11. Callaghan, E. G., and J. Colton, "Building Sustainable & Resilient Communities: A Balancing of Community Capital," *Environmental Development Sustainability* 10 (2008): 931–42; Dynes, R. R., "Finding Order in Disorder: Continuities in the 9/11 Response," *Mid-South Sociological Society*, October 18, 2002: 1–22; Haque, C. E., and D. Etkin, "People and Community as Constituent Parts of Hazards: The Significance of Societal Dimensions in Hazards Analysis," *Natural Hazards* 41 (2007): 271–82; Walter, C., "Community Building Practice," in *Community Organizing and Community Building for Health*, edited by M. Minkler, New Brunswick, NJ: Rutgers University Press, 2004.

12. Beeton, R. J. S., *Society's Forms of Capital: A Framework for Renewing Our Thinking*, Canberra: Department of the Environment and Heritage, Australian State of the Environment Committee, 2006; Walter, "Community Building Practice."

13. See, for example, Bourdieu, P., "The Forms of Capital," in *Handbook of Theory and Research for the Sociology of Education*, edited by J. G. Richardson, 110–20, New York: Greenwood, 1986; Coleman, J. S., *Foundations of Social Theory*, Cambridge, MA: Harvard University Press, 1990; Putnam, R. D., "Bowling Alone: America's Declining Social Capital," *Journal of Democracy*, 1995: 65–78; Putnam, R. D., *Bowling Alone: The Collapse and Revival of American Community*, New York: Simon and Schuster Paperbacks, 2000.

14. Green, G. P., and A. Haines, *Asset Building and Community Development*, Thousand Oaks, CA: Sage Publications, 2002.

15. Walter, "Community Building Practice."

16. Dynes, "Finding Order in Disorder"; Walter, "Community Building Practice."

17. Dynes, "Finding Order in Disorder"; Lindell, M. K., and C. S. Prater, "Assessing Community Impacts of Natural Disasters," *Natural Hazards Review* 4, no. 4 (2003): 176–85.

18. Mileti, D. S., *Disasters by Design: A Reassessment of Natural Hazards in the United States*, Washington, DC: Joseph Henry Press, 1999.

19. National Research Council (NRC), *Facing Hazards and Disasters: Understanding Human Dimensions*, Washington, DC: National Academies Press, 2006; Walter, "Community Building Practice."

20. Dynes, "Finding Order in Disorder."

21. Berke, P. R., J. Kartez, and D. Wenger, "Recovery after Disaster: Achieving Sustainable Development, Mitigation and Equity," *Disasters*, 1993: 93–109.

22. Department for International Development (DFID), *Sustainable Livelihoods and Poverty Elimination*, London: Author, 1999; Smith, R., C. Simard, and A. Sharpe, *A Proposed Approach to Environment and Sustainable Development Indicators Based on Capital*, Ottawa, ON: The National Round Table on the Environment and the Economy's Environment and Sustainable Development Indicators Initiative, 2001.

23. Mileti, *Disasters by Design*; Walter, "Community Building Practice."

24. Lindell and Prater, "Assessing Community Impacts of Natural Disasters."

25. Buckle, P., G. Mars, and S. Smale, "New Approaches to Assessing Vulnerability and Resilience," *Australian Journal of Emergency Management* 15, no. 2 (2000): 8–15; Walter, "Community Building Practice."

26. Burby, R. J., *Cooperating with Nature: Confronting Natural Hazards with Land-Use Planning for Sustainable Communities*, Washington, DC: Joseph Henry Press, 1998; Godschalk, D. R., T. Beatley, P. Berke, D. Brower, and E. Kaiser, *Natural Hazard Mitigation: Recasting Disaster Policy and Planning*, Washington, DC: Island Press, 1999.

27. DFID, *Sustainable Livelihoods and Poverty Elimination*; Walter, "Community Building Practice."

28. Bates and Peacock, *Living Conditions, Disasters, and Development*; Peacock, W. G., D. Dash, and Y. Zhang, "Shelter and Housing Recovery Following Disaster," in *The Handbook of Disaster Research*, edited by H. Rodriquez, E. L. Quarantelli, and R. Dynes, 258–74, New York: Springer, 2006; Zhang, Y., and W. G. Peacock, "Planning for Housing Recovery?" *Journal of the American Planning Association* 76, no. 1 (2010): 5–24.

29. Walter, "Community Building Practice."

30. Smith, R., C. Simard, and A. Sharpe, *A Proposed Approach to Environment and Sustainable Development Indicators*.

31. DFID, *Sustainable Livelihoods and Poverty Elimination*; Smith, Simard, and Sharpe, *A Proposed Approach to Environment and Sustainable Development Indicators*; Walter, "Community Building Practice."

32. Smith, Simard, and Sharpe, *A Proposed Approach to Environment and Sustainable Development Indicators*.

33. Burby, R. J. *Cooperating with Nature*; Godschalk et al., *Natural Hazard Mitigation*; Walter, "Community Building Practice."

34. Walter, "Community Building Practice"; Burby, R. J., *Cooperating with Nature*; Godschalk et al., *Natural Hazard Mitigation*.

35. Mileti, *Disasters by Design*.
36. Berke, P. R., and T. Beatley, *After the Hurricane: Linking Recovery to Sustainable Development in the Caribbean*, Baltimore, MD: Johns Hopkins University Press, 1997; NRC, *Facing Hazards and Disasters*.

Chapter 3

1. Godschalk, D. R., T. Beatley, P. Berke, D. Brower, and E. Kaiser, *Natural Hazard Mitigation: Recasting Disaster Policy and Planning*, Washington, DC: Island Press, 1999; Lindell, M. K., and R. W. Perry, *Behavioral Foundations of Community Emergency Planning*, Washington, DC: Hemisphere Publishing, 1992.
2. Lindell, M. K., and R. W. Perry, "Household Adjustment to Earthquake Hazard: A Review of Research," *Environment and Behavior*, 2000: 461–501.
3. Lindell and Perry have been some of the most prolific researchers and writers on emergency management and environmental hazard management for more than 30 years. They along with Prater have written two wonderful books: Lindell, M. K., C. S. Prater, and R. W. Perry, *Introduction to Emergency Management*, Hoboken, NJ: Wiley, 2007; Lindell, M. K., C. Prater, and R. P. Perry, *Emergency Management*, Hoboken, NJ: Wiley, 2006. See also Federal Emergency Management Agency (FEMA), *Making Mitigation Work: A Handbook for State Officials*, Washington, DC: Author, 1986.
4. Mileti, D. S., *Disasters by Design: A Reassessment of Natural Hazards in the United States*, Washington, DC: Joseph Henry Press, 1999; Godschalk et al., *Natural Hazard Mitigation*.
5. Brody, S. D., W. E. Highfield, and J. E. Kang, *Rising Waters: The Causes and Consequences of Flooding in the United States*, Cambridge, England: Cambridge University Press, 2011.
6. Lindell, Prater, and Perry, *Emergency Management*, p. 244.
7. Lindell and Perry, *Behavioral Foundations*.
8. Lindell, Prater, and Perry, *Introduction to Emergency Management*; Lindell, Prater, and Perry, *Emergency Management.*, pp. 250–52.
9. FEMA has wonderful guidelines and support for starting your own CERT program. See http://www.fema.gov/community-emergency-response-teams.
10. Lindell and Perry, *Behavioral Foundations*.
11. Mileti, *Disasters by Design*.
12. Lindell, Prater, and Perry, *Introduction to Emergency Management*; Lindell, Prater, and Perry, *Emergency Management*.
13. Lindell, Prater, and Perry, *Emergency Management*, p. 246.
14. Tierney, K. J., M. K. Lindell, and R. W. Perry. *Facing the Unexpected: Disaster Preparedness and Response in the United States*, Washington, DC: Joseph Henry Press, 2001; Bates, F. L., and W. G. Peacock. "Long-Term [Disaster] Recovery," *International Journal of Mass Emergencies and Disasters* 7, no. 3 (1989): 349–65.
15. Peacock, W. P., B. H. Morrow, and H. Gladwin, *Hurricane Andrew: Ethnicity, Gender, and the Sociology of Disasters*, New York: Routledge, 1997.
16. Lindell and Perry, *Behavioral Foundations*.
17. Bolin, R., "Disaster Characteristics and Psychological Impacts," in *Disasters and Mental Health: Selected Contemporary Perspectives*, edited by B. Sowder, 3–28, Rockville, MD: National Institute of Mental Health, 1985; Peacock, W. G., and A. K. Ragsdale, "Social Systems, Ecological Networks and Disasters: Toward a Socio-Political Ecology of Disasters," in *Hurricane Andrew: Ethnicity, Gender, and the Sociology of Disasters*, edited by W.

G. Peacock, B. H. Morrow, and H. Gladwin, New York: Routledge, 1997; Comerio, M. C., *Disaster Hits Home: New Policy for Urban Housing Recovery*, Berkeley: University of California Press, 1998; Bolin, R., *Household and Community Recovery after Earthquakes*, Boulder, CO: Institute of Behavioral Science, 1993.

18. Bolin, R. C., *Long-Term Family Recovery from Disaster*, Boulder: University of Colorado, 1982; Bolin, R., "Disaster Characteristics"; Bates and Peacock, "Long-Term [Disaster] Recovery."

19. Bolin, R. C., *Long-Term Family Recovery*; Bolin, "Disaster Characteristics"; Bolin, R. C., and L. Stanford, "Shelter, Housing and Recovery: A Comparison of U.S. Disasters," *Disasters*, 1991: 24–34; Peacock and Ragsdale, "Social Systems"; Bolin, R., and L. Stanford, *The North-bridge Earthquake: Vulnerability and Disaster*, London: Routledge, 1998; Zhang, Y., and W. G. Peacock, "Planning for Housing Recovery? Lessons Learned from Hurricane Andrew," *Journal of the American Planning Association*, 2010: 5–24; Van Zandt, S., Y. Zhang, W. Highfield, and W. G. Peacock, "Inequities in Long Term Housing Recovery," 2013, http://hrrc.arch.tamu.edu/media/cms_page_media/561/Long-term%20recovery_NHC_13.pdf.

20. Peacock, W. G., D. Dash, and Y. Zhang, "Shelter and Housing Recovery following Disaster," in *The Handbook of Disaster Research*, edited by H. Rodriquez, E. L. Quarantelli, and R. Dynes, 258–74, New York: Springer, 2006.

21. The importance of considering all four phases of disasters when considering disaster impacts and ultimately recovery has been clearly articulated in a series of articles and books by Lindell, Prater, and Perry: Lindell, Prater, and Perry, *Emergency Management*; Lindell, M. K., and R. P. Perry, *Communicating Environmental Risk in Multiethnic Communities*, Thousand Oaks, CA: Sage, 2004; Lindell, Prater, and Perry, *Introduction to Emergency Management*; Lindell, M. K., and C. S. Prater, "Assessing Community Impacts of Natural Disasters," *Natural Hazards Review* 4, no. 4 (2003): 176–85.

22. Blaikie, P. M., T. Cannon, I. Davis, and B. Wisner, *At Risk: Natural Hazards, People's Vulnerability and Disasters*, London: Routledge, 1994.

23. For a more complete introductory discussion of different disaster agents we recommend Keller, E. A., and D. DeVecchio, *Natural Hazards: Earth's Processes as Hazards Disasters, and Catastrophes*, Upper Saddle River, NJ: Prentice Hall, 2011. In addition, the U.S. Geological Survey website (www.usgs.gov) maintains a series of wonderful Web pages and links for information on all kinds of hazards (http://www.usgs.gov/natural_hazards/), with a particular focus on geologically based hazards. The NOAA also maintains a wonderful website (www.noaa.gov) called Weather-Ready Nation (http://www.nws.noaa.gov/com/weatherreadynation/#.UyM3ql6pqAI) that has a wealth of information on weather- and climate-related hazards.

24. Lindell, Prater, and Perry, *Emergency Management*; Lindell, Prater, and Perry, *Communicating Environmental Risk*; Lindell, Prater, and Perry, *Introduction to Emergency Management*; Lindell, and Prater, "Assessing Community Impacts."

25. FEMA, *A Whole Community Approach to Emergency Management: Principles, Themes, and Pathways for Action*, FDOC 104-008-1, Washington, DC: Author, 2011.

Chapter 4

1. Peacock, W. G., J. E. Kang, Y. S. Lin, H. Grover, R. Husein, and G. R. Burns, *Status and Trends of Coastal Hazard Exposure and Mitigation Policies for the Texas Coast: The Mitigation Policy Mosaic of Coastal Texas*, College Station, TX: Hazard Reduction & Recovery Center, 2009.

2. Henson, B., "Hurricane Storm Surge: In a Category of Its Own," *Atmos News*, September 4, 2012.

3. The USGS Flood Inundation Mapping Program works with local communities to create flood inundation map libraries to assist with cost-effective mitigation decision making. See http://water.usgs.gov/osw/flood_inundation/ for more information.

4. Peacock et al., *Status and Trends of Coastal Hazard Exposure*.

Chapter 5

1. Schwab, J., ed., "Planning for Post-Disaster Recovery and Reconstruction," Planning Advisory Service report 483/484. Chicago: American Planning Association, 1998; Burby, R. J., *Cooperating with Nature: Confronting Natural Hazards with Land-Use Planning for Sustainable Communities*, Washington, DC: Joseph Henry Press, 1998; Godschalk, D. R., T. Beatley, P. Berke, D. Brower, and E. Kaiser, *Natural Hazard Mitigation: Recasting Disaster Policy and Planning*, Washington, DC: Island Press, 1999; Daniels, T., and K. Daniels, *The Environmental Planning Handbook: For Sustainable Communities and Regions*, Chicago: Planners Press, 2003.

2. Highfield, W., W. G. Peacock, and S. Van Zandt, "Mitigation Planning: Why Hazard Exposure, Structural Vulnerability, and Social Vulnerability Matter," *Journal of Planning Education & Research* 34, no. 3 (2014): 287–300.

3. Ibid.

4. Mileti, D. S., *Disasters by Design: A Reassessment of Natural Hazards in the United States*, Washington, DC: Joseph Henry Press, 1999.

5. Frostin, P., and A. G. Holtmann, "The Determinants of Residential Property Damage Caused by Hurricane Andrew," *Southern Economic Journal* 61, no. 2 (1994): 387–97.

6. Highfield, Peacock, and Van Zandt, "Mitigation Planning."

7. Ibid.

8. Xiao, Y., and S. Van Zandt, "Building Community Resiliency: Spatial Links between Household and Business Post-disaster Return," *Urban Studies* 49, no. 11 (2013): 2523–42.

9. Godschalk, D., "Urban Hazard Mitigation: Creating Resilient Cities," *Natural Hazards Review* 4, no. 3 (2003): 136–43.

10. http://www.planning.org/nationalcenters/hazards/coastalzonemanagement/datatools.htm.

11. Godschalk, "Urban Hazard Mitigation."

12. Holling, C., "The Resilience of Terrestrial Ecosystems," in *Foundations of Ecological Resilience*, edited by L. Gunderson, C. Allen, and C. Holling, 67–108, Washington, DC: Island Press, 2010, p. 72.

13. Beatley, T., *Planning for Coastal Resilience*, Washington, DC: Island Press, 2009.

Chapter 6

1. Deyle, R. E., S. P. French, R. A. Olshansky, and R. G. Paterson, "Hazard Assessment: The Factual Basis for Planning and Mitigation," in *Cooperating with Nature: Confronting Natural Hazards with Land-Use Planning for Sustainable Communities*, edited by R. Burby, Washington, DC: Joseph Henry Press/National Academy Press, 1998; National Research Council (NRC), *Facing Hazards and Disasters: Understanding Human Dimensions*, Washington, DC: National Academies Press, 2006.

2. Similar lines of thought were evident in what has been called environmental justice research: Bullard, R. D., *Dumping in Dixie: Race, Class, and Environmental Quality*,

Boulder, CO: Westview Press, 1990; Bryant, B. I., and P. Mohai, *Race and the Incidence of Environmental Hazards*, Boulder, CO: Westview Press, 1992; Pastor, M., R. Bullard, J. K. Boyce, A. Fothergill, R. Morello-Frosch, and B. Wright, "Environment, Disaster, and Race after Katrina," *Race, Poverty & the Environment* 13, no. 1 (2006): 21–26.

3. Blaikie, P. M., T. Cannon, I. Davis, and B. Wisner, *At Risk: Natural Hazards, People's Vulnerability and Disasters*, London: Routledge, 1994, p. 9.

4. Morrow, B. H., "Identifying and Mapping Community Vulnerability," *Disasters* 23, no. 1 (1999): 1–18.

5. Perry, R. W., and M. K. Lindel, "The Effects of Ethnicity on Evacuation Decision-Making," *International Journal of Mass Emergency Disasters* 9, no. 1 (1991): 47–68; Morrow, B. H., "Stretching the Bonds: The Families of Andrew," in *Hurricane Andrew: Ethnicity, Gender, and the Sociology of Disasters*, edited by W. G. Peacock, B. H. Morrow, and H. Gladwin, London: Routledge, 1997.

Chapter 7

1. Lyles, W., P. Berke, and G. Smith, "A Comparison of Local Hazard Mitigation Plan Quality in Six States, USA," *Landscape and Urban Planning*, 2014: 89–99.

2. Federal Emergency Management Agency (FEMA), *State Multi-Hazard Mitigation Planning Guidance* (Mitigation Planning "Blue Book"), Washington, DC: Author, January 2008.

3. Ibid.

4. Ibid.

5. These recommendations and an implicit acknowledgment that the FEMA guidelines focus on what is necessary to develop a minimal mitigation plan, not necessarily a fully robust comprehensive mitigation plan. This is perfectly reasonable, given that these guidelines are designed to be applied across the country, in diverse areas with varying planning capabilities.

6. Federal Emergency Management Agency (FEMA), *Mitigation Ideas: Possible Mitigation Measures by Hazards Type*, Washington, DC: FEMA Region V, 2002.

7. Godschalk, D. R., T. Beatley, P. Berke, D. Brower, and E. Kaiser, *Natural Hazard Mitigation: Recasting Disaster Policy and Planning*, Washington, DC: Island Press, 1999.

8. Berke, P. R., E. Roenigk, E. Kaiser, and R. Burby, "Enhancing Plan Quality: Evaluating the Role of State Planning Mandates for Natural Hazard Mitigation," *Journal of Environmental Planning and Management*, 1996: 79–96.

9. Peacock, W. G., J. E. Kang, Y. S. Lin, H. Grover, R. Husein, and G. R. Burns, *Status and Trends of Coastal Hazard Exposure and Mitigation Policies for the Texas Coast: The Mitigation Policy Mosaic of Coastal Texas*, College Station, TX: Hazard Reduction & Recovery Center, 2009; Kang, J. E., W. G. Peacock, and R. Husein, "An Assessment of Coastal Zone Hazard Mitigation Plans in Texas," *Journal of Disaster Research*, 2010: 520–28.

10. Lyles, Berke, and Smith, "A Comparison of Local Hazard Mitigation Plan Quality."

11. Berke, P. R., "Evaluating Environmental Plan Quality: The Case of Planning for Sustainable Development in New Zealand," *Journal of Environmental Planning and Management*, 1994: 155–69; Berke, P. R., and S. P. French, "The Influence of State Planning on Local Plan Quality," *Journal of Planning Education and Research*, 1994: 237–50; Burby, R. J., and L. C. Dalton, "Plans Can Matter! The Role of Land Use Plans and State Planning Mandates in Limiting the Development of Hazardous Areas," *Public Administration Review*, 1994: 229–38; Berke et al., "Enhancing Plan Quality."

12. Peacock et al., *Status and Trends of Coastal Hazard Exposure*; Kang, Peacock, and Husein, "An Assessment of Coastal Zone Hazard Mitigation Plans."

13. For a more detailed discussion of their assessment protocol, see Lyles, Berke, and Smith, "A Comparison of Local Hazard Mitigation Plan Quality."

14. Ibid.

15. Berke, P., W. Lyles, and G. Smith, "Impacts of Federal and State Hazard Mitigation Policies on Local Land Use Policy," *Journal of Planning Education and Research*, 2014: 60–76.

Chapter 8

1. Lyles, W., P. Berke, and G. Smith, "A Comparison of Local Hazard Mitigation Plan Quality in Six States, USA," *Landscape and Urban Planning*, 2014: 89–99.

2. Hyndman, D., and D. Hyndman, *Natural Hazards and Disasters*, Boston: Cengage Learning, 2006.

3. Burby, R. J., R. E. Deyle, D. R. Godschalk, and R. B. Olshansky, "Creating Hazard Resilient Communities through Land-Use Planning," *Natural Hazards Review*, 2000: 96–106; Berke, P., J. Crawford, and N. Eriksen, "Do Cooperative Environmental Planning Mandates Produce Good Plans? Empirical Results from the New Zealand Experience," *Environment and Planning*, 1999: 643–64; Burby, R., and M. May, "Making Building Codes an Effective Tool for Earthquake Hazard Mitigation," *Environmental Hazards*, 1999: 27–37; Godschalk, D. R., D. J. Brower, and T. Beatley, *Catastrophic Coastal Storms: Hazard Mitigation and Development Management*, Durham, NC: Duke University Press, 1989; Henstra, D., and G. McBean, "The Role of Government in Services for Natural Disaster Mitigation," *Institute for Catastrophic Loss Reduction Research Paper Series*, 2004.

4. Daniels, T., and K. Daniels, *The Environmental Planning Handbook: For Sustainable Communities and Regions*, Chicago: Planners Press, 2003; Lindell, M. K., C. S. Prater, and R. W. Perry, *Introduction to Emergency Management*, Hoboken, NJ: Wiley, 2007; Beatley, T., "Planning for Sustainability in European Cities: A Review of Practices in Leading Cities," in *The Sustainable Urban Development Reader*, edited by S. M. Wheeler and T. Beatley, 249–58, London: Routledge, 2003; Godschalk, D. R., T. Beatley, P. Berke, D. Brower, and E. Kaiser, *Natural Hazard Mitigation: Recasting Disaster Policy and Planning*, Washington, DC: Island Press, 1999.

5. Godschalk, D. R., D. J. Brower, and T. Beatley, *Catastrophic Coastal Storms: Hazard Mitigation and Development Management*, Durham, NC: Duke University Press, 1989.

6. Peacock, W. G., and R. Husein, *The Adoption and Implementation of Hazard Mitigation Policies and Strategies by Coastal Jurisdictions in Texas: The Planning Survey Results*, submitted to the Texas General Land Office, the National Oceanic and Atmospheric Administration, and the Coastal Coordination Council, College Station, TX: Hazard Reduction & Recovery Center, 2011.

7. Burby and May, "Making Building Codes an Effective Tool"; Godschalk, Brower, and Beatley, *Catastrophic Coastal Storms*.

8. Burby, R. J., *Cooperating with Nature: Confronting Natural Hazards with Land-Use Planning for Sustainable Communities*, Washington, DC: Joseph Henry Press, 1998; May, P., "Mandate Design and Implementation: Enhancing Implementation Efforts and Shaping Regulatory Styles," *Journal of Policy Analysis and Management* , 1993: 634–63; Godschalk et al., *Natural Hazard Mitigation*.

9. Burby, R. J., *Cooperating with Nature*; Deyle, R. E., S. P. French, R. A. Olshansky, and R. G. Paterson, "Hazard Assessment: The Factual Basis for Planning and Mitigation," in *Cooperating with Nature: Confronting Natural Hazards with Land-Use Planning for Sustainable Communities*, edited by R. Burby, 199–66, Washington, DC: Joseph Henry Press/ National Academy Press, 1998.

10. Olshansky, R. B., and J. D. Kartez, "Managing Land Use to Build Resilience," in *Cooperating with Nature: Confronting Natural Hazards with Land-Use Planning for Sustainable Communities*, by R. J. Burby, 167–202, Washington, DC: National Academies Press, 1998.

11. Deyle et al., "Hazard Assessment"; Olshansky and Kartez, "Managing Land Use."

12. Godschalk, Brower, and Beatley, *Catastrophic Coastal Storms*; Beatley, T., D. J. Brower, and A. K. Schwab, *An Introduction to Coastal Zone Management*, 2nd ed., Washington, DC: Island Press, 2002.

13. Beatley, T., *Planning for Coastal Resilience*, Washington, DC: Island Press, 2009.

14. Klee, G., *The Coastal Environment: Toward Integrated Coastal and Marine Sanctuary Management*, Upper Saddle River, NJ: Prentice Hall, 1999, p. 106.

15. Olshansky and Kartez, "Managing Land Use."

16. Beatley, *Planning for Coastal Resilience*.

17. Burby, R. J., *Cooperating with Nature*.

18. Ibid.; Tang, Z., "Evaluating Local Coastal Zone Land Use Planning Capacities in California," *Ocean and Coastal Management*, 2008: 544–55.

19. Mileti, D. S., *Disasters by Design: A Reassessment of Natural Hazards in the United States*, Washington, DC: Joseph Henry Press, 1999.

20. Klee, *The Coastal Environment*; Williams, A., and A. Micallef, *Beach Management: Principles and Practice*, Sterling, VA: Earthscan, 2009; Beatley, *Planning for Coastal Resilience*.

21. Williams and Micallef, *Beach Management*.

22. Brody, S. D., S. Zahran, A. Vedlitz, and H. Grover, "Examining the Relationship between Physical Vulnerability and Public Perceptions of Global Climate Change in the United States," *Environment and Behavior* 40, no. 1 (2008): 72–95; Brody, S. D., J. E. Kang, and S. Bernhardt, "Identifying Factors Influencing Flood Mitigation at the Local Level in Texas and Florida: The Role of Organizational Capacity," *Natural Hazards*, 2010: 167–84; Brody, S. D., W. E. Highfield, and J. E. Kang, *Rising Waters: The Causes and Consequences of Flooding in the United States*, New York: Cambridge University Press, 2011.

23. Hyndman and Hyndman, *Natural Hazards and Disasters*.

24. Beatley, *Planning for Coastal Resilience*.

25. Brody, S. D., D. R. Godschalk, and R. J. Burby, "Mandating Citizen Participation in Plan Making: Six Strategic Planning Choices," *Journal of the American Planning Association*, 2003: 245–64; Peacock, W. G., "Hurricane Mitigation Status and Factors in Influencing Mitigation Status among Florida's Single-Family Homeowners," *Natural Hazards Review*, 2003: 149–58.

26. Norton, R. K., "More and Better Local Planning," *Journal of the American Planning Association*, 2005: 55–71; Robin, L., "Capacity Building for Natural Resource Management: Lessons from Risk and Emergency Management," *Australasian Journal of Environmental Management*, 2008: 6.

27. Beatley, *Planning for Coastal Resilience*; Berke, P. R., E. Roenigk, E. Kaiser, and R. Burby, "Enhancing Plan Quality: Evaluating the Role of State Planning Mandates for Natural Hazard Mitigation," *Journal of Environmental Planning and Management*, 1996: 79–96;

Brody, S. D., and W. E. Highfield, "Does Planning Work?: Testing the Implementation of Local Environmental Planning in Florida," *Journal of the American Planning Association*, 2005: 159–75; Burby, R. J., *Cooperating with Nature*; Godschalk et al., *Natural Hazard Mitigation*; Olshansky and Kartez, "Managing Land Use"; Srivastava, R., and L. Laurian, "Natural Hazard Mitigation in Local Comprehensive Plans: The Case of Flood, Wildfire and Drought Planning in Arizona," *Disaster Prevention and Management*, 2006: 461–83.

28. Tang, Z., M. K. Lindell, C. Prater, T. Wei, and C. M. Hussey, "Examining Local Coastal Zone Management Capacity in US Pacific Coastal Counties," *Coastal Management*, 2011: 105–32; Daniels and Daniels, *The Environmental Planning Handbook*.

29. Beatley, *Planning for Coastal Resilience*.

30. Ibid.

31. Schwab, J., *Hazard Mitigation: Integrating Best Practices into Planning*, 560, Planning Advisory Service Report, Chicago, IL: American Planning Association, 2010.

32. Holway, J. M., and R. J. Bubry, "The Effects of Floodplain Development Controls on Residential Land Values," *Land Economics*, 1990: 259–71.

33. Federal Emergency Management Agency (FEMA), *Local Multi-Hazard Mitigation Planning Guidance*, Washington, DC: Author, 2007.

34. Schwab, A., K. Eschelbach, and D. Brower, *Hazard Mitigation and Preparedness*, Danvers, MA: Wiley, 2007.

35. Brody, S. D., S. Zahran, P. Maghelal, H. Grover, and W. E. Highfield, "The Rising Costs of Floods: Examining the Impact of Planning and Development Decisions in Property Damage in Florida," *Journal of the American Planning Association* 73, no. 1 (2007): 330–45.

36. Brody et al., *Rising Waters*.

37. Schwab, Eschelbach, and Brower, *Hazard Mitigation and Preparedness*.

38. Davis, B. C., "Regional Planning in the US Coastal Zone: A Comparative Analysis of 15 Special Area Plans," *Ocean and Coastal Management*, 2004: 79–94; Hershman, M. J., J. W. Good, T. Bernd-Cohen, R. F. Goodwin, V. Lee, and P. Pogue, "The Effectiveness of Coastal Zone Management in the United States," *Coastal Management*, 1999: 113–38; Tang, "Evaluating Local Coastal Zone Land Use Planning Capacities in California."

39. Beatley, *Planning for Coastal Resilience*.

40. Olshansky and Kartez, "Managing Land Use"; Tang, "Evaluating Local Coastal Zone Land Use Planning Capacities in California."

41. Deyle et al., "Hazard Assessment"; Olshansky and Kartez, "Managing Land Use"; Tang, "Evaluating Local Coastal Zone Land Use Planning Capacities in California."

42. Deyle et al., "Hazard Assessment"; Olshansky and Kartez, "Managing Land Use."

43. Godschalk, Brower, and Beatley, *Catastrophic Coastal Storms*.

44. Dodson, D., J. Thomasson, and L. Totten, *Building Community by Design: A Resource Guide for Community Change Leaders*, Chapel Hill, NC: MDC, 2002.

Chapter 9

1. Merriam-Webster, *Learner's Dictionary*, http://www.learnersdictionary.com/ (accessed April 1, 2014).

2. Schick, F., "Consistency," *The Philosophical Review*, 1966: 467–95.

3. Argandona, A., "Consistency in Decision Making in Companies," in *Humanizing the Firm and the Management Profession*, Barcelona: IESE Business School, 2008.

4. Gibbs, D., and A. E. G. Jonas, "Governance and Regulation in Local Environmental Policy: The Utility of a Regime Approach," *Geoforum*, 2000: 299–313.

5. Lopez, J. A. Perez, "I Am the Boss, Why Should I Be Ethical?" *People in Corporations*, 1990: 179–88.

6. Sun, L. G., "Smart Growth in Dumb Places: Sustainability, Disaster, and the Future of the American City," *Brigham Young University Law Review* (2011): 2157.

7. Mandelker, D. R., "The Role of the Local Comprehensive Plan in Land Use Regulation," *Michigan Law Review*, 1976: 899–973.

8. Morgan, T. D., and J. W. Shonkwiler, "Urban Development and Statewide Planning: Challenging of the 1980s," *Oregon Law Review*, 61 (1982): 351; Meck, S., "Legislative Requirement That Zoning and Land Use Controls Be Consistent with an Independently Adopted Local Comprehensive Plan: A Model Statute," *Washington University Journal of Law & Policy*, 2000: 295.

9. Burby, R. J., R. E. Deyle, D. R. Godschalk, and R. B. Olshansky, "Creating Hazard Resilient Communities through Land-Use Planning," *Natural Hazards Review*, 2000: 99–106.

10. Godschalk, D., D. Parham, D. Porter, W. Potapchuk, and S. Schukraft, "Pulling Together: A Planning and Development Consensus Building Manual," in *Ensuring Success: Meeting and Management*, Washington, DC: Urban Land Institute, 1994.

11. Dickey, J. W., *Metropolitan Transportation Planning*, Boca Raton, FL: CRC Press, 1983.

12. Potter, J. R., and M. J. Savonis, "Transportation in an Age of Climate Change: What Are the Research Priorities?" *TR News*, 2003: 227.

13. Savonis, M., V. R. Burkett, J. R. Potter, R. Kafalenos, R. Hyman, and K. Leonard, "The Impact of Climate Change on Transportation in the Gulf Coast," *TCLEE 2009: Lifeline Earthquake Engineering in a Multihazard Environment*, 2009.

14. Stecker, R., A. Pechan, J. M. Steinhauser, M. Rotter, G. Scholl, and K. Eisenack, "Why Are Utilities Reluctant to Adapt to Climate Change?" Report, Odenburg/Berlin, 2011; Rubin, J. "Transportation and Climate Change," *Maine Policy Review*, 2008: 115–19; Greene, D. L., and M. Wegener, "Sustainable Transport," *Journal of Transport Geography*, 1997: 177–90.

15. Xiao, Y., and W. G. Peacock, "Do Hazard Mitigation and Preparedness Reduce Physical Damage to Businesses in Disasters?: The Critical Role of Business Disaster Planning," *Natural Hazards Review* 15, no. 3 (2014).

16. City of Galveston Comprehensive Plan. 2011. Page 17. Available online at: http://www.cityofgalveston.org/DocumentCenter/View/1711..

17. Dodson, D., J. Thomasson, and L. Totten, *Building Community by Design: A Resource Guide for Community Change Leaders*, Chapel Hill, NC: MDC, 2002.

Chapter 10

1. Mileti, D. S., *Disasters by Design: A Reassessment of Natural Hazards in the United States*, Washington, DC: Joseph Henry Press, 1999.

2. Habermas, J., *Theory of Communicative Action*, Boston: Beacon Press, 1984.

3. Gawande, A., *The Checklist Manifesto: How to Get Things Right*, New York: Metropolitan Books, 2009.

Bibliography

Adger, W. N. "Social and Ecological Resilience: Are They Related?" *Progress in Human Geography* 24, no. 3 (2000): 347–64.

Advisory Council for Historic Preservation website. http://www.achp.gov (accessed November 2013).

Alba, Richard D., and John R. Logan. "Analyzing Locational Attainments: Constructing Individual-Level Regression Models Using Aggregate Data." *Sociological Methods and Research* 20 (1992): 367–97.

Argandona, A. "Consistency in Decision Making in Companies." In *Humanizing the Firm and the Management Profession*. Barcelona: IESE Business School, 2008.

Arnstein, Sherry R. "A Ladder of Citizen Participation." In *The City Reader*, edited by Richard T. Gates and Frederic Stout, 240–52. London: Routledge, 1996.

Bates, F. L., and W. G. Peacock. *Living Conditions, Disasters, and Development: An Approach to Cross-Cultural Comparisons*. Athens: University of Georgia Press, 2008.

Bates, F. L., and W. G. Peacock. "Long-Term [Disaster] Recovery." *International Journal of Mass Emergencies and Disasters* 7, no. 3 (1989): 349–65.

Beatley, Timothy. "Applying Moral Principles to Growth Management." *APA Journal*, 1984: 459–69.

Beatley, Timothy. *Planning for Coastal Resilience*. Washington, DC: Island Press, 2009.

Beatley, Timothy. "Planning for Sustainability in European Cities: A Review of Practices in Leading Cities." In *The Sustainable Urban Development Reader*, edited by S. M. Wheeler and T. Beatley, 249–58. London: Routledge, 2003.

Beatley, Timothy. "Preserving Biodiversity: Challenges for Planners." *Journal of the American Planning Association* 66, no. 1 (2000): 5–20.

Beatley, T., D. J. Brower, and A. K. Schwab. *An Introduction to Coastal Zone Management*. 2nd ed. Washington, DC: Island Press, 2002.

Beeton, R. J. S. *Society's Forms of Capital: A Framework for Renewing Our Thinking*. Canberra: Department of the Environment and Heritage, Australian State of the Environment Committee, 2006.

Berke, P. R. "Evaluating Environmental Plan Quality: The Case of Planning for Sustainable Development in New Zealand." *Journal of Environmental Planning and Management*, 1994: 155–69.

Berke, P. R., and T. Beatley. *After the Hurricane: Linking Recovery to Sustainable Development in the Caribbean*. Baltimore, MD: Johns Hopkins University Press, 1997.

Berke, P. R., and T. J. Campanella. "Planning for Postdisaster Resiliency." *Annals of the American Academy of Political and Social Science* 604, no. 1 (2006): 192–207.

Berke, P., J. Crawford, and N. Eriksen. "Do Cooperative Environmental Planning Mandates Produce Good Plans? Empirical Results from the New Zealand Experience." *Environment and Planning*, 1999: 643–64.

Berke, P. R., and S. P. French. "The Influence of State Planning on Local Plan Quality." *Journal of Planning Education and Research*, 1994: 237–50.

Berke, P. R., J. Kartez, and D. Wenger. "Recovery after Disaster: Achieving Sustainable Development, Mitigation and Equity." *Disasters*, 1993: 93–109.

Berke, P., W. Lyles, and G. Smith. "Impacts of Federal and State Hazard Mitigation Policies on Local Land Use Policy." *Journal of Planning Education and Research*, 2014: 60–76.

Berke, P. R., E. Roenigk, E. Kaiser, and R. Burby. "Enhancing Plan Quality: Evaluating the Role of State Planning Mandates for Natural Hazard Mitigation." *Journal of Environmental Planning and Management*, 1996: 79–96.

Blaikie, P. M., T. Cannon, I. Davis, and B. Wisner. *At Risk: Natural Hazards, People's Vulnerability and Disasters*. London: Routledge, 1994.

Bolin, R. "Disaster Characteristics and Psychological Impacts." In *Disasters and Mental Health: Selected Contemporary Perspectives*, edited by B. Sowder, 3–28. Rockville, MD: National Institute of Mental Health, 1985.

Bolin, R. *Household and Community Recovery after Earthquakes*. Boulder, CO: Institute of Behavioral Science, 1993.

Bolin, R. C. *Long-Term Family Recovery from Disaster*. Boulder, CO: University of Colorado, 1982.

Bolin, R., and L. Stanford. *The Northbridge Earthquake: Vulnerability and Disaster*. London: Routledge, 1998.

Bolin, R. C., and L. Stanford. "Shelter, Housing and Recovery: A Comparison of U.S. Disasters." *Disasters*, 1991: 24–34.

Bourdieu, P. "The Forms of Capital." In *Handbook of Theory and Research for the Sociology of Education*, edited by J. G. Richardson, 110–20. New York: Greenwood, 1986.

Bratt, R., C. Hartman, and A. Meyerson. *Critical Perspectives on Housing*. Philadelphia: Temple University Press, 1986.

Brody, Samuel D., Stephen E. Davis, Wesley E. Highfield, and Sarah P. Bernhardt. "A Spatial–Temporal Analysis of Section 404 Wetland Permitting in Texas and Florida: Thirteen Years of Impact along the Coast." *Wetlands* 28, no. 1 (2008): 107–16.

Brody, S. D., D. R. Godschalk, and R. J. Burby. "Mandating Citizen Participation in Plan Making: Six Strategic Planning Choices." *Journal of the American Planning Association* 69, no. 3 (2003): 245–64.

Brody, S. D., and W. E. Highfield. "Does Planning Work?: Testing the Implementation of Local Environmental Planning in Florida." *Journal of the American Planning Association*, 2005: 159–75.

Brody, Samuel D., Wesley E. Highfield, and Jung Eun Kang. *Rising Waters: The Causes and Consequences of Flooding in the United States*. Cambridge, England: Cambridge University Press, 2011.

Brody, S. D., W. E. Highfield, H. C. Ryu, and L. Spanel-Weber. "Examining the Relationship between Wetland Alteration and Watershed Flooding in Texas and Florida." *Natural Hazards* 40, no. 2 (2007): 413–28.

Brody, S. D., J. E. Kang, and S. Bernhardt. "Identifying Factors Influencing Flood Mitigation at the Local Level in Texas and Florida: The Role of Organizational Capacity." *Natural Hazards*, 2010: 167–84.

Brody, S. D., and S. Zahran. "Estimating Flood Damage in Texas Using GIS: Predictors, Consequences, and Policy Implications." In *Geospatial Technologies and Homeland Security: Research Frontiers and Challenges*, edited by Daniel Sui, 171–88. New York: Springer, 2008.

Brody, S. D., S. Zahran, W. E. Highfield, H. Grover, and A. Vedlitz. "Identifying the Impact of the Built Environment on Flood Damage in Texas." *Disasters* 32, no. 1 (2007): 1–18.

Brody, Samuel D., Sammy Zahran, Praveen Maghelal, Himanshu Grover, and Wesley E. Highfield. "The Rising Costs of Floods: Examining the Impact of Planning and Development Decisions in Property Damage in Florida." *Journal of the American Planning Association* 73, no. 1 (2007): 330–45.

Brody, Samuel D., Sammy Zahran, Arnold Vedlitz, and Himanshu Grover. "Examining the Relationship between Physical Vulnerability and Public Perceptions of Global Climate Change in the United States." *Environment and Behavior* 40, no. 1 (2008): 72–95.

Bruneau, Michel, Stephanie E. Chang, Ronald T. Eguchi, George C. Lee, Thomas D. O'Rourke, Andrei M. Reinhorn, Masanobu Shinozuka, Kathleen Tierney, William A. Wallace, and Detlof von Winterfeldt. "A Framework to Quantitatively Assess and Enhance the Seismic Resilience of Communities," *Earthquake Spectra* 19, no. 4 (November 2003): 733–52; Tierney, K., and M. Bruneau, "Conceptualizing and Measuring Resilience," *Transportation News* , May–June 2007: 14–17.

Bryant, B. I., and P. Mohai. *Race and the Incidence of Environmental Hazards*. Boulder, CO: Westview Press, 1992.

Buckle, P. "Re-defining Community and Vulnerability in the Context of Emergency Management." *Australian Journal of Emergency Management*, 2000: 8–14.

Buckle, P., G. Mars, and S. Smale. "New Approaches to Assessing Vulnerability and Resilience." *Australian Journal of Emergency Management* 15, no. 2 (2000): 8–15.

Bullard, R. D. *Dumping in Dixie: Race, Class, and Environmental Quality*. Boulder, CO: Westview Press, 1990.

Burby, Raymond J. *Cooperating with Nature: Confronting Natural Hazards with Land-Use Planning for Sustainable Communities*. Washington, DC: Joseph Henry Press, 1998.

Burby, R. J. "Hurricane Katrina and the Paradoxes of Government Disaster Policy: Bringing About Wise Governmental Decisions for Hazardous Areas." *Annals of the American Academy of Political and Social Science* 604, no. 1 (2006): 171–91.

Burby, R. J., and L. C. Dalton. "Plans Can Matter! The Role of Land Use Plans and State Planning Mandates in Limiting the Development of Hazardous Areas." *Public Administration Review*, 1994: 229–38.

Burby, R. J., R. E. Deyle, D. R. Godschalk, and R. B. Olshansky. "Creating Hazard Resilient Communities through Land-Use Planning." *Natural Hazards Review*, 2000: 99–106.

Burby, R., and M. May. "Making Building Codes an Effective Tool for Earthquake Hazard Mitigation." *Environmental Hazards*, 1999: 27–37.

Callaghan, E. G., and J. Colton. "Building Sustainable & Resilient Communities: A Balancing of Community Capital." *Environmental Development Sustainability* 10 (2008): 931–42.

Chaskin, R. J. "Defining Community Capacity: A Framework and Implications from a Comprehensive Community Initiative." *Urban Affairs Association Annual Meeting*. Chicago: The Chapin Hall Center for Children at the University of Chicago, 1999.

Coleman, J. S. *Foundations of Social Theory*. Cambridge, MA: Harvard University Press, 1990.

Comerio, M. C. *Disaster Hits Home: New Policy for Urban Housing Recovery*. Berkeley: University of California Press, 1998.

Comfort, L., et al. "Reframing Disaster Policy: The Global Evolution of Vulnerable Communities." *Environmental Hazards* 1, no. 1 (1999): 39–44.

Costanza, R., O. Perez-Maqueo, M. L. Martinez, P. Sutton, S. J. Anderson, and K. Mulder. "The Value of Coastal Wetlands for Hurricane Protection." *AMBIO: A Journal of the Human Environment* 37, no. 4 (2008): 241–8.

Craig, William J., and Sarah A. Elwood. "How and Why Community Groups Use Maps and Geographic Information." *Cartography and Geographic Information Systems*, 1998: 95–104.

Dahrendorf, Ralf. "Citizenship and Beyond: The Social Dynamics of an Idea." *Social Research*, no. 41 (1974): 673–701.

Daniels, T., and K. Daniels. *The Environmental Planning Handbook: For Sustainable Communities and Regions*. Chicago: Planners Press, 2003.

Davidoff, Paul. "Advocacy and Pluralism in Planning." *Journal of the American Institute of Planners*, 1966: 400–10.

Davis, B. C. "Regional Planning in the US Coastal Zone: A Comparative Analysis of 15 Special Area Plans." *Ocean and Coastal Management*, 2004: 79–94.

Department for International Development (DFID). *Sustainable Livelihoods and Poverty Elimination*. London: Author, 1999.

Dewey, John. *Liberalism and Social Action*. New York: Capricorn Books (Orig. 1935), 1963.

Deyle, R. E., S. P. French, R. A. Olshansky, and R. G. Paterson. "Hazard Assessment: The Factual Basis for Planning and Mitigation." In *Cooperating with Nature: Confronting Natural Hazards with Land-Use Planning for Sustainable Communities*, edited by R. Burby, 119–66. Washington, DC: Joseph Henry Press/National Academy Press, 1998.

Dickey, J. W. *Metropolitan Transportation Planning*. Boca Raton, FL: CRC Press, 1983.

Dodson, D., J. Thomasson, and L. Totten. *Building Community by Design: A Resource Guide for Community Change Leaders*. Chapel Hill, NC: MDC, 2002.

Dunn, Christine E. "Participatory GIS--a People's GIS?" *Progress in Human Geography* 2007: 616–37.

Dynes, R. R. "Finding Order in Disorder: Continuities in the 9/11 Response." *Mid-South Sociological Society*, October 18, 2002: 1–22.

EM-DAT. *The OFDA/CRED International Disaster Database*, 2009. http://www.emdat.be/database (accessed November 2011).

Feagin, J. R., and M. P. Sikes. *Living with Racism: The Black Middle Class Experience*. Boston: Beacon, 1994.

Federal Emergency Management Agency (FEMA). "Homeowner's Guide to Retrofitting: Six Ways to Protect Your House from Flooding." Washington, DC: Author, 1998.

Federal Emergency Management Agency (FEMA). *Local Multi-Hazard Mitigation Planning Guidance*. Washington, DC: Author, 2007.

Federal Emergency Management Agency (FEMA). *Making Mitigation Work: A Handbook for State Officials*. Washington, DC: Author, 1986.

Federal Emergency Management Agency (FEMA). *Mitigation Ideas: Possible Mitigation Measures by Hazards Type*. Washington, DC: FEMA Region V, 2002.

Federal Emergency Management Agency (FEMA). "National Disaster Recovery Framework: Strengthening Disaster Recovery for the Nation." Washington, DC: Author, 2011.

Federal Emergency Management Agency (FEMA). "Standard Operating Procedure: Historic Review, 9570.9 SOP." Washington, DC: Public Assistance Program, Federal Emergency Management Agency, 2001.

Federal Emergency Management Agency (FEMA). *State Multi-Hazard Mitigation Planning Guidance* (Mitigation Planning "Blue Book"). Washington, DC: Author, January 2008.

Federal Emergency Management Agency (FEMA). *A Whole Community Approach to Emergency Management: Principles, Themes, and Pathways for Action*. FDOC 104-008-1, Washington, DC: Author, 2011.

Flippen, Chenoa. "Unequal Returns to Housing Investments? A Study of Real Housing Appreciation among Black, White, and Hispanic Households." *Social Forces* (University of North Carolina Press) 82, no. 4 (June 2004): 1523–51.

Folke, C., S. R. Carpenter, T. Elmqvist, L. Gunderson, C. S. Holling, and B. Walker. "Resilience and Sustainable Development: Building Adaptive Capacity in a World of Transformations." *Ambio* 31 (2002): 437–40.

Friedman, John. *Planning in the Public Domain*. Princeton, NJ: Princeton University Press, 1987.

Frostin, P., and A. G. Holtmann. "The Determinants of Residential Property Damage Caused by Hurricane Andrew." *Southern Economic Journal* 61, no. 2 (1994): 387–97.

Galveston, The City of. "City of Galveston Comprehensive Plan." Public document, HDR Engineering, Inc., Galveston, adopted October 27, 2011.

Gawande, A. *The Checklist Manifesto: How to Get Things Right*. New York: Metropolitan Books, 2009.

Gibbs, D., and A. E. G. Jonas. "Governance and Regulation in Local Environmental Policy: The Utility of a Regime Approach." *Geoforum*, 2000: 299–313.

Godschalk, D. "Urban Hazard Mitigation: Creating Resilient Cities." *Natural Hazards Review* 4, no. 3 (2003): 136–43.

Godschalk, D. R., T. Beatley, P. Berke, D. Brower, and E. Kaiser. *Natural Hazard Mitigation: Recasting Disaster Policy and Planning*. Washington, DC: Island Press, 1999.

Godschalk, D. R., D. J. Brower, and T. Beatley. *Catastrophic Coastal Storms: Hazard Mitigation and Development Management*. Durham, NC: Duke University Press, 1989.

Godschalk, D., D. Parham, D. Porter, W. Potapchuk, and S. Schukraft. "Pulling Together: A Planning and Development Consensus Building Manual." In *Ensuring Success: Meeting and Management*. Washington, DC: Urban Land Institute, 1994.

Green, G. P., and A. Haines. *Asset Building and Community Development*. Thousand Oaks: Sage Publications, 2002.

Greene, D. L., and M. Wegener. "Sustainable Transport." *Journal of Transport Geography*, 1997: 177–90.

Guy, R. F., L. G. Pol, and R. Ryker. "Discrimination in Mortgage Lending: The Mortgage Disclosure Act." *Population Research and Policy Review*, 1982: 283–96.

Gyourko, J., and P. Linneman. "The Affordability of the American Dream: An Examination of the Last 30 Years." *Journal of Housing Research* 4, no. 1 (1993): 39–72.

Haar, C. M. "In Accordance with a Comprehensive Plan." *Harvard Law Review*, 1955: 1154–75.

Habermas, Jurgen. *Theory of Communicative Action.* Boston: Beacon Press, 1984.

Haque, C. E., and D. Etkin. "People and Community as Constituent Parts of Hazards: The Significance of Societal Dimensions in Hazards Analysis." *Natural Hazards* 41 (2007): 271–82.

Hazards & Vulnerability Research Institute. The Spatial Hazard Events and Losses Database for the United States, Version 12.0 [Online Database]. Columbia: University of South Carolina, 2013.

Henson, B. "Hurricane Storm Surge: In a Category of Its Own." *Atmos News*, September 4, 2012.

Henstra, D., and G. McBean. "The Role of Government in Services for Natural Disaster Mitigation." *Institute for Catastrophic Loss Reduction Research Paper Series*, 2004.

Hershman, M. J., J. W. Good, T. Bernd-Cohen, R. F. Goodwin, V. Lee, and P. Pogue. "The Effectiveness of Coastal Zone Management in the United States." *Coastal Management*, 1999: 113–38.

Highfield, W. E., W. G. Peacock, and S. S. Van Zandt. "Determinants and Characteristics of Damage in Single-Family Island Households from Hurricane Ike 1." *Association of Collegiate Schools of Planning Conference*, Minneapolis, 2010.

Highfield, W., W. G. Peacock, and S. Van Zandt. "Mitigation Planning: Why Hazard Exposure, Structural Vulnerability, and Social Vulnerability Matter." *Journal of Planning Education & Research* 34, no. 3 (2014): 287–300.

Holling, C. S. "Resilience and Stability of Ecological Systems." *Annual Review of Ecology and Systematics* 4 (1973): 1–23.

Holling, C. "The Resilience of Terrestrial Ecosystems." In *Foundations of Ecological Resilience*, edited by L. Gunderson, C. Allen, and C. Holling, 67–108. Washington, DC: Island Press, 2010.

Holling, C. S. "What Barriers? What Bridges?" In *Barriers and Bridges to the Renewal of Ecosystems and Institutions*, edited by L. H. Gunderson, C. S. Holling, and S. S. Light, 3–34. New York: Columbia University Press, 1995.

Holling, C. S., D. W. Schindler, B. W. Walker, and J. Roughgarden. "Biodiversity in the Functioning of Ecosystems: An Ecological Synthesis." In *Biodiversity Losses: Economic and Ecological Issues*, edited by C. Perrings, K. G. Maler, C. Folke, B. O. Jansson, and C. S. Holling, 44–83. New York: Cambridge University Press, n.d.

Holloway, Steven R., and Elvin K. Wyly. "'The Color of Money' Expanded: Geographically Contingent Mortgage Lending in Atlanta." *Journal of Housing Research* 12, no. 1 (2001): 55–90.

Holway, J. M., and R. J. Bubry. "The Effects of Floodplain Development Controls on Residential Land Values." *Land Economics*, 1990: 259–71.

Horton, H. D. "Race and Wealth: A Demographic Analysis of Black Homeownership." *Sociological Inquiry*, 1992: 480–89.

Hyndman, D., and D. Hyndman. *Natural Hazards and Disasters.* Boston: Cengage Learning, 2006.

Innes, Judith E. "Planning Theory's Emerging Paradigm: Communicative Action and Interactive Practice." *Journal of Planning Education and Research*, 1995: 183–89.

Innes, Judith E., and David E. Booher. "Reframing Public Participation: Strategies for the 21st Century." *Planning Theory & Practice* 5, no. 4 (2004): 419–36.

International Federation of Red Cross and Red Crescent Societies. *World Disasters Report 2004: Focus on Community Resilience*. West Hartford, CT: Kumarian Press, 2004.

Isserman, Andrew M. "Projection, Forecast, and Plan on the Future of Population Forecasting." *Journal of the American Planning Association* 50, no. 2 (1984): 208–21.

Jacob, J. S., and S. Showalter. "The Resilient Coast: Policy Frameworks for Adapting the Built Environment to Climate Change and Growth in Coastal Areas of the U.S. Gulf of Mexico." *Sea Grant*, 2007. http://nsglc.olemiss.edu/TheBuiltEnvironment08-sm_000.pdf (accessed April 2014).

Kang, J. E., W. G. Peacock, and R. Husein. "An Assessment of Coastal Zone Hazard Mitigation Plans in Texas." *Journal of Disaster Research*, 2010: 520–28.

Kaufmann, Robert. *FEMA Disaster Photo Library*, Galveston, TX, 2008. https://www.fema.gov/media-library (accessed March 1, 2014).

Keller, E. A., and D. DeVecchio. *Natural Hazards: Earth's Processes as Hazards Disasters, and Catastrophes*. Upper Saddle River, NJ: Prentice Hall, 2011.

Klee, G. *The Coastal Environment: Toward Integrated Coastal and Marine Sanctuary Management*. Upper Saddle River, NJ: Prentice Hall, 1999.

Klein, Richard J. T., Robert J. Nicholls, and Frank Thomalla. "Resilience To Natural Hazards: How Useful Is This Concept?" *Environmental Hazards*, 2003: 35–45.

Lake, R. W. "Racial Transition and Black Homeownership in American Suburbs." In *America's Housing*, edited by G. Sternlieb and J. W. Hughes, 419–38. New Brunswick, NJ: Center for Urban Policy Research, 1980.

Lebel, L. "Resilience and Sustainability of Landscapes." *ASB Partnership*, 2001. http://www.asb.cgiar.org/docs (accessed August 5, 2007).

Lebel, L., et al. "Governance and the Capacity to Manage Resilience in Regional Social–Ecological Systems." *Ecology and Society* 11, no. 1 (2006): 1–15.

Lindell, M. K., and R. W. Perry. *Behavioral Foundations of Community Emergency Planning*. Washington, DC: Hemisphere Publishing, 1992.

Lindell, M. K., and R. W. Perry. *Communicating Environmental Risk in Multiethnic Communities*. Thousand Oaks, CA: Sage, 2004.

Lindell, M. K., and R. W. Perry. "Household Adjustment to Earthquake Hazard: A Review of Research." *Environment and Behavior*, 2000: 461–501.

Lindell, M. K., and R. W. Perry. "The Protective Action Decision Model: Theoretical Modifications and Additional Evidence." *Risk Analysis* 32, no. 4 (April 2012): 616–32.

Lindell, M. K., and C. S. Prater. "Assessing Community Impacts of Natural Disasters." *Natural Hazards Review* 4, no. 4 (2003): 176–85.

Lindell, M. K., C. Prater, and R. P. Perry. *Emergency Management*. Hoboken, NJ: Wiley, 2006.

Lindell, M. K., C. S. Prater, and R. W. Perry. *Introduction to Emergency Management*. Hoboken, NJ: Wiley, 2007.

Logan, J. R., and H. Molotch. *Urban Fortunes: The Political Economy of Place*. Berkeley: University of California Press, 1987.

Lopez, J. A. Perez. "I Am the Boss, Why Should I Be Ethical?" *People in Corporations*, 1990: 179–88.

Lyles, W., P. Berke, and G. Smith. "A Comparison of Local Hazard Mitigation Plan Quality in Six States, USA." *Landscape and Urban Planning*, 2014: 89–99.

Maguire, B., and P. Hagan. "Disasters and Communities: Understanding Social Resilience." *Australian Journal of Emergency Management* 22 (2007): 16–20.

Mandelker, D. R. "The Role of the Local Comprehensive Plan in Land Use Regulation." *Michigan Law Review*, 1976: 899–973.

Manyena, Siambabala Bernard. "The Concept of Resilience Revisited." *Disasters* 30, no. 4 (December 2006): 434–50.

Mao Tse-tung. *On Practice. In Four Essays on Philosophy*. Peking: Foreign Languages Press (Orig. 1937), 1968.

May, P. "Mandate Design and Implementation: Enhancing Implementation Efforts and Shaping Regulatory Styles." *Journal of Policy Analysis and Management*, 1993: 634–63.

McCall, Michael, K. "Seeking Good Governance in Participatory-GIS: A Review of Processes and Governance Dimensions in Applying GIS to Participatory Spatial Planning." *Habitat International*, 2003: 549–73.

McCall, Michael K., and Peter A. Minang. "Assessing Participatory GIS for Community-Based Natural Resource Management: Claiming Community Forests in Cameroon." *Geographical Journal*, 2005: 340–56.

Meck, S. "Legislative Requirement That Zoning and Land Use Controls Be Consistent with an Independently Adopted Local Comprehensive Plan: A Model Statute." *Washington University Journal of Law & Policy*, 2000: 295.

Mileti, D. S. *Disasters by Design: A Reassessment of Natural Hazards in the United States*. Washington, DC: Joseph Henry Press, 1999.

Morgan, T. D., and J. W. Shonkwiler. "Urban Development and Statewide Planning: Challenging of the 1980s." *Oregon Law Review*, 61 (1982): 351.

Morrow, B. H. "Identifying and Mapping Community Vulnerability." *Disasters* 23, no. 1 (1999): 1–18.

Morrow, B. H. "Stretching the Bonds: The Families of Andrew." In *Hurricane Andrew: Ethnicity, Gender, and the Sociology of Disasters*, edited by W. G. Peacock, B. H. Morrow, and H. Gladwin, 1–19. London: Routledge, 1997.

Mumford, Lewis. *The Culture of Cities*. New York: Harcourt, Brace, 1938.

Munich Reinsurance Company. *Topics Geo: Natural Catastrophes 2010, Analysis, Assessments, and Positions*. Munich: Author, 2011.

Murphy, Michael D. *Landscape Architecture Theory: An Evolving Body of Thought*. Long Grove, CA: Waveland Press, 2005.

National Historic Preservation Act of 1966. 16 U.S. Code 470, amended 2006.

National Oceanic and Atmospheric Administration (NOAA). *The Deadliest, Costliest, and Most Intense United States Tropical Cyclones from 1851 to 2004 (and Other Frequently Requested Hurricane Facts)*. Miami, FL: Author, 2005.

National Oceanic and Atmospheric Administration (NOAA). *State of the Climate: Tornadoes for Annual 2009*. Asheville, NC: National Climatic Data Center, NOAA, 2009.

National Research Council (NRC). *Facing Hazards and Disasters: Understanding Human Dimensions*. Washington, DC: National Academies Press, 2006.

Nelson, Carl L. *Protecting the Past from Natural Disasters*. Washington, DC: Preservation Press, National Trust for Historic Preservation, 1991.

Norris, F. H., S. P. Stevens, B. Pfefferbaum, K. F. Wyche, and R. L. Pfefferbaum. "Community Resilience as a Metaphor, Theory, Set of Capacities, and Strategy for Disaster Readiness." *American Journal of Community Psychology* 41, no. 1–2 (March 2008): 127–50.

Norton, R. K. "More and Better Local Planning." *Journal of the American Planning Association*, 2005: 55–71.

Oliver, M., and T. Shapiro. *Black Wealth/White Wealth: A New Perspective on Racial Inequality*. New York: Routledge, 1997.

Olshansky, R., L. Hopkins, and L. Johnson. "Disaster and Recovery: Processes Compressed in Time." *Natural Hazards Review* 13, no. 3 (2012): 173–78.

Olshansky, R. B., and J. D. Kartez. "Managing Land Use to Build Resilience." In *Cooperating with Nature: Confronting Natural Hazards with Land-Use Planning for Sustainable Communities*, edited by R. J. Burby, 167–202. Washington, DC: National Academies Press, 1998.

Pastor, M., R. Bullard, J. K. Boyce, A. Fothergill, R. Morello-Frosch, and B. Wright. "Environment, Disaster, and Race after Katrina." *Race, Poverty & the Environment* 13, no. 1 (2006): 21–26.

Paton, D., and D. M. Johnston. *Disaster Resilience*. Springfield, IL: Charles C. Thomas, 2006.

Peacock, W. G. "Hurricane Mitigation Status and Factors in Influencing Mitigation Status among Florida's Single-Family Homeowners." *Natural Hazards Review*, 2003: 149–58.

Peacock, W. G., D. Dash, and Y. Zhang. "Shelter and Housing Recovery Following Disaster." In *The Handbook of Disaster Research*, edited by H. Rodriquez, E. L. Quarantelli, and R. Dynes, 258–74. New York: Springer, 2006.

Peacock, W. G., H. Grover, J. Mayunga, S. Brody, S. D. Van Zandt, and H. J. Kim. *The Status and Trends of Population Social Vulnerabilities along the Texas Coast with Special Attention to the Coastal Management Zone and Hurricane Ike: The Coastal Planning*. College Station, TX: College of Architecture, Texas A&M University, Hazard Reduction & Recovery Center, 2011.

Peacock, W. G., and R. Husein. *The Adoption and Implementation of Hazard Mitigation Policies and Strategies by Coastal Jurisdictions in Texas: The Planning Survey Results*. Submitted to the Texas General Land Office, the National Oceanic and Atmospheric Administration, and the Coastal Coordination Council. College Station, TX: Hazard Reduction & Recovery Center, 2011.

Peacock, W. G., J. E. Kang, Y. S. Lin, H. Grover, R. Husein, and G. R. Burns. *Status and Trends of Coastal Hazard Exposure and Mitigation Policies for the Texas Coast: The Mitigation Policy Mosaic of Coastal Texas*. College Station, TX: Hazard Reduction & Recovery Center, 2009.

Peacock, W. G., H. Kunreuther, W. H. Hooke, S. L. Cutter, S. E. Chang, and P. R. Berke. *Toward a Resiliency and Vulnerability Observatory Network: RAVON*. HRRC reports: 08-02R, 2008.

Peacock, W. P., B. H. Morrow, and H. Gladwin. *Hurricane Andrew: Ethnicity, Gender, and the Sociology of Disasters*. New York: Routledge, 1997.

Peacock, W. G., and A. K. Ragsdale. "Social Systems, Ecological Networks and Disasters: Toward a Socio-Political Ecology of Disasters." In *Hurricane Andrew: Ethnicity, Gender, and the Sociology of Disasters*, edited by W. G. Peacock, B. H. Morrow, and H. Gladwin, 20–35. New York: Routledge, 1997.

Perry, R. W., and M. K. Lindel. "The Effects of Ethnicity on Evacuation Decision-Making." *International Journal of Mass Emergency Disasters* 9, no. 1 (1991): 47–68.

Pielke, Roger A., Mary W. Downton, and J. Zoe Barnard Miller. *Flood Damage in the United States, 1926–2003: A Reanalysis of National Weather Service Estimates*. Boulder, CO: UCAR, 2002.

Pimm, S. L. "The Complexity and Stability of Ecosystems." *Nature*, 1984: 321–26.

Potter, J. R., and M. J. Savonis. "Transportation in an Age of Climate Change: What Are the Research Priorities?" *TR News*, 2003: 227.

Poumadre, M., C. Mays, S. Le Mer, and R. Blong. "The 2003 Heat Wave in France: Dangerous Climate Change Here and Now." *Risk Analysis*, 2005: 1483–94.

Putnam, R. D. "Bowling Alone: America's Declining Social Capital." *Journal of Democracy*, 1995: 65–78.

Putnam, R. D. B*owling Alone: The Collapse and Revival of American Community*. New York: Simon and Schuster Paperbacks, 2000.

Ramirez-Gomez, Sara, and Christian Martinez. "Indigenous Communities in Suriname Identify Key Local Sites." *ArcNews*, n.d.

Randolph, John. *Ecosystem and Watershed Management*. Washington, DC: Island Press, 2003.

Rawls, John. *A Theory of Justice*. Cambridge, MA: Harvard University Press, 1971.

Resilience Alliance. *Assessing and Managing Resilience in Social-Ecological Systems: A Practitioners Workbook*. Stockholm: Author, 2007.

Rittel, Horst W. J., and Melvin M. Webber. "Dilemmas in a General Theory of Planning." *Policy Sciences*, 1973: 155–69.

Robin, L. "Capacity Building for Natural Resource Management: Lessons from Risk and Emergency Management." *Australasian Journal of Environmental Management* , 2008: 6.

Rubin, J. "Transportation and Climate Change." *Maine Policy Review*, 2008: 115–19.

Sagalyn, Lynne B. "Mortgage Lending in Older Urban Neighborhoods: Lessons from Past Experience." *Annals of the American Academy of Political and Social Scienc*e 465 (1983): 98–108.

Savonis, M. J., V. R. Burkett, and J. R. Potter. "Impacts of Climate Change and Variability on Transportation Systems and Infrastructure: Gulf Coast Study, Phase I." A report by the U.S. Climate Change Science Program and the Subcommittee on Global Change Research, 2008.

Savonis, M. J., V. R. Burkett, J. R. Potter, R. Kafalenos, R. Hyman, and K. Leonard. "The Impact of Climate Change on Transportation in the Gulf Coast." *TCLEE 2009: Lifeline Earthquake Engineering in a Multihazard Environment*, Washington, DC: US Department of Transportation, 2009.

Schick, F. "Consistency." *Philosophical Review*, 1966: 467–95.

Schlossberg, Marc, Cody Evers, Ken Kato, and Christo Brehm. "Active Transportation, Citizen Engagement and Liveability: Coupling Citizens and Smartphones to Make the Change." *Journal of the Urban & Regional Information Systems Association* 24, no. 2 (2012).

Schwab, A., K. Eschelbach, and D. Brower. *Hazard Mitigation and Preparedness*. Danvers, MA: Wiley, 2007.

Schwab, J. *Hazard Mitigation: Integrating Best Practices into Planning*. Planning Advisory Service Report 560. Chicago: American Planning Association, 2010.

Schwab, J., ed. "Planning for Post-Disaster Recovery and Reconstruction." Planning Advisory Service Report 483/484. Chicago: American Planning Association, 1998.

Shapiro, T. M. *The Hidden Cost of Being African American: How Wealth Perpetuates Inequality*. Oxford, England: Oxford University Press, 2004.

Smith, G., and D. Wenger. "Sustainable Disaster Recovery: Operationalizing an Existing Agenda." In *Handbook of Disaster Research*, edited by H. Rodriguez, E. Quarantelli, and R. Dynes, 234–57. New York: Springer, 2006.

Smith, Robert, Claude Simard, and Andrew Sharpe. *A Proposed Approach to Environment and Sustainable Development Indicators Based on Capital*. Ottawa, ON: The National Round Table on the Environment and the Economy's Environment and Sustainable Development Indicators Initiative, 2001.

South, S. J., and K. D. Crowder. "Escaping Distressed Neighborhoods: Individual, Community, and Metropolitan Influences." *American Journal of Sociology* 102 (1997): 1040–84.

Squires, G. D. "Why an Insurance Regulation for Prohibit Redlining?" *John Marshall Law Review*, 1998: 489–511.

Squires, Gregory D., and Sunwoong Kim. "'Does Anybody Who Works Here Look Like Me?' Mortgage Lending, Race, and Lender Employment." *Social Science Quarterly* 76, no. 4 (1995): 821–38.

Squires, G. D., S. O'Connor, and J. Silver. "The Unavailability of Information on Insurance Unavailability: Insurance Redlining and the Absence of Geocoded Disclosure Data." *Housing Policy Debate*, 2001: 347–72.

Squires, G. D., and W. Velez. "Insurance Redlining and the Transformation of an Urban Metropolis." *Urban Affairs Quarterly*, 1987: 63–83.

Srivastava, R., and L. Laurian. "Natural Hazard Mitigation in Local Comprehensive Plans: The Case of Flood, Wildfire and Drought Planning in Arizona." *Disaster Prevention and Management*, 2006: 461–83.

Stecker, R., A. Pechan, J. M. Steinhauser, M. Rotter, G. Scholl, and K. Eisenack. "Why Are Utilities Reluctant to Adapt to Climate Change?" Report, Odenburg/Berlin, 2011.

Stinchcomb, A. L. "Social Structure and Organizations." In *Handbook of Organizations*, edited by J. G. March, 142–93. Chicago: Rand McNally, 1965.

Sun, L. G. "Smart Growth in Dumb Places: Sustainability, Disaster, and the Future of the American City." *Brigham Young University Law Review* (2011): 2157.

Tang, Z. "Evaluating Local Coastal Zone Land Use Planning Capacities in California." *Ocean and Coastal Management*, 2008: 544–55.

Tang, Z., M. K. Lindell, C. Prater, T. Wei, and C. M. Hussey. "Examining Local Coastal Zone Management Capacity in US Pacific Coastal Counties." *Coastal Management* 2011: 105–32.

Teaford, Jon. "Urban Renewal and Its Aftermath." *Housing Policy Debate* 11, no. 2 (2000): 443–65.

Texas A&M University Galveston. *Ike Dike*, 2010. http://www.tamug.edu/ikedike/index.html (accessed August 2013).

Texas State Data Center. *Texas Population Projections Program*, 2000–2040. http://txsdc.utsa.edu/ (accessed December 2012).

Tierney, K., and M. Bruneau. "Conceptualizing and Measuring Resilience." *Transportation News*, May–June 2007: 14–17.

Tierney, K. J., M. K. Lindell, and R. W. Perry. *Facing the Unexpected: Disaster Preparedness and Response in the United States*. Washington, DC: Joseph Henry Press, 2001.

Timmerman, P. "Vulnerability, Resilience and the Collapse of Society." *Environmental Monograph 1* (Institute For Environmental Studies, University of Toronto), 1981.

United Nations Office for Disaster Risk Reduction (UN/ISDR). "Hyogo Framework for 2005–2015: Building the Resilience of the Nations and Communities to Disasters," 2005. www.unisdr.org/wcdr/intergover/official-docs/Hyogo-framework-action-english.pdf (accessed January 4, 2007).

U.S. Army Corps of Engineers. *Waterborne Commerce Statistics Center*, 2004. http://www
    .iwr.usace.army.mil/About/TechnicalCenters/WCSCWaterborneCommerceStatistics
    Center.aspx (accessed December 2012).

U.S. Census Bureau. *2007 Economic Census*, 2007. https://www.census.gov/econ
    /census07/www/get_data.html (accessed December 2012).

U.S. Census Bureau. U.S. Census data, 2010.

Van Zandt, S., Y. Zhang, W. Highfield, and W. G. Peacock. "Inequities in Long Term Hous-
    ing Recovery," 2013. http://hrrc.arch.tamu.edu/media/cms_page_media/561/Long
    -term%20recovery_NHC_13.pdf.

Walker, B., and D. Salt. *Resilience Thinking: Sustaining Ecosystems and People in a Changing
    World*. Washington, DC: Island Press, 2006.

Walker, B., et al. "Resilience Management in Social–Ecological Systems: A Working
    Hypothesis for a Participatory Approach." *Conservation Ecology*, 2002.

Walter, C. "Community Building Practice." In *Community Organizing and Community
    Building for Health*, edited by M. Minkler. New Brunswick, NJ: Rutgers University Press,
    2004.

Whyte, David. "Mameen." In *River Flow* 286. Langley, WA: Many Rivers Press, 2007.

Wilbanks, T. J. "Enhancing the Resilience of Communities to Natural and Other Hazards:
    What We Know and What We Can Do." *Natural Hazards Observer* 32 (2008): 10–11.

Wildavsky, A. *Searching for Safety*. New Brunswick, NJ: Transaction, 1991.

Wildavsky, A. *The Rise of Radical Egalitarianism*. Washington, DC: American University
    Press, 1991.

Williams, A., and A. Micallef. *Beach Management: Principles and Practice*. Sterling, VA:
    Earthscan, 2009.

Xiao, Y., and W. G. Peacock. "Do Hazard Mitigation and Preparedness Reduce Physical
    Damage to Businesses in Disasters?: The Critical Role of Business Disaster Planning."
    Natural Hazards Review 15, no. 3 (2014).

Xiao, Y., and S. Van Zandt. "Building Community Resiliency: Spatial Links between House-
    hold and Business Post-disaster Return." *Urban Studies* 49, no. 11 (2013): 2523–42.

Zahran, S., S. D. Brody, W. G. Peacock, A. Vedlitz, and H. Grover. "Social Vulnerability and
    the Natural and Built Environment: A Model of Flood Casualties in Texas." *Disasters*
    32, no. 4 (2008): 537–60.

Zhang, Y., and W. G. Peacock. "Planning for Housing Recovery? Lessons Learned from
    Hurricane Andrew." *Journal of the American Planning Association* 76, no. 1 (2010): 5–24.

About the Authors

Jaimie Hicks Masterson, MUP, is program coordinator of Texas Target Communities at Texas A&M University. Her work centers on collaboratively engaging communities in order to build capacity, guide wise development decisions, and mitigate hazards. She has developed training materials for communities on urban and land use planning, environmental hazards, and community capacity. Her background is in landscape architecture, education and outreach to underrepresented populations, and disaster and environmental planning. She holds a master of urban planning degree from Texas A&M University.

Walter Gillis Peacock, PhD, is professor and director of the Hazard Reduction & Recovery Center at Texas A&M University. Peacock's research, which has been funded by the NSF, the NOAA, and the Texas General Land Office, among others, focuses primarily on natural hazards and human system responses to hazards and disaster. Having authored more than 100 journal articles, book chapters, and books on disaster recovery and mitigation, Peacock is one of the world's leading experts on planning for socially vulnerable populations. His current research focuses on the capacity of local communities to implement mitigation plans in Texas. His graduate-level planning courses include courses in statistical methods and hazard mitigation. He holds a PhD in sociology from the University of Georgia.

Shannon S. Van Zandt, PhD, AICP, is associate professor and coordinator of the Master of Urban Planning Program as well as director of the Center for Housing and Urban Development at Texas A&M University. Her work centers on the spatial distribution of housing and its consequences for vulnerable populations. Van Zandt connects her research to both the education of planning graduate students and the planning profession through engagement with real communities along the Texas Coast and elsewhere. She is a faculty fellow of the Hazard Reduction & Recovery Center and the Center for

Texas Beaches & Shores. Her graduate-level planning courses include courses in land use planning methods, planning theory, professional communications, and housing policy. She holds a PhD in city and regional planning from the University of North Carolina at Chapel Hill.

Himanshu Grover, PhD, AICP, is assistant professor at the Urban and Regional Planning Department at the University at Buffalo (SUNY). His research focuses on planning policies and design of sustainable and resilient communities. Grover examines and evaluates the impact of local planning policies on the ability of at-risk communities to understand, analyze, and respond to environmental threats. He has more than six years of professional planning experience and has been associated with numerous internationally funded projects. His courses include planning for climate change, urban infrastructure management, design of cities, and introduction to urban planning. He holds a PhD in urban and regional sciences from the Texas A&M University at College Station.

Lori Feild Schwarz, AICP, is the comprehensive planning manager for the City of Plano, Texas. She oversees the First Choice Neighborhoods program and heritage preservation and long-range planning for the city. Before this position, she was the assistant director of planning and special projects for the City of Galveston. She managed the planning division and also serves as historic preservation officer for the city. Schwarz was hired by the city in 2001 and participated in numerous citywide planning efforts, including the 2001 Comprehensive Plan, Beach Access Plan, Hazard Mitigation Plan, Disaster Response Plan for Historic Properties, and Long-Term Recovery Plan for the City of Galveston. She supervised the large-scale Progress Galveston project, which includes a comprehensive revision of the city's land development regulations and numerous specialized plans. Schwarz holds a master of historic preservation degree from the University of Georgia.

John T. Cooper Jr., PhD, is professor of practice, director of outreach for the Hazard Reduction and Recovery Center, and director of Texas Target Communities at Texas A&M University. His research and practice focus on promoting principles of inclusive planning and plan quality and helping planners mitigate threats to economy, environment, and culture by transforming communities from high-risk and low-opportunity to equitable, resilient, and adaptive. Before returning to A&M, John managed a $2.5-million FEMA-funded effort to understand barriers to increased disaster awareness and preparedness in marginalized communities. He currently serves on the advisory board for the DHS Center of Excellence–Natural Disasters, Coastal Infrastructure, and Emergency Management (DIEM) at the University of North Carolina at Chapel Hill. He holds a PhD in city and regional planning from the University of North Carolina at Chapel Hill.

Index